Exploring the American Civil War through 50 Historic Treasures

AASLH

Exploring America's Historic Treasures

About the Organization

The American Association for State and Local History (AASLH) is a national history membership association headquartered in Nashville, Tennessee, that provides leadership and support for its members who preserve and interpret state and local history in order to make the past more meaningful to all people. AASLH members are leaders in preserving, researching, and interpreting traces of the American past to connect the people, thoughts, and events of yesterday with the creative memories and abiding concerns of people, communities, and our nation today. In addition to sponsorship of this book series, AASLH publishes the *History News* magazine, a newsletter, technical leaflets and reports, and other materials; confers prizes and awards in recognition of outstanding achievement in the field; supports a broad education program and other activities designed to help members work more effectively; and advocates on behalf of the discipline of history. To join AASLH, go to www.aaslh.org or contact Membership Services, AASLH, 2021 21st Ave. South, Suite 320, Nashville, TN 37212.

About the Series

The American Association for State and Local History publishes the Exploring America's Historic Treasures series to bring to life topics and themes from American history through objects from museums and other history organizations. Produced with full-color photographs of historic objects, books in this series investigate the past through the interpretation of material culture.

Exploring the American Civil War through 50 Historic Treasures

JULIE L. HOLCOMB

ROWMAN & LITTLEFIELD
Lanham • Boulder • New York • London

Published by Rowman & Littlefield
An imprint of The Rowman & Littlefield Publishing Group, Inc.
4501 Forbes Boulevard, Suite 200, Lanham, Maryland 20706
www.rowman.com

6 Tinworth Street, London SE11 5AL, United Kingdom

British Library Cataloguing in Publication Information Available

Library of Congress Cataloging-in-Publication Data

Names: Holcomb, Julie L., 1963- author.
Title: Exploring the American Civil War through 50 historic treasures /
   Julie L. Holcomb.
Other titles: Exploring the American Civil War through fifty historic
   treasures
Description: Lanham : Rowman & Littlefield, [2021] | Series: AASLH:
   exploring America's historic treasures | Includes bibliographical
   references and index. | Summary: "This book will deploy a wide range of
   material culture objects, artwork, and landscapes to the tell the story
   of the American Civil War. The objects will document the war's history
   from its beginnings in the fierce debates over slavery through its
   legacy, including recent debates about Confederate monuments"-- Provided
   by publisher.
Identifiers: LCCN 2020052923 (print) | LCCN 2020052924 (ebook) | ISBN
   9781538118559 (cloth) | ISBN 9781538118566 (epub)
Subjects: LCSH: United States—History—Civil War, 1861–1865—Sources. |
   Material culture—United States—History—19th century. | United
   States—History—Civil War, 1861–1865—Causes—Sources. |
   Slavery—United States—History—19th century—Sources. | United
   States—History—Civil War, 1861–1865—Campaigns.
Classification: LCC E464 .H59 2021 (print) | LCC E464 (ebook) | DDC
   973.7—dc23
LC record available at https://lccn.loc.gov/2020052923
LC ebook record available at https://lccn.loc.gov/2020052924

For Noah and Paige

Contents

List of Figures

Preface

Twenty-eight-year-old Samuel N. Kennerly joined the Edisto Rifles (later the 1st South Carolina Infantry, Company A) in April 1861. A physician from Orangeburg, South Carolina, Kennerly mustered in as a common soldier. In April 1862, after twelve months of service, all members of the Rifles, including Kennerly, reenlisted for another three years, this time as part of the 25th South Carolina Infantry. That same month Kennerly returned home and married Julia Culler. Their son Samuel was born the following year. Kennerly, along with 70 percent of his regiment, died at the Battle of Weldon Railroad, Virginia, in August 1864. Although she later remarried, Julia Culler Kennerly saved her husband's letters, eventually passing them on to their son.[1]

In 2001, the Pearce Civil War Collection at Navarro College in Corsicana, Texas, acquired the collection of Kennerly's wartime correspondence. Elderhostel volunteers transcribed the more than one hundred letters written by Kennerly to his wife between 1861 and 1864. As they worked on the letters, the volunteers followed Kennerly's story, reading passages aloud and sympathizing with Kennerly's desire to return to the safety of home and family.[2]

The Pearce Civil War Collection, like many museums and archives, relies on the work of volunteers who help transcribe and research the collections. For nearly ten years, the Pearce Collection hosted Elderhostel service projects each summer, bringing in groups of mostly retired men and women to work with historical documents such as the Kennerly letters. These volunteers paid to participate in these projects. Many of these volunteers returned each year, drawn by the stories that could be found in the Civil War collection.[3]

Historic treasures are "a virtual time machine" taking us "into the lives of those persons in culture and history whose genius has touched us, whose lives and accomplishments have inspired us, whose efforts have created our heritage and influenced our present." Although Kenneth Rendell is speaking of historical letters and documents, his words apply equally well to artifacts. As Rendell explains, historical materials "are the most direct link we can have to the heroes and heroines, villains, and ordinary people of the past." From these objects—both two and three dimensional—we can relate to the men and women of the past and "appreciate that their lives may not be all that different from our own."[4] For more than a century, individuals and institutions have collected the treasures of the American Civil War—letters, diaries, documents, photographs, artifacts, souvenirs, and relics. As historian Teresa Barnett notes, "Collecting Civil War artifacts [is] a mass pastime in a way that no American relic collection tradition has been before or since."[5]

Collecting Civil War objects began during the war as soldiers sent home curiosities. Encountering the exotic vegetation of the South for the first time, Northern soldiers collected specimens to send home, including persimmons, magnolia blossoms, grains of "Georgia rice," and bolls of cotton. Not limiting themselves to the natural world, soldiers also ransacked homes and scavenged curiosities from enemy camps. Letters home might be written on "rebel" or "Yankee" paper. Soldiers also sent home the personal effects of wounded and dead comrades or even strangers. In 1862, after the Battle of Antietam in Sharpsburg, Maryland, Union soldier Robert Gould Shaw sent his sister a letter he had found on the battlefield. In his accompanying note, he described the dead soldier: "It looked as if he had been reading them both [the letter and his Bible] before he died."[6]

Civil War battlefields often saw large numbers of visitors as soon as the fighting ended.[7] Contemporary descriptions noted not only the unburied bodies but also the profusion of discarded items scattered across the battlefield, including knapsacks, canteens, clothing, ammunition boxes, rifles, Bibles, letters, and photographs. Three weeks after the Battle of Gettysburg, in July 1863, the Gettysburg *Adams Sentinel* published an account of the battle, "Touching Incident of the Battle-Field," that described the collection from the battlefield of "a small paper, which contained two separate locks of hair attached thereto." The writer surmised that "these tender mementoes of . . . home and children had been sent to [the soldier] by his attached wife, to cheer his heart in the far distant land to which the fortunes of war had brought him; and probably he wore the tender testimonials near his heart, when the fatal missile of death separated him from those he loved."[8] Journalist John Trow-bridge, who visited the site of the Battle of the Wilderness, Virginia, several years after the fighting there, described the battlefield as still strewn with "knapsacks, haversacks, pieces of clothing, fragments of harness, tin plates, canteens, some pierced with balls, fragments of shells, with here and there a round-shot, or a shell unexploded, straps, buckles, cartridge-box, socks, old shoes, rotting letters."[9]

Collecting Civil War treasures continued after the war. Veterans saved letters, diaries, and other souvenirs as evidence of their service. Individuals and families who had lost someone in the war saved their soldier's letters and other relics as mementos. In the North, exhibiting these relics began almost as soon as the war ended. For example, in the 1870s, the collector Joel A. Danner opened a museum at Gettysburg, the first of many at that battlefield. Similar museums opened at other battle sites. In the late 1880s, Northern entrepre-neur and former Confederate soldier Charles F. Gunther moved the build-ing that had housed Libby Prison, a notorious Union prisoner-of-war site, from Richmond, Virginia, to Chicago, Illinois. The building was dismantled and loaded onto 132 freight cars for shipment. Once in Chicago it was reas-sembled, albeit missing a few stones, which had been carried off as souvenirs after a rail accident in Kentucky. The Libby War Prison Museum exhibited Gunther's extensive collection of wartime artifacts. In the North, veterans led efforts to collect and display Civil War objects. As a result, the collections and the exhibitions focused on military details: "the particulars of individual battles, the convolutions of military strategy, the specialized knowledge of firearms." Catalog entries, as Barnett notes, focused "on statistics, tactical de-scriptions, and the minutiae of military hardware."[10]

In contrast, in the South, war relics were not exhibited until the late 1880s and 1890s when Southern commemoration moved from its "bereavement" phase to its "celebration" phase. In the immediate postwar period, as Barnett writes, "Southern memorial activities focused very directly on burying and honoring the war dead." Public commemoration efforts remained within the cemetery walls. Although Southerners did not display relics in this early period, they did continue to collect and preserve them. When these objects were brought into the public sphere, Southerners used them to support the ideology of the Lost Cause. Using Civil War artifacts, Southerners asserted the importance of the experience of the war as the basis of Southern iden-tity. The material culture of the Civil War—letters, documents, artifacts, photographs—was deployed to celebrate the Lost Cause: the South's bid for political independence, the heroism of its supporters, and its defeat as the result of superior Northern resources. For example, the founders of Richmond's Confederate Museum, established by the Confederate Memorial Literary Society in 1896, appealed to "every man and woman in the South" to "rescue the fragments of individual heroism and endurance, fast floating away to oblivion, to gather in the tattered, rusty mementoes of our Lost Cause, and commit them to the keeping of the Confederate Memorial Literary Society." In the South, the collection and preservation of Civil War objects was led primarily by women. As a result, collection and interpretation tended to focus on the individual, inviting viewers to gather these individual stories into a collective memory of the war.[11]

Today these two impulses—the tactical and the sentimental—are still apparent in discussions of Civil War objects. Often when we talk about the objects of the Civil War, the focus is on the military material of the war. Similarly, books that present collections of Civil War objects tend to focus on the military aspects of the war, including weapons, uniforms, and the equipment of the common soldier. However, two recent volumes, both published during the Civil War sesquicentennial, take a broader view, featuring objects of Civil War military history alongside objects that document slavery, women's history, and politics. *The Civil War in 50 Objects* by Harold Holzer explores the collections of the New York Historical Society, while *Smithsonian Civil War: Inside the National Collection*, edited by Neil Kagan and Stephen G. Hyslop, examines the collections of the various Smithsonian institutions.[12]

Although *Exploring the American Civil War through 50 Historic Treasures* continues the focus of these two texts by examining a wide variety of objects that help tell the military, social, religious, political, and gender history of the war, it also charts a different course. First, in this book, objects are broadly defined. The chapters that follow feature historic objects, documents, and photographs; political and literary works; artworks; and landscapes. Care was also taken to balance familiar objects with lesser-known artifacts by selecting treasures from a variety of institutional and private collections rather than focusing on the collections of a single institution. Readers will find objects from large institutions, such as the American Civil War Museum, the New York Public Library, the Library of Congress, and the National Museum of African American History and Culture, as well as treasures from smaller institutions such as the Pearce Civil War Museum, the Texas Heritage Museum, and the New Hampshire Historical Society. The institutions represented here include museums, libraries, and archives. In four instances, permission to include an object or image in this book came directly from the individual artist, photographer, or collector.

ORGANIZATION OF THE BOOK

Exploring the American Civil War through 50 Historic Treasures adopts a broad view of the Civil War. The book begins with the war's origins in the fierce debates about slavery and concludes with recent challenges to Confederate monuments. Discussions of race and gender may be found throughout the text rather than segregated into the sections that discuss slavery, emancipation, and the home front.

The fifty objects selected for this project are organized into ten thematic sections, each comprised of four to six chapters. The first two sections focus on the antebellum and early war period, exploring the expansion of the slave labor economy, the election of Abraham Lincoln, and the unfolding secession crisis. In the next four sections, the emphasis shifts to the wartime period, highlighting objects that reveal the military and home front experience. In the seventh and eighth sections, the objects selected reflect a broader time period, highlighting the symbols and the technology of the Civil War era. The final two sections focus on the process of emancipation and the legacy of the war.

The objects presented here do not appear in strictly chronological order. Those who wish to read the chapters in chronological order are encouraged to consult the timeline of objects available in this book. A Civil War timeline is also included to provide greater context for the objects.

The objects featured in this text represent just a small fraction of the historic treasures related to the Civil War that may be in found in museums, libraries, archives, and other cultural institutions. Moreover, the chapters and the topics presented here reflect *a* story of the Civil War. A different set of objects would tell a different story of the war. I hope the stories presented here will spark a desire to learn more about the Civil War.

The Civil War still matters to our nation, as the current debates about Confederate monuments makes clear. These debates remind us that as a nation we have failed to take the war seriously, particularly when it comes to the "tough stuff" of Civil War history: the war's causes and consequences.[13] It is an opportune time for a book that explores the historic treasures of the American Civil War in ways that engage both the difficult aspects of the war and the ongoing challenge of addressing the war's legacy.

Timeline of Objects

1920
Let Us Have Peace, 1865, oil painting by
Jean-Leon Gerome Ferris, page 99

1938
A Union soldier and a Confederate
soldier shake hands at the 75th
anniversary reunion of the Battle of
Gettysburg, page 262

2019
Stone Mountain, Georgia, page 270

2020
George Floyd mural, page 273

Timeline of the American Civil War, 1860–1865

1860

November

6   Abraham Lincoln is elected sixteenth president of the United States.

December

17   The first secession convention meets in Columbia, South Carolina. The vote to secede passes unanimously.

1861

January

9   Mississippi secedes from the Union.
10   Florida secedes from the Union.
11   Alabama secedes from the Union.
19   Georgia secedes from the Union.
26   Louisiana secedes from the Union.

February

1   Texas secedes from the Union.
8–9   Representatives from the seceded Southern states meet in Montgomery, Alabama, to create a new government.
18   Jefferson Davis is appointed the first president of the Confederate States of America.

March

4   Abraham Lincoln is inaugurated in Washington, DC.

April

12   Southern forces fire on Fort Sumter, South Carolina. The Civil War begins.

15   President Abraham Lincoln issues a public declaration that an insurrection exists. He calls for seventy-five thousand militia to stop the rebellion.

17   Virginia secedes from the Union.

May

3   President Lincoln calls for additional volunteers to serve for three years.

6   Arkansas secedes from the Union.

20   North Carolina secedes from the Union.

23   Voters in Virginia approve the ordinance of secession.

June

8   Tennessee secedes from the Union.

July

21   First Battle of Bull Run (also known as the First Manassas).

August

10   Battle of Wilson's Creek, Missouri.

28–29   Fort Hatteras at Cape Hatteras, North Carolina, falls to Union naval forces, marking the beginning of Union efforts to block Southern ports along the Carolina coast.

October

21   Battle of Ball's Bluff, Virginia.

1862

February

6   Confederates surrender Fort Henry, Tennessee, creating an opportunity for Union forces to gain control of the Tennessee River.

16   The Confederate surrender of Fort Donelson, Tennessee, places the Cumberland River in Union hands.

22   Jefferson Davis is inaugurated as president of the Confederate States of America.

March

7–8   Battle of Pea Ridge, Arkansas.

9   The naval battle between the USS *Monitor* and the CSS *Virginia* (formerly the USS *Merimack*) is fought in Hampton Roads, Virginia.

April

6–7   Battle of Shiloh (also known as Pittsburg Landing)

24–27   Union forces gain control of New Orleans and the mouth of the Mississippi River.

May

31–June 1 Battle of Seven Pines, Richmond, Virginia.

June

25–July 1 The Seven Days' Battles, Richmond, Virginia.

July

1   President Lincoln issues a call for three hundred thousand volunteers to serve for three years.

August

30–31   The Second Battle of Bull Run (or Second Manassas).

September

17   The Battle of Antietam (or Sharpsburg), Maryland.

22   President Lincoln issues the preliminary Emancipation Proclamation.

December

13   Battle of Fredericksburg, Virginia.

1863

January

1   Emancipation Proclamation takes effect.

March

3   Draft begins in the North.

May

1–4   Battle of Chancellorsville, Virginia.

18   Siege of Vicksburg, Mississippi, begins.

June

9   Battle of Brandy Station, Virginia.

9	Gettysburg campaign begins.
14–15	Battle of Second Winchester, Virginia.
28	Gettysburg campaign continues.

July

1–3	The Battle of Gettysburg, Pennsylvania.
4	Vicksburg, Mississippi, surrenders to Union forces under command of General Ulysses S. Grant.
10–11	Union naval and land forces attack Confederate defenses near Charleston, South Carolina. Union forces include the 54th Massachusetts, the first African American regiment to see combat.
13–16	Draft riots break out in New York City and other Northern cities.
14	Gettysburg campaign concludes when the Army of Northern Virginia crosses the Potomac River.
18	Second assault on Battery Wagner, South Carolina. The 54th Massachusetts leads the charge. Their commander, Colonel Robert Gould Shaw, is killed and buried with the dead of his regiment.

August

21	Lawrence, Kansas, is sacked by Confederate and Missouri guerrillas under William Clarke Quantrill.

September

9	Union army occupies Chattanooga, Tennessee. The Siege of Chattanooga begins soon afterward when Confederate forces under Braxton Bragg surround the city. The siege will last through November.
19–20	Battle of Chickamauga, Georgia.

November

19	The Soldiers' National Cemetery at Gettysburg, Pennsylvania, is dedicated. President Lincoln delivers the Gettysburg Address.
23–25	Battle for Chattanooga with the Battle of Lookout Mountain on November 24 and the Battle of Missionary Ridge on November 25.
26–Dec. 1	Mine Run Campaign.
27–Dec. 3	Siege of Knoxville, Tennessee.

December

8	President Lincoln issues his Proclamation of Amnesty and Reconstruction.

1864

February

9   More than one hundred Union prisoners escape from Libby Prison in Richmond, Virginia.

27   Andersonville Prison opens in Georgia.

March

3   General Grant assumes command of all Union armies.

10   The Red River campaign begins.

April

8   Battle of Sabine Crossroads or Mansfield, Louisiana, the first major battle of the Red River Campaign.

9   Battle of Pleasant Hill, Louisiana.

12   Confederate cavalry under the command of Nathan Bedford Forrest capture Fort Pillow, Tennessee, which is defended by African American troops, many of whom were murdered by Forrest's troops after they had surrendered.

May

4–5   Battle of the Wilderness, Virginia. This was the opening battle of the Overland Campaign, also known as the Wilderness Campaign.

7   The Atlanta campaign begins as General William T. Sherman marches south from Tennessee into Georgia.

8–21   Battle of Spotsylvania Court House, Virginia.

11   Battle of Yellow Tavern, Virginia.

14–15 Battle of Resaca, Georgia.

June

1–3   Battle of Cold Harbor, Virginia.

8   President Lincoln is nominated by his party for a second term as president.

15–18 Assault on Petersburg, Virginia.

27   Battle of Kennesaw Mountain, Georgia.

July

9   Battle of Monocacy, Maryland.

17   General John Bell Hood replaces General Joseph Johnston as commander of the Army of Tennessee.

20   Battle of Peachtree Creek, the first major battle around the city of Atlanta, Georgia.

21   Battle of Atlanta.

30   Battle of the Crater, Petersburg, Virginia.

August

5   Battle of Mobile Bay.

18–19   Battles on the Weldon Railroad near Petersburg, Virginia.

25   Battle of Ream's Station.

31–Sept. 1   Battle of Jonesborough, Georgia.

September

1   Fall of Atlanta, Georgia.

19   Third Battle of Winchester, Virginia.

22   Battle of Fisher's Hill, Virginia.

October

19   Battle of Cedar Creek, Virginia.

November

8   President Lincoln is reelected.

16   General William T. Sherman's army begins its "March to the Sea."

30   Battle of Franklin, Tennessee.

December

10   Sherman's Army of Georgia arrives in Savannah, completing his "March to the Sea."

15–16   Battle of Nashville, Tennessee.

1865

February

17   Sherman's army captures Columbia, South Carolina, and parts of the city are destroyed by fire.

March

4   President Lincoln is inaugurated for his second term.

11   Sherman's army occupies Fayetteville, North Carolina.

25   Attack on Fort Stedman, Petersburg, also known as "Lee's last offensive."

April

1   Battle of Five Forks, Virginia.

2   Fall of Petersburg and Richmond, Virginia.

9	Confederate surrender at Appomattox Court House, Virginia. In the parlor of William McLean, General Robert E. Lee signs the document of surrender.
12	Army of Northern Virginia formally surrenders and is disbanded.
14	President Lincoln is assassinated by actor John Wilkes Booth at Ford's Theater in Washington, DC. That same day Union troops reoccupy Fort Sumter, South Carolina.
26	Confederate General Joseph Johnston signs the surrender document for the Confederate Army of Tennessee.

May

4	General Richard Taylor surrenders Confederate forces in the Department of Alabama, Mississippi, and East Louisiana.
10	Confederate president Jefferson Davis is captured near Irwinville, Georgia.
12	Final battle of the Civil War takes place at Palmito Ranch, Texas.
23	Grand Review of the Army of the Potomac in Washington, DC.
24	Grand Review of General Sherman's Army in Washington, DC.

June

2	Civil War ends when General Simon Bolivar Buckner enters into terms for the surrender of the Army of the Trans-Mississippi.
19	Union forces land at Galveston, Texas, with the news that the war had ended and the enslaved were now free.

Introduction

CAUSES

In the decades after the American Revolution, Northern states began to pass laws either abolishing slavery outright or enacting laws to gradually free the enslaved. In the South, states continued their development of a slave-intensive agriculture. As lands were opened to settlement in areas like Alabama and Mississippi, Southerners developed a lucrative domestic trade in slaves, selling thousands of enslaved men, women, and children from the Upper to the Lower South. In the first half of the nineteenth century, slave-grown cotton became the single largest source of value in the American economy. In part I, the selected historic treasures focus on slavery, the slave trade, and the slave labor economy. This part also explores the protests against slavery that began in the eighteenth century and became more aggressive in the nineteenth century.

POLITICS

The expansion of the slave labor economy triggered vigorous debates about slavery, its place in the new territories and states of the West, and its protection in the free states of the North. In the 1840s, as the abolitionist movement and opposition to slavery grew, these debates intensified.

From the beginning, slaveholders' property rights were recognized and protected. The Constitutional Convention of 1787 affirmed the property rights of slaveholders by granting slaveholders the right to retrieve their fugitive slaves from neighboring states. The Fugitive Slave Clause, in Article IV, Section 2 of the U.S. Constitution, made it clear that slavery would be tolerated even in states where it had been made illegal. The Fugitive Slave Law of 1793 clarified the constitutional obligation of slave rendition and established a process for the return of fugitive slaves. It also made slave rendition a federal rather than a state matter. Because of the Fugitive Slave Law, Black inhabitants of free states were vulnerable to kidnapping by slave catchers who claimed them as fugitives for the purpose of selling them south for profit. Northern states, such as Indiana (1824), Connecticut (1828), and Vermont (1840), responded by passing personal liberty laws, emphasizing their right to reject the claims of slaveholders and to protect the inhabitants of their state. Southern states denounced personal liberty laws as unconstitutional.

In 1842, in *Prigg v. Pennsylvania*, the Supreme Court addressed the constitutionality of the Fugitive Slave Law of 1793 and the personal liberty laws passed by Northern states. The Supreme Court upheld the constitutionality of the Fugitive Slave Law; however, it also ruled that it was the responsibility of the federal government, rather than the state, to return fugitive slaves. Northern states exploited this distinction, passing new personal liberty laws forbidding state officials from aiding in slave rendition and barring the use of state prisons and buildings for the imprisonment of fugitives. With few federal officials in place in the North and no federal jails, Southerners found it difficult to successfully retrieve their fugitive slaves. Although fugitive slaves were technically vulnerable to rendition under the Fugitive Slave Law of 1793, Northern state laws that forbid the use of local resources to assist in the capture of fugitive slaves made the law difficult to enforce. Southerners began to demand a stronger Fugitive Slave Law, one that included a provision for an increased federal presence in the North to aid with slave rendition.

Debates about the extension of slavery into the territories furthered tensions between North and South. With the end of the Mexican War, the United States acquired more than one-half million square miles of Mexican territory extending westward from the Rio Grande River to the Pacific Ocean. Pro- and antislavery forces each tried to stake claims for this territory. In 1846 David Wilmot, a Democratic congressman from Pennsylvania, introduced an amendment to an appropriation bill for the war with Mexico seeking a ban on slavery in all territory acquired through the war. The Wilmot Proviso thrust the demand for "free soil" and the curtailment of the "slave power" into the center of American politics. Despite repeated attempts, the amendment never passed.

In 1850, pro-slavery politicians were successful in gaining passage of the Fugitive Slave Act. The act was the most controversial bill in a series of five individual bills that were known collectively as the Compromise of 1850. The war with Mexico, which had ended in 1848, added more than one million square miles of new territory to the United States, increasing the size of the country by almost 68 percent. In 1849 California requested permission to join the Union as a free state. Adding California as a free state threatened to destroy the tenuous political balance between slave and free states that had existed since the Missouri Compromise of 1820. The bitter debates over that earlier compromise had led to the admission of Missouri as a slave state and Maine as a free state; it also excluded slavery from the Louisiana Purchase lands north of latitude 36°30'. After the Mexican War, Southern slaveholders insisted on their right to take their slave property anywhere in the new territories, while Northerners insisted just as urgently that slavery should not be allowed to spread beyond the states where it existed. After months of debate, Congress passed the Compromise of 1850. The compromise admitted California as a free state, provided for slavery to be decided by popular vote in the territories of New Mexico and Utah, prohibited the slave trade (but not slavery) in the District of Columbia, settled a boundary dispute between Texas and New Mexico, and established a stricter Fugitive Slave Law. Of the five acts, the Fugitive Slave Act was the most hated.

The Fugitive Slave Law of 1850 was the most comprehensive statement by the federal government to that time of the rights of slaveholders to reclaim their fugitive slaves. The new law strengthened procedural protections for slaveholders while further stripping away protections for Blacks claimed as slaves. Under the new law, federal commissioners were appointed to determine the status of fugitive slaves. Commissioners received ten dollars for each fugitive returned to slavery and only five dollars for each fugitive freed, creating an incentive for commissioners to rule against any Black claimed as a slave. Alleged fugitives were denied both a jury trial and the right to testify in their own behalf. The Fugitive Slave Law of 1850 also required citizens to assist in the recapture of fugitive slaves and threatened severe penalties for those who rescued or attempted to rescue fugitives: "Any person obstructing the arrest of a fugitive or attempting his or her rescue, or aiding him or her to escape, or harboring and concealing a fugitive, knowing him to be such, shall be subject to a fine of not exceeding one thousand dollars, and be imprisoned not exceeding six months, and shall also forfeit and pay the sum of one thousand dollars for each fugitive so lost." The Fugitive Slave Law of 1850 confirmed that slaveholders' claims would continue to trump Black claims for freedom.[1]

In 1857, Chief Justice Roger B. Taney, in the Supreme Court decision *Dred Scott v. Sandford*, declared the Missouri Compromise (1820) unconstitutional. According to Taney, Congress did not possess the power to legislate the limits of slavery's expansion. Taney also declared that Blacks had no rights before the law that whites were "bound to respect."

The 1850s were a watershed moment for many Northerners, weary of Southern demands for more protection and more territory for slavery. The Fugitive Slave Act, *Dred Scott*, and the Kansas-Nebraska Act of 1854 demonstrated just how fiercely Southerners intended to defend their "peculiar institution" and how vehemently some Northerners would fight a law they believed unjust. Focusing on the political context of the Civil War era, part II begins by examining resistance to the Fugitive Slave Act. The rest of the part examines the presidential campaign and election of Abraham Lincoln, the ensuing secession crisis, and the political efforts of the newly formed Confederate States of America to secure their borders and to identify their international allies.

MILITARY HISTORY

In parts III, IV, and V, the objects highlight the military history of the war. Part III focuses on the battlefield, exploring the Eastern and Western theaters of war, the enlistment of Black soldiers, and the care of the wounded and dead after the fighting ended. Part IV focuses on important military leaders: Ulysses S. Grant, Robert E. Lee, Stonewall Jackson, Benjamin Butler, and Martin Delany. In part V, the focus shifts to the common soldier and his experience of the war. This part opens with two well-known brigades—the Iron Brigade (Union) and Hood's Texas Brigade (Confederate)—before turning to prisoner of war camps, the draft, and the cavalry.

HOME FRONT

The home front is the focus of part VI. Because the home-front experience varied widely depending on geographic location, class, race, and gender, this part adopts a multivocal approach by exploring the many experiences of the home front. The historic treasures in this part document the home front in the North, South, and West, as well as borderlands areas like Missouri and Arkansas.

SYMBOLS AND TECHNOLOGY

Parts VII and VIII explore the symbols and the technology that developed in the Civil War era. In part VII, the first two chapters focus on the visual and literary symbolism of the abolitionist movement while the last two chapters examine the use of flags and songs as symbols of nationalism. Part VIII focuses on the deployment of different forms of technology, including military technology and medical care.

EMANCIPATION

The Civil War resulted in the abolition of slavery. However, abolition was not a war objective for the Union until the second year of the war. This part examines the Northern debate over the war's purpose; the efforts of enslaved men, women, and children to make the abolition of slavery a war aim; the recruitment of Black soldiers; and the passage of the Thirteenth Amendment. Emancipation was not a singular event but instead a process that continued long after the war ended.

LEGACY

Continuing this exploration of the ongoing impact of the war, the final part brings the history of the Civil War into the twenty-first century by examining objects related to the legacy of the war. This part focuses on both the immediate aftermath of the war and the ongoing influence of the war in American society, including depictions of the war in popular culture and recent debates over the removal of Confederate monuments.

Acknowledgments

Growing up in Oregon, the history of the American West rather than the history of the Civil War figured prominently in my coursework and my reading in high school and as a young adult. In my thirties, as a nontraditional undergraduate student at Pacific University, I took my first Civil War history course. Taught by Larry Lipin, the course challenged my assumptions and encouraged me to think more critically about the Civil War and its significance. Later, as a graduate student at the University of Texas at Arlington, I took Stephen Maizlish's Civil War historiography course. The reading load was brutal, especially for someone who held a full-time job in addition to being a part-time graduate student. Still, that course and the books we read remain among my favorites from my doctoral program, perhaps because it was so closely related to my work with the Pearce Civil War and Western Art Museum.

For nearly eight years, I worked at the Pearce Museum, located on the campus of Navarro College in Corsicana, Texas. Serving first as the college and special collections archivist and then as director of the museum, I had an unusual position. During my years at the Pearce Museum, my day generally began with a meeting over coffee with the Pearces. Usually it was Charles, but at times his wife Peggy would join the group. The Pearces' interest in the Civil War era began a decade before I arrived at Navarro. Peggy had read *The Killer Angels*, Michael Shaara's novel about the Battle of Gettysburg, and become infatuated with Union officer Joshua Lawrence Chamberlain. Sometime after this Chuck bought Peggy a letter written by Chamberlain to his wife Fanny from the Battle of Antietam. For several years, Chuck and Peggy built a small but impressive collection of Civil War documents. In the late 1990s, the Pearces gave their collection to Navarro College. By the time I was hired, the collection had grown to three thousand documents and plans were being developed to construct a museum to exhibit the Civil War collection as well as the Pearces' collection of contemporary Western art. At our morning meetings, we reviewed catalogs and other offerings from auction houses and individual dealers, quickly building a collection that within eight years numbered nearly twenty thousand documents and artifacts.

I owe a debt of gratitude to Charles (1919–2008) and Peggy Pearce (1918–2005) and their children Vivian Pearce and Sumner Pearce as well as Darrell Beauchamp, who served as dean of learning resources and special collections at Navarro. The coffee group varied over the years. In addition to Charles, Peggy, and Darrell, the group included Mary Hayes, Amanda Morrison, and Rosalie Meier. Volunteers Holly Brickhouse and her daughter Lee Brickhouse Becher amazed (and continue to amaze) me with their incredible knowledge of the Civil War.

I extend my appreciation to several individuals who helped me identify objects to include in this book. Susannah Ural graciously shared her knowledge of Hood's Texas Brigade and the James Rodgers Loughridge Papers, which are part of the Pearce Civil War Collection. My thanks also to John Versluis, Texas Heritage Museum; Paul Fisher and Benna Vaughan, Texas Collection, Baylor University; Andrea Turner and Beth Farwell, Central Libraries, Baylor University; and Ann Zembala and Christina Lucas, Pearce Civil War Collection.

Curators, archivists, and collections managers at many institutions provided research assistance and photography services. Clayton Crenshaw, former music librarian, Baylor University; Shannon Simpson and Sylvia Smith, Ellis County Museum, Waxahachie, Texas; Michelle Metzger, Dallas Historical Society; Lisa Marine, Wisconsin Historical Society; Terre Heydari, Degolyer Library, Southern Methodist University; Doug Remley, National Museum of African American History and Culture; Patrick Walsh, Texas General Land Office; Meredith McDonough, Alabama Department of Archives and History; Katelyn Allen, Mount Holyoke College Art Museum; Elizabeth Borja and Kate Igoe, National Air and Space Museum; Carolyn Sautter, Gettysburg College; Graham Dozier, Virginia Museum of History and Culture; Dean Hargett, State Historical Society of Missouri; Jennifer Loredo, U.S. Army Heritage and Education Center; Dustin Klein, Southern Museum of Civil War and Locomotive History; and Andrea Hoffman, Department of Veterans Affairs, Wisconsin.

I am grateful to Thomas Breakey and Rutger Breakey. For the second time, they have supported my work by sharing their amazing collection of 24th Michigan materials. I met Andy Thomas while I worked at the Pearce Museum. I am thrilled to include one of his paintings in this book. Mary H. Farmer graciously agreed to let me use her photograph of Stone Mountain. I also extend thanks to my friend Loraine Schmitt for allowing me to use her image of the George Floyd mural in Portland, Oregon.

My appreciation goes out to my editor at Rowman & Littlefield, Charles Harmon, and to editorial assistant Erinn Slanina. I appreciate Charles's guidance and his patience, especially as COVID-19 temporarily delayed my revision schedule. My thanks also go out to Aja Bain, at AASLH, for her guidance.

Portions of this book were written on Friday afternoons during sessions of Baylor University's Women's Faculty Writing Program (WFWP). Started by Baylor English professor Lisa Shaver in 2017, the WFWP brings together women associate professors from across the campus to work on their research and writing. By creating space and time for scholarship, the WFWP helps women work toward promotion to full professor. The program has grown from one group to three. Although group membership has changed over the past three years, I am especially grateful to Lisa Shaver, Beth Allison Barr, Julie deGraffenried, Andrea Turpin, and Lenore Wright. And a special thanks to Kimberly Kellison, who encouraged me to join the group.

Finally, I extend my gratitude to the friends and family who have cheered me on for the past two years. My friends Sarah Canby Jackson and Michael and Alice Mattick deserve special mention. Mike, the book is finally done! The support of my family was critical: David Holcomb, Mark Holcomb, Sara Eckel, Keith and Evona Parsley, and Steven and Debra Holcomb. Of particular note are my daughter and son-in-law Jennifer and Eric Sfetku and my grandchildren Noah and Paige. They never fail to bring joy and balance into my life. I dedicate this book to Noah and Paige. Although their interests run more to the scientific and the artistic than the historic, they share my love of museums.

No one deserves more thanks than my husband Stan Holcomb. He is my greatest supporter. Stan keeps me fed. He keeps me sane. And he keeps me centered. Stan's unwavering, unconditional love sustained me for the past two years as I finished this book. Words can never convey how much his love and faith mean to me.

Part I

CAUSES

From the beginning, North American colonists relied on enslaved labor to produce crops such as tobacco, rice, and indigo. By the end of the seventeenth century, there were nearly thirty thousand enslaved Africans in British North America. By the time of the American Revolution, that number had increased to nearly one-half million, or about one-fifth of the total colonial population. In 1787, after much debate, the Founding Fathers agreed to a compromise that protected all citizens' property interests in slaves and protected the foreign slave trade until 1808.

Resistance to slavery was also present from the beginning. Slave resistance formed the core of what would become an organized movement for the abolition of slavery. Enslaved men and women led shipboard insurrections, organized revolts, and ran away. The violence of enslavement and resistance led some members of the Religious Society of Friends, or the Quakers, to question the slave trade and slavery. By the late eighteenth century, Quakers took the extraordinary step of banning slaveholding by its members, the first denomination to do so. Quakers were also influential in the development of antislavery activism. Beginning with Pennsylvania in 1780, states in New England and the mid-Atlantic region began to pass abolition measures.

Despite resistance to slavery, Black slavery remained deeply entrenched in American society, so much so that antislavery activists were denounced as troublemakers who incited slaves to rebel. In the 1830s, abolitionists were frequently threatened by anti-abolitionist mobs even in Northern states. Southern slaveholders defended slavery against abolitionists' attacks and pointed out the economic benefits of slavery. In the 1850s, Southern defensiveness over slavery took an even more sinister turn when Congressman Preston S. Brooks of South Carolina brutally attacked Massachusetts Senator Charles S. Sumner on the Senate floor. For many Americans, violence in the halls of Congress was evidence of just how far Southerners were willing to go in defense of slavery.

For Sale—"A Day I'll Never Forgit"

Bill of sale for four slaves: twenty-year-old Milly, five-year-old Ann, two-year-old Jack, and eight-month-old Mary. Sold by James and Josiah Huie to Samuel Guy, March 31, 1824.

In March 1824, Samuel Guy, a planter from Iredell County, North Carolina, purchased four slaves: twenty-year-old Milly, five-year-old Ann, two-year-old Jack, and an infant named Mary. The slave traders James and Josiah Huie drew up the bill of sale documenting the transfer of ownership and affirming that the four slaves were "Sound, Sensible and healthy and Slaves for Life." Guy paid $777 for Milly and the three children, an amount that would equal nearly $20,000 today. Although the receipt provides no clue to the relationship between the four slaves, it is probable that Milly was the mother of all three children.[1]

As the property of Samuel Guy, Milly and her children had limited control over their lives. Instead their lives were structured by the work of the plantation and the demands of their owner. In the words of historian Thavolia Glymph, enslaved women like Milly

> mopped [the] floors, dusted [the] mahogany tables, made [the] beds, ironed, wet-nursed, and bathed and powdered their owners. In [the] yard and outbuildings—from kitchens, smokehouses, loom and weaving houses to spring and ice houses, wood sheds, dairies, and chicken houses—enslaved women scoured dishes, made biscuits and pies from scratch, churned butter, turned vegetables cultivated in gardens they worked and freshly-killed chickens into breakfast, supper, and evening meals, and fruits into jams and jellies. They washed damask tablecloths and every piece of clothing their owners wore, raised and fattened the poultry, and fetched wood. They were expected to do these things in silence and reverence, barefooted and ill-clothed.[2]

Milly may have also labored in the field assisting in the cultivation of corn, the primary food staple, and cotton, the major cash crop. The quantity and quality of the food Milly ate, the clothes she wore, the punishments she received, and the quarters where she lived were all determined by Guy.

Between 1810 and 1828, Guy acquired at least twenty slaves, including Milly and her children. Thirteen of these slaves may be identified in extant bills of sale: Silvey (1811); Nancy and her child Serena (1816); Amy and her child Sindy (1817); Esther (1818); Milly, Ann, Jack, and Mary (1824); Dave (1824); Beck (1824); and Timpy (1828). From Guy's probate inventory, we can identify six more slaves who were his property: Tom, Dick, Bob, Jude, Charles, and Beck's unnamed child. A search of North Carolina newspapers for the period reveals one more slave owned by Guy. In 1823, Guy posted a notice in the *Western Carolinian* offering a reward for the capture of his runaway slave

Bill. He offered an additional reward for the identity of the person who helped Bill escape.[3]

Of the thirteen slaves identified in the bills of sale, most were purchased privately from individuals or estates. Two of these sales are noteworthy. In 1818, Guy traveled to Pittsylvania County, Virginia, to purchase twenty-year-old Esther, paying the considerable sum of $500, or nearly $10,000 today, for the young enslaved woman. The circumstances surrounding Esther's purchase are unknown. We do not know, for example, whether Esther was particularly beautiful, or if she possessed highly valuable labor skills, both characteristics that would have influenced her value to her seller and her buyer.[4] As historian Daina Ramey Berry points out, "the market value of individual women var[ied] according to the buyer's desires, year of sale, and location of the market" as well as the buyer's preference for particular physical attributes or labor skills.[5] Guy's purchase of Milly and her children also stands out from his other slave purchases because it is the only known transaction involving slave dealers. James and Josiah Huie were active in the domestic slave trade, offering "a liberal price in cash" for enslaved men, women, and even children in North Carolina to sell in the slave markets of the Lower South.[6]

For the enslaved, the slave auction was a staple of slave life. The traumatic separation of slave families was remembered long after the event, as evidenced by the frequent references to sales, separations, and prices in slave testimonies. For example, Georgia slave Esther Brown, who was "so little when dey bid me off, dey had to hold me up so folkses could see me," remembered clearly the day she and her siblings went to "de block" and were "sold off to diffunt parts of de county, and us never heared from 'em no more."[7] In his autobiography, former Kentucky slave Josiah Henson recalled his first experience with the auction block:

> We were all put at auction and sold to the highest bidder, and scattered over various parts of the country. My brothers and sisters were bid off one by one, while my mother, holding my hand, looked on in an agony of grief, the cause of which I but ill understood at first, but which dawned on my mind, with dreadful clearness, as the sale proceeded. My mother was then separated from me, and put up in her turn. She was bought by a man named Isaac R. . . . and then I was offered to the assembled purchasers. My mother, half distracted with the parting forever from all her children, pushed through the crowd, while the bidding for me was going on, to the spot where R. was standing. She fell at his feet, and clung to his knees, entreating him in tones that a mother only could command,

to buy her *baby* as well as herself, and spare to her one of her little ones at least. Will it, can it be believed that this man, thus appealed to, was capable not merely of turning a deaf ear to her supplication, but of disengaging himself from her with such violent blows and kicks, as to reduce her to the necessity of creeping out of his reach, and mingling the groan of bodily suffering with the sob of a breaking heart?[8]

No. 660.

HASTY S GRIEF

Unattributed full-page illustration by Hammatt Billings for *The Child's Anti-Slavery Book: Containing a Few Words about American Slave Children* (New York: Carlton and Porter, 1859). This illustration originally appeared in *Uncle Tom's Cabin* (The Splendid Edition). Billings drew it to illustrate the heart-rending moment when enslaved mother Hasty is sold away from her son Albert. Heartbroken, Hasty pleads with her master, saying, "O Albert! O, my boy! you's my last baby."

For enslaved men, women, and children, the day they were separated from their family was, in the words of Georgia slave Mary Ferguson, "a day I'll never forgit."[9]

What happened to Milly and her children? The family is mentioned in passing in a letter dated November 29, 1827, written by North Carolina planter Benjamin C. West to Guy. Two years later the children Ann and Jack appear in the historical record a third time as part of Guy's estate. There among the furniture, the bushels of corn, the farm equipment, and the clothing and household goods, executor Rufus Reid listed twelve slaves, including Ann and Jack. Milly and Mary are noticeably absent, leaving us to wonder what became of them.[10]

2

Good Credit, Good Prices, and Good Profits

The Domestic Slave Trade

In this photograph taken by Andrew J. Russell during the Civil War, a Union army guard stands while two other men sit in front of the slave trading firm Price, Birch, and Company. The premises were formerly owned by the slave trading firm Franklin and Armfield. During the war, the Union army used the building to house Confederate prisoners.

In 1828 Isaac Franklin and John Armfield purchased this three-story home to serve as the East Coast headquarters of their slave trading firm. Located at 1315 Duke Street in Alexandria, Virginia, the home had been built for Robert Young, a brigadier general in the District of Columbia militia. Franklin and Armfield constructed on the property a kitchen, a tailor's shop, an infirmary, and a two-story rear wing with grated doors to hold slaves awaiting sale and transfer. The entire property was bounded by high walls of whitewashed brick. The site was strategically located with easy access to the inland plantations where agents purchased their human merchandise, who were then transported to Franklin and Armfield's pen to await shipment either by overland routes or by sea to slave markets in the Deep South.[1]

From this site, Franklin and Armfield built arguably the largest slave trading firm in American history. The two men recognized the enormous profits to be made from the interstate slave trade by purchasing slaves cheaply in Maryland and Virginia and selling them at great profit in the burgeoning markets of the Deep South. At its peak, the firm had agents in almost every important Southern city, buying and selling thousands of slaves annually. Franklin was, as historian Calvin Schermerhorn notes, "the apotheosis of slavery's capitalist." Together Franklin and Armfield "built an expansive domestic interlocking partnership that was vertically organized and fiercely competitive." The firm kept slave jails at both ends of the trade. They owned ships for transporting slaves between Alexandria and New Orleans, Louisiana, and Natchez, Mississippi. Armfield oversaw the business in Alexandria while Franklin handled matters in the South. In New Orleans, Franklin developed connections with the banking community to ease the problem of interstate remittances. In 1832 alone, 5 percent of all commercial credit available through the Second Bank of the United States had been extended to Franklin and Armfield.[2]

The interstate slave trade fed the insatiable demand for enslaved labor in newly opened areas of the Deep South. More and more slaveholders hoped to capitalize on the global demand for cotton, which had increased from no cotton production to speak of in 1790 to making almost two billion pounds by 1860. Slavery was indispensable to the growth of the American economy even in the North, as historian Edward E. Baptist illustrates in a discussion of the first-, second-, and third-order effects of slave-grown cotton. The first-order effect was the cotton crop itself. Cotton sales in 1836 totaled 5 percent of the entire U.S. domestic product. It was the single largest source of value in the American economy. Second-order effects resulted from the goods and services necessary to produce cotton, including items such as financial transactions (that is, slave sales, land sales, and lines of credit) and provisions (that is, pork, corn, and cloth). Third-order effects included the money spent by individuals like textile workers in New England and hog farmers in Illinois whose labor provided the goods slaveholders purchased. The purchases made by these workers and farmers fueled local economies throughout the so-called free labor North. As Baptist concludes, "All told, more than $600 million, or almost half of the economic activity in the United States in 1836, derived directly or indirectly from cotton produced by the million-odd slaves— 6 percent of the total US population—who toiled in labor camps on slavery's frontier."[3]

The slave trade was the most fiercely contested aspect of slavery. Enslaved men, women, and children were stripped of their humanity and categorized as merchandise: "first rate house servants," "likely men," "field wom[e]n large & likely," and "fancy maid[s]," the last offered for sexual exploitation.[4] Franklin and Armfield's success, as well as their location in the District of Columbia, meant they were often the focus of abolitionists' ire. In 1837, Henry B. Stanton denounced Franklin and Armfield before a committee of Massachusetts lawmakers:

> Franklin & Armfield are extensive dealers in human flesh, at the Capital. They have a regular line of "Packets" running from Alexandria to New Orleans, whose chief business is the transportation of slaves. I present their case only as a *specimen* of the trade in the District. Ay, sir, there is a keen competition in this brokerage in human blood. Franklin & Armfield are but one of the many firms, who drive this trade at the seat of the Federal Government.

As visitors to the nation's capital encountered the harsh realities of the slave trade, many began to envision enslaved men, women, and children not as property to be exploited but as people who should be freed.[5]

By 1836, when Franklin and Armfield began to dismantle their business, the two men had amassed great wealth. Franklin, who had invested his earnings in land and slaves, retired to Tennessee. In addition to his Tennessee holdings, Franklin owned several plantations in Louisiana and more than five hundred slaves. Franklin died in 1846. Armfield retired from the slave trade in the 1850s. He too invested his wealth in land. Armfield made large donations to the University of the South before his death in 1871.[6]

Franklin and Armfield agent George Kephart purchased the Duke Street property in 1836. He operated his slave trading firm on the site until he sold out to the slave trading firm of Price, Birch, and Company in 1858. That firm operated until 1861 when Alexandria fell to Union troops. The photograph at the beginning of this chapter shows the property during the Civil War, when the site was used as a prison for Confederate soldiers.

For more than thirty years, 1315 Duke Street bore witness to the worst abuses of slavery as tens of thousands of enslaved men, women, and children moved through the site on a forced migration to the Deep South. Designated a National Historic Landmark in 1978, 1315 Duke Street continues to bear witness to the slave trade. Purchased by the Northern Virginia Urban League in 1996 and the City of Alexandria in 2020, the site houses the Freedom House Museum, a small but powerful museum that documents the story of the domestic slave trade.[7]

Buy for the Sake of the Slave!

Quakers and the Boycott of Slave Labor

Label used by the American Free Produce Association.

This seemingly inconsequential label, measuring six by three inches and made of low-quality rag paper with no watermark, is evidence of an early and consistent form of antislavery activism. The American Free Produce Association (AFPA) organized in 1838 to encourage consumers to purchase goods produced by compensated labor. Made up of primarily Quakers, the AFPA worked to provide consumers with free labor alternatives to slave labor goods such as cotton and sugar. Glue marks and fibers on the back of this label suggest it was attached to a bolt of black cotton. Bearing the iconic image of the kneeling slave, the label reminded consumers why it was important to purchase goods untainted by slave labor.[1]

By the time Quakers helped organize the AFPA, Quakers had been antislavery activists for more than one hundred years. Originating in the political turmoil of the English Civil War in the mid-1600s, the Society of Friends believed individuals, even those who had not been exposed to Christianity, possessed an inner light, or the spirit of God within. The presence of the divine in each individual led Friends to espouse the Golden Rule—"Whatsoever ye would that men should do to you, do ye even so to them." While Quakers' belief in the Golden Rule did not distinguish them from other Christians or even other religious groups, their practice of using the Golden Rule as a fundamental guiding principle did. As a result of this belief, Quakers rejected physical violence and coercion, practices that provided the foundation for Quakers' antislavery testimony.[2]

Quakers questioned whether it was right for Christians to trade in slaves or to own slaves. Some suggested that Quakers should also forgo anything produced by slave labor. Philadelphia Quaker Benjamin Lay was one of the first Quakers to urge his co-religionists to reject slavery. Lay's tactics were as striking as his appearance. Standing just over four feet tall, hunch-backed, and oddly proportioned, Lay dressed in coarse clothes and refused to eat with slaveholders or to be served by slaves. His diet was simple and excluded sugar, which was grown by slaves. At a Quaker meeting in Burlington, New Jersey, Lay splattered Quakers with fake blood to protest slavery. On another occasion, he kidnapped the child of a neighboring slave owner so he might experience the loss slave mothers and fathers experienced.[3]

In the 1750s, the Seven Years' War led many colonial Quakers, including New Jersey Quaker minister John Woolman, to view the political crisis as a moral crisis caused by Friends' continued support of slavery. Citing the Golden Rule, Woolman claimed slavery violated Christian principles of universal brotherhood. He urged Quakers to reject slave labor goods, describing slaves and the proceeds of their labor as "prize goods" that had been seized by force as an act of war. "Prize goods" were contrary to Quaker teachings about violence and coercion. Moreover, Woolman believed that continued reliance on slaves and the products of their labor made Quakers more comfortable with other oppressive economic habits, such as the consumption of fashionable clothing or the relentless pursuit of wealth. Unless Quakers changed their economic habits, they would become separated from God. Woolman, like many American Quaker ministers, traveled in England where he shared his ideas about abstention from slave labor goods with British Quakers.[4]

In 1791, the Quaker practice of abstaining from slave labor goods was transformed into a nationwide boycott in Britain when the Baptist printer William Fox wrote a short pamphlet calling for a boycott of slave-grown sugar. Fox calculated that if just one family abstained from sugar, that family could save the life of one slave in the West Indies. Although the boycott attracted support from more than four hundred thousand British consumers, it failed to bring about the abolition of the slave trade or slavery. Britons staged a similar protest in the 1820s.

The boycott of slave labor goods did not gain much momentum in the United States until the 1820s when Quaker abolitionists organized free produce associations in cities such as Philadelphia, Pennsylvania; Wilmington, Delaware; and Salem, Ohio. Urging abstinence from slave labor goods and the substitution of free labor goods, these groups used their collective power to locate and to procure for interested consumers cotton, sugar, and other goods produced by compensated labor.

In 1837, the Clarkson Anti-Slavery Society (Pennsylvania) sent out a call for abolitionists to join in a general convention of men and women committed to abstinence from the products of slave labor. The Requited Labor Convention met in May 1838 at the newly constructed Pennsylvania Hall. Although the convention was disrupted by the destruction of the hall by anti-abolitionist mobs, the group gathered that fall to organize the American Free Produce Association.

From the beginning, the AFPA focused on both the moral and the economic aspects of the boycott of slave labor goods. The AFPA issued *An Address to Abolitionists* laying out the moral foundation of the free produce movement. By purchasing slave labor goods, the consumer sanctioned slavery and withheld a "very important testimony against slavery as a sin." The *Address* reminded supporters of the importance of moral consistency.

Membership in the AFPA peaked in 1839 and began a steady decline in the 1840s. There were several reasons for the organization's decline. Internal divisions over antislavery activism and external opposition from anti-abolitionist mobs weakened Quakers' support of the free produce and antislavery movements. Many non-Quaker abolitionists found it too difficult and too time consuming to locate free labor goods. Instead they believed they should focus on other more effective abolitionist strategies rather than wasting their time worrying about yards of cotton and pounds of sugar. Unitarian minister Samuel J. May summed up the view of many abolitionists when he compared the use of free produce as the principal weapon against slavery to "bailing the Atlantic with a spoon."[5]

In 1845, Quakers George W. Taylor, Abraham Pennock, and Samuel Rhoads organized the Free Produce Association of Friends of Philadelphia Yearly Meeting. Similar groups were organized among Quakers in New York (1845), Ohio (1846), and New England (1848). Taylor also opened a free labor store in Philadelphia. For the next twenty years, Taylor maintained an extensive correspondence with suppliers and supporters throughout the United States, including Ohio, Indiana, and Texas, as well as the Caribbean and England. In the 1850s, he opened a cotton mill in Chester County, Pennsylvania, and sent agents into the South to locate free labor cotton.[6]

In the collection of the Friends Historical Association there is a child-sized pinafore. It looks like an ordinary garment, most likely meant to be worn over a young girl's dress. A closer look reveals that it bears its original tag identifying the fabric as "free labour cotton." Although the garment's full provenance is unclear, it (or at least the cloth from which it is made) may well have been purchased in Taylor's free labor store, perhaps from a bolt of cloth bearing an American Free Produce Association label.[7]

The boycott of slave labor goods, such as cotton and sugar, did not result in a widespread consumer movement against slavery in the United States. At the height of its popularity, the American boycott attracted five to six thousand individuals, while free produce societies attracted about fifteen hundred members. Although consumer protests did not force slave labor goods from the antebellum marketplace, consumer activism did make explicit the connection between enslaved labor and consumer goods. Labels such as this one from the American Free Produce Association reminded consumers to buy for the sake of the slave.[8]

Striking a Blow for Freedom

Black Activism and the Abolitionist Movement

Appeal to the Coloured Citizens of the World by David Walker.
SOURCE: THE LIBRARY COMPANY OF PHILADELPHIA

D avid Walker's *Appeal to the Coloured Citizens of the World*, published in
1829, marked a significant shift in Black activism. His was the first abolitionist pamphlet of the second wave of abolitionism. Walker's *Appeal* "was not
the lone voice of black abolitionism," historian Manisha Sinha notes; rather it
was "its most effective statement." Walker called the fight against slavery and
for Black rights a "holy cause." Cataloging the political and civil rights denied
to free Blacks, he called for Blacks to resist slavery by whatever means necessary, including violence. Published in three editions between 1829 and 1831,
Walker's *Appeal* influenced white and Black activists, including William Lloyd
Garrison, Maria Stewart, and Henry Highland Garnet.[1]

Black resistance to enslavement took many forms, none more frightening
to slaveholders than armed resistance. For example, in 1721, an unnamed
African woman on board the English slaver *Robert* instigated a shipboard
rebellion killing three sailors before being subdued by the rest of the crew.
The successful slave rebellion in Haiti in the 1790s and subsequent uprisings
in places like Barbados (1816), Demerara (1823), and Virginia (1831) were
evidence of ongoing Black resistance to enslavement. Even when slaveholders were successful in putting down conspiracies such as Gabriel's (1800) and
Denmark Vesey's (1822), slaveholders worried about abolitionist agitation.

However, Black activism was not limited to armed resistance. In the eighteenth century, Black Americans filed freedom suits and submitted petitions,
using the legal system to gain their freedom. Quaker activists like Anthony
Benezet and Warner Mifflin assisted slaves in their quest for freedom.

In the late eighteenth century, the growth of free Black communities in the
North contributed to the rise of Black institutions and Black print culture.
Organizing independent churches, Masonic lodges, insurance organizations,
and mutual aid societies, Black Americans focused on community building
and racial uplift. The rise of religious egalitarianism and evangelical Christianity in this period provided the foundation for an antiracist construction of
Christianity, which Black Americans used to challenge enslavement and racism. Early Black texts supported these efforts by expressing for the first time
a corporate consciousness. These so-called Black Founders shaped civil rights
activism well into the nineteenth century.

Nineteenth-century Black activism built on this foundation and refined
its arguments in the fight against colonization in the 1810s and 1820s after
the organization of the American Colonization Society (ACS). The ACS
promoted African colonization for freed slaves and free Blacks claiming
slaveholders would be encouraged to free their slaves if they were relocated to

Africa. In addition to ending slavery, colonization would resolve racial problems and provide racial uplift. Many abolitionists, including Walker, believed
colonization was anti-Black rather than antislavery.[2]

Walker was born in Wilmington, North Carolina, in 1796 or 1797 to a free
Black woman and an enslaved father. Free as a result of his mother's status,
Walker traveled throughout the South where he witnessed firsthand the horrors of slavery and the harsh consequences of slave resistance. In Charleston,
South Carolina, he observed the discovery and the violent suppression of the
slave insurrection conspiracy led by free Black carpenter Denmark Vesey.
Afterward, Walker moved to Boston where he opened a secondhand clothing
store. He learned to read and write and became a leader in the Black community, joining the Massachusetts General Colored Association, an organization
devoted to "racial betterment and slave abolition." Walker also began writing
for *Freedom's Journal*, the first African American newspaper in the United
States. *Freedom's Journal* became the voice of Black protest.[3]

By 1829, Walker had grown impatient with the gradualist approach of the
antislavery movement. In his *Appeal*, Walker urged Black resistance to slavery,
criticized the American Republic and the colonization movement, and challenged the racist, anti-Christian views of Americans. Walker described the
oppressed condition of America's Black population, claiming African Americans were "the most wretched, degraded, and abject set of beings that ever
lived since the world began." Walker believed education, religion, and political
unity were the keys to African American liberation. Free Black people had a
responsibility to the enslaved to *go to work and enlighten your brethren*." According to Sinha, Walker's *Appeal* was "a powerful indictment of American
slaveholding republicanism and a revolutionary call for abolition."[4]

Walker's familiarity with Black communication networks helped him distribute his pamphlet throughout the South despite white resistance. He sewed
copies of the pamphlet into the linings of the clothing that he sold to sympathetic sailors who were sailing for Southern ports. On December 29, 1829,
police in Savannah, Georgia, seized sixty copies of the *Appeal* that Walker
had sent to Reverend Henry Cunningham. Another twenty copies were inter-
cepted in Atlanta, Georgia, the following month. And in August 1830, copies
were found in Wilmington, North Carolina. In response, Southern whites
placed a bounty on Walker's head. Additionally, Southern states passed more
restrictive laws, limiting slave literacy and restricting the dissemination of
antislavery literature. Southern whites' reaction to Walker's *Appeal* reflected
their fears that slave literacy was dangerous and that Black preachers posed

a real threat. White Southerners' response also reflected their fear of slave insurrection. Nine years after Vesey's failed insurrection and just two years after the publication of Walker's *Appeal*, Nat Turner led the bloodiest slave revolt in antebellum America, resulting in the deaths of nearly sixty whites in Southampton County, Virginia.

The response to Walker's *Appeal* and his mysterious, premature death in 1830 led some to speculate he had been poisoned. However, official records show he died of tuberculosis.[5]

Walker was an early, important voice in the Black abolitionist movement. In the decades before the Civil War, Black abolitionists established formal and informal networks to resist enslavement and racism. Nineteenth-century Black activists, including William Wells Brown, Frederick Douglass, Henry Highland Garnet, James W. C. Pennington, David Ruggles, Sojourner Truth, Harriet Tubman, and Samuel Ringgold Ward (to name just a few), propelled antislavery from the margins to the center of the political debate about slavery. Black activism also pushed many white abolitionists to embrace equal rights and full citizenship for Black Americans.

5

"I *will be* harsh as truth, and as uncompromising as justice"

The Antebellum Antislavery Movement

Destruction by Fire of Pennsylvania Hall,
On the night of the 17th May, 1838

Destruction by Fire of Pennsylvania Hall. On the Night of May 17, 1838. Hand-colored lithograph by J. C. Wild.

On May 14, 1838, abolitionists celebrated the grand opening of Pennsylvania Hall, located at the corner of 6th and Haines Streets in Philadelphia. The women of the Philadelphia Female Anti-Slavery Society had been instrumental in raising forty thousand dollars for construction of the building. Standing sixty-two feet wide, one hundred feet deep, and forty-two feet high, Pennsylvania Hall housed the offices of the eastern district of the Pennsylvania Anti-Slavery Society (not to be confused with the Pennsylvania Abolition Society), a free produce store, an antislavery reading room, the offices of the antislavery newspaper the *Pennsylvania Freeman*, several meeting rooms, and a lecture hall. Above the stage in the hall was the motto "Virtue, Liberty, and Independence."[1]

To celebrate the building's grand opening, abolitionists planned a series of meetings, sending invitations to men and women regardless of race. Outside the hall, on the day of the dedication, anti-abolitionists began to gather. Placards opposing the abolitionists were distributed. By the third day, May 17, a growing group of men began to gather around the building "prowling about the doors, examining the gas-pipes, and talking in an 'incendiary' manner to groups which they collected around them in the street." That evening the mob smashed windows and broke into the meeting. To protect the more vulnerable members of their meeting, the abolitionists left the hall in racially mixed groups. The violence continued for several days, destroying other nearby property, including the Colored Orphans' Asylum.[2]

The image at the start of this chapter illustrates the destruction of Pennsylvania Hall. Several key details are noteworthy. On the left side of the image, firefighters spray nearby buildings with water to prevent the fire from spreading but do not attempt to extinguish the blaze consuming Pennsylvania Hall. Notice, too, how calm the crowd appears. Witnesses estimated the crowd to be between ten and fifteen thousand people, but only two to three hundred people participated in the attack on the hall. Once the fire began, most spectators stood back to watch, most of them blocking the fire companies and keeping them from putting out the fire.

The Boston abolitionist William Lloyd Garrison later described the conflagration as a "legal lynching." Indeed, the destruction of Pennsylvania Hall happened in a period of increasing anti-abolitionist and racially motivated mob violence. For example, in 1836, in St. Louis, Missouri, Francis McIntosh, "an African American of light complexion due to mixed ancestry was beaten and then slowly burned to death in front of a large crowd of onlookers." Elijah Lovejoy, a white abolitionist newspaper editor from Alton, Illinois, reported the lynching of McIntosh in his newspaper. In 1837, Lovejoy fell victim to anti-abolitionist violence. Lovejoy and his supporters gathered in his office to protect his printing press from anti-abolitionist mobs. When the mobs set the building on fire, Lovejoy ran from the building. He was shot and killed.[3]

In the 1830s, Black and white abolitionists launched a more aggressive, more radical antislavery movement. The publication of David Walker's *Appeal*, which is discussed in the previous chapter; the launch of Garrison's abolitionist newspaper *The Liberator*; and the antislavery activism of Blacks and women led many Americans to denounce abolitionists as troublemakers. Certainly the abolitionism of the 1830s marked a significant shift from the antislavery movement of the eighteenth century when elite white men formed societies in opposition to the slave trade and slavery. The Pennsylvania Abolition Society (PAS), the nation's first and best-known antislavery organization, was first organized in 1775. Focusing on legal and political action, the PAS recruited prominent men like John Jay and Benjamin Franklin to enhance the society's credibility. PAS members focused on legal and political action, defending free Blacks in court and drafting legislative petitions. The men who participated in the PAS advocated gradual emancipation because they believed gradualism to be the most judicious and moral course of action. Gradual emancipation respected the property rights of slaveholders and allowed time to prepare the enslaved for freedom.

In 1780, the PAS had helped secure Pennsylvania's gradual abolition law, the first in the nation. Although the Pennsylvania legislation helped many enslaved people become emancipated, the legislation failed to help many others, including York, who was the human property of the Kinzer family of Lancaster County, Pennsylvania. York was born in 1776, four years before the passage of the gradual abolition law, and as a result, the law did not apply to him. Instead he was passed from generation to generation of the Kinzer family. At the time of his death in 1845 at the age of sixty-nine, York was still enslaved, the human property of William Penn Kinzer.[4]

Radical abolitionists like Garrison condemned such gradualist measures, demanding the immediate abolition of slavery and calling for racial equality. In July 1829, in a speech at Boston's Park Street Church, Garrison rewrote the Declaration of Independence to include African Americans. Two years later, with the publication of the first issue of *The Liberator*, Garrison declared: "I *will be* harsh as truth, and as uncompromising as justice. On this subject [slavery] I do not wish to think, or speak, or write with moderation." Garrison promised, "I am in earnest,—I will not equivocate,—I will not excuse,—I will not retreat a single inch—AND I WILL BE HEARD." In language that echoed the religious revivals of the 1820s, Garrison denounced slavery as a sin against God and censured slaveholders as sinners. Garrison believed the abolition of slavery had to happen without delay.[5]

To coordinate the work of antislavery, abolitionists formed organizations. In 1832, Garrison helped found the New England Anti-Slavery Society, the first of many antislavery organizations to take an uncompromising stand against slavery. A year later, abolitionists from nine states gathered in Philadelphia to organize the American Anti-Slavery Society. Among the delegates to the founding convention were the well-known Black abolitionists Robert Purvis and James McCrummell. A committee of delegates approved a Declaration of Sentiments that affirmed their break with gradualist measures and their commitment to the immediate abolition of slavery and racial equality.

In the days following the AASS convention, Philadelphia Quaker Lucretia Mott called on McCrummell to assist in organizing the interracial Philadelphia Female Anti-Slavery Society. At its peak, the PFASS had more than two hundred members. It was one of dozens of female antislavery societies formed in this period, including the Salem (Massachusetts) Female Anti-Slavery Society (1832) and the Boston Female Anti-Slavery Society (1833). Female antislavery organizations challenged gender norms by encouraging women to join in the public debate about slavery. The interracial character of some organizations, like the PFASS, invoked fears of racial "amalgamation" (mixing) and social equality. The PFASS was among the more radical of the women's groups.[6]

In addition to organizing associations and recruiting women into the movement, abolitionists organized postal campaigns and circulated petitions. The postal campaign targeted ministers, politicians, and newspaper editors throughout the South. Flooding the South with thousands of pieces of abolitionist literature, reformers believed they could convince slaveholders to voluntarily end slavery. Instead abolitionists' postal campaign sparked a wave of mob violence throughout the North and the South. In 1835, angry residents of Charleston, South Carolina, broke into the post office and confiscated abolitionist literature that they later burned along with an effigy of Garrison. That fall, in Boston, a mob looking for British abolitionist George Thompson instead found Garrison and dragged him through the streets.

The abolitionists' antislavery petition campaign, also launched in 1835, encouraged women to go door to door gathering signatures. No congressional action was taken on these petitions, however; they were automatically tabled because of the "gag rule." Implemented in 1836, the "gag rule" was passed in response to increasing anti-abolitionist violence. Northern and Southern politicians hoped to calm sectional hostilities by refusing to debate any anti-slavery petition. Abolitionists persisted, sending more than 415,000 petitions to Congress by May 1838. The "gag rule" accelerated the growing sectionalism of American politics and did much to politicize the abolitionist movement.

Thus by 1838 many Americans believed abolitionists were a disruptive minority determined to destroy the social order. Increasingly, churches and Quaker meetinghouses refused to lend their facilities for abolitionist meetings. With the opening of Pennsylvania Hall, abolitionists believed they would have a space "wherein liberty and equality of civil rights can be freely discussed, and the evils of slavery fearlessly portrayed."

The fire at Pennsylvania Hall left only smoldering ruins. The Hall's board of directors filed suit, seeking damages. City officials claimed the abolitionists had incited the violence by holding a racially mixed meeting. Finally, in 1841, the Pennsylvania Supreme Court granted the board a nominal financial award.

The destruction of Pennsylvania Hall did not end the abolitionist movement. Instead abolitionists used the hall's destruction to rally more people to the cause. Two days after escaping from Philadelphia, Garrison observed, "Awful as is this occurrence in Philadelphia, it will do incalculable good to our cause." Pennsylvania Hall "will rise like a Phoenix out of its ashes," another abolitionist observed. Abolitionists described the burning of Pennsylvania Hall as an attack on free speech, demonstrating to indifferent Americans how closely their own freedom was linked to the freedom of others.[7]

6

Bleeding Kansas,
Bleeding Sumner

Challenges to the Expansion
of Slavery in the West

Southern Chivalry—Argument versus Club's. Lithograph by John L. Magee.
SOURCE: BOSTON ATHENAEUM.

John L. Magee's dramatic lithograph *Southern Chivalry—Argument versus Club's* depicts one of the most violent episodes in the political fight over slavery. On Thursday, May 22, 1856, Congressman Preston S. Brooks of South

Carolina entered the nearly empty chamber of the U.S. Senate and approached the desk of Senator Charles Sumner of Massachusetts. Two days earlier, in the Senate, Sumner had challenged the "Slave oligarchy" in his "Crime against Kansas" speech. In his speech Sumner had taken personal and political aim at Andrew Butler, a senator from South Carolina and the uncle of Brooks. Declaring Sumner's speech a libel against the state of South Carolina and a slander against Butler, Brooks beat Sumner over the head with his gold-headed cane until Sumner collapsed bleeding and insensible on the Senate floor.[1]

At least eight prints were created, depicting the event, all appearing in the North and all supporting Sumner. Magee's lithograph is the best-known representation of the event. In the foreground of the print, Brooks is looming over Sumner, who lies prone and bleeding from the head, grasping a pen in one hand and "Kansas" papers in the other. Laurence Keitt, who was a friend of Brooks, is seen in the background waving a cane at a legislator. Other members of Congress are present in the background, some laughing and some scowling. The use of the word "chivalry" in the title is a sarcastic expression of the widely held Northern view that the manners and courtliness of the Southern gentleman were a hypocrisy. In Magee's print "reason [is] overcome by violent impulse, gentility overcome by ruffianism, and indeed, all civilized values overwhelmed by brute barbarism."[2]

The Thirty-Fourth Congress, which was seated in December 1855, has been described as the most violent Congress in U.S. history. Sectional tensions ran high as the session began. Five years earlier, the passage of the Compromise of 1850, including the controversial Fugitive Slave Law, had injected even more forcefully the issue of slavery into the everyday lives of many Northerners. The Kansas-Nebraska Act, introduced in 1854, further divided the United States into two opposing factions over the issue of slavery. Brooks's attack on Sumner in the hallowed hall of the Capitol was, as one scholar notes, "a virtual sloshing of kerosene into already dangerously overheated furnaces of partisan rancor on the issue" of slavery. For many Northern opponents of slavery, the caning of Sumner confirmed beyond a doubt the presence of a "slave power" conspiracy.[3]

The rancor over the Kansas-Nebraska Act began as soon as it was introduced by Stephen Douglas of Illinois in January 1854. Douglas introduced the bill to organize the territory of Nebraska in hopes of securing a northern route for the transcontinental railroad. Southern senators objected to the bill. Under the terms of the Missouri Compromise of 1820, Nebraska would enter as a free state. In 1819, when Missouri applied for statehood, Northern politicians protested. The heated debate about the place of slavery in the nation's westward expansion led to the passage of the Compromise in 1820, allowing Missouri to be admitted as a slave state and Maine, formerly part of Massachusetts, as a free state, thus maintaining a delicate political balance between Northern and Southern interests. The compromise also prohibited slavery in Louisiana Purchase lands north of 36°30'. To appease his Southern critics, Douglas proposed repealing the Missouri Compromise and replacing it with the principle of popular sovereignty, leaving the question of whether states would be slave or free to the settlers of the state. The act also proposed the creation of two territories: Kansas and Nebraska. Antislavery politicians, like Sumner, attacked Douglas and his supporters for breaking a sacred compact by repealing the Missouri Compromise.

The opening of the Kansas and Nebraska territories under the principle of popular sovereignty provoked a protracted political crisis in both Kansas and the nation. By 1855, two rival governments were established in Kansas, one backed by pro-slavery Missourians and the other backed by antislavery groups. Political polarization and civil strife increased as each side brought in settlers hoping to sway the vote. On May 21, 1856, one day after Sumner concluded his speech in the Senate, events in Kansas turned violent when pro-slavery Missourians sacked the town of Lawrence, a free state stronghold. In response, abolitionist John Brown, along with his four sons, orchestrated the murder of five pro-slavery settlers along Pottawatomie Creek. Brown justified his action as obedience to the will of a just God. He became a hero in the eyes of Northern extremists. The political firestorm in Kansas became so violent that Horace Greeley, editor of the *New York-Tribune*, is said to have coined the term "Bleeding Kansas."

Sumner's speech, "Crime against Kansas," took five hours over May 19 and 20, 1856, and filled 112 printed pages. Before he gave his speech, Sumner had the speech printed and prepared for mass mailing, intending to reach a broad national audience and not just his fellow senators. Sumner denounced the brutal "rape of Kansas" by pro-slavery forces. He condemned Southern "plantation manners" and his Southern colleagues' habit of "trampling" congressional rules "under foot." He outlined remedies for the Kansas problem, demanding that the state be admitted as a free state. Sumner took aim at three senators: Douglas, Butler, and James Mason (of Virginia). Of Butler, Sumner said,

> The Senator from South Carolina has read many books of chivalry, and believes himself a chivalrous knight, with sentiments of honor and courage. Of course,

he has chosen a mistress to whom he has made his vows, and who, though ugly to others, is always lovely to him; though polluted in the sight of the world, is chaste in his sight;—I mean the harlot, Slavery.

Southern politicians were outraged by Sumner's speech. Douglas was heard to mutter, "That damn fool will get himself killed by some other damn fool." Two days after Sumner's speech, Brooks entered the Senate chamber and beat Sumner over the head, inflicting more than a dozen blows before his cane shattered. Keitt, also a representative from South Carolina, prevented intervention by the onlookers. A bloodied and barely conscious Sumner was carried from the chamber.[4]

The Northern press interpreted the event as an attack on free speech and as evidence of a Southern conspiracy to expand the slaveholding empire by any means, including violence and murder. "No reasonable man should doubt that the Slave power have unalterably determined to extend the area of their now merely *local* institution [slavery]; and if possible to render it *National*. The bowie-knife, the pistol and the bludgeon . . . to be used in effecting the result," concluded James Watson Webb, editor of the *New York Courier and Enquirer*. In the moments after the attack, Sumner told New York senator William Seward he hoped the attack would further the antislavery cause. Although Sumner was not universally admired in the North, there was close to universal disapprobation of the attack on him.[5]

The House of Representatives voted against expelling Brooks. Nonetheless, Brooks resigned his office and returned home. However, Brooks was reelected to office later that same year. Sumner survived the attack, but his recovery took over three years. By the time he returned to the Senate in 1859, Brooks and Butler had both died.[6]

For many, the caning of Sumner on the Senate floor represented how far Southerners were willing to go to protect their "peculiar institution." The incident galvanized Northerners in opposition to the slave interest, further escalating sectional tensions.

Part II

POLITICS

As slavery deepened sectional tensions between the North and the South, politicians worked out a series of compromises meant to maintain a balance of power between the nonslaveholding and the slaveholding states. However, by the 1840s, many Northerners had grown weary of Southern demands. The passage of the Fugitive Slave Act in 1850 was a watershed moment, demonstrating how fiercely Southerners intended to defend their peculiar institution and how vehemently some Northerners would fight a law they believed unjust. The political battles about the protection of slave property made slavery the major issue of the election of 1860. After Lincoln was elected president, eleven states seceded from the Union. As Lincoln noted in 1865, in his second inaugural address, "One eighth of the whole population were colored slaves. Not distributed generally over the Union, but localized in the Southern part of it. These slaves constituted a peculiar and powerful interest. All knew that this interest was, somehow, the cause of the war." The protection of slavery informed the choices made by the Confederate government, while the protection of the Union preoccupied Lincoln for the first two years of the war.

"A Man Kidnapped!"

Northern Resistance to the
Fugitive Slave Act of 1850

Broadside publicizing the arrest of the fugitive slave Anthony
Burns, who escaped from Richmond, Virginia, and made his way
to Boston, Massachusetts, where, in May 1854, he was arrested.

On May 26, 1854, the Boston Vigilance Committee (BVC) held a public meeting at Faneuil Hall to protest the arrest of Anthony Burns, a twenty-three-year-old fugitive slave from Virginia. To publicize the meeting, as well as the arrest of Burns, the members of the BVC had this broadside printed and distributed. Broadsides were single sheets of paper, printed on one side only, that could be produced quickly and crudely in larger numbers to inform the public about important events. In Boston in the 1850s, Black and white abolitionists used broadsides such as this one to organize resistance to the Fugitive Slave Law of 1850.[1]

The meeting brought out a large crowd—an estimated five thousand men and women—packing the hall "far beyond the capacity of the building." Abolitionists Wendell Phillips and Theodore Parker addressed the crowd. The meeting adjourned abruptly when someone in the balcony announced that "a mob of negroes" had gathered outside the courthouse where Burns was jailed. A riotous crowd soon attempted to storm the courthouse, but it was stopped by the men defending the building. In the melee, one defender, James Batchelder, was shot and killed. At a hearing the next day, Burns was ordered returned to Virginia. Thousands of Bostonians watched as Burns was marched under heavy guard to the wharf where he was placed on a ship bound for Virginia. It was a rare failure for Bostonians.

Boston had a history as a haven for fugitive slaves. No slave had ever been returned to slavery from Boston under the Fugitive Slave Law of 1793. At great personal risk, Black and white Bostonians protected the fugitives in their midst. In 1827, Black Bostonians John and Sophia Robinson were convicted of withholding five-year-old Elizabeth from her white guardian. The couple received four months in jail for their actions. Officials were unable to recover Elizabeth, who disappeared into the African American community. Bostonians established their first vigilance committee in 1841. The following year, after the arrest of George Latimer, a fugitive slave from Virginia, Boston's abolitionist citizens launched a protest campaign and began publishing the first fugitive slave abolitionist newspaper, *Latimer Journal and North Star*. The paper featured an interview with Latimer who outlined his master's abuses. In 1848, when William and Ellen Craft arrived in Boston, after staging their dramatic escape from slavery in Georgia, the African American community in Boston provided the couple refuge.[2]

In 1850, as President Millard Fillmore prepared to sign the Fugitive Slave Act into law, Northerners in cities like Boston began organizing to oppose the new law. On October 14, 1850, several thousand Bostonians met in Faneuil

Hall vowing to stand with the fugitives who lived in Boston. If the "law be put into operation," Black abolitionist Frederick Douglass warned, "the streets of Boston . . . would be running with blood."[3]

To better coordinate their efforts, Black and white abolitionists reorganized the Boston Vigilance Committee with two hundred members, including Black abolitionists, Garrisonians, political abolitionists, and working-class men. The members of the BVC used a variety of legal and extralegal maneuvers to thwart slave catchers. When slave catchers arrived in Boston in 1850 searching for the Crafts, opponents of the new law posted handbills and broadsides throughout the city warning residents of the presence of slave catchers in Boston.[4] The slave catchers were so harassed, they eventually gave up and left Boston emptyhanded. The Crafts fled first to Canada and then to Great Britain. In 1851, when Shadrach Minkins, a fugitive from Norfolk, Virginia, was arrested in Boston, hundreds of protestors gathered outside the courthouse. A group of twenty to thirty Blacks stormed the courthouse, seizing Minkins and carrying him off to Beacon Hill where much of Boston's African American community lived. Minkins was eventually sent on to Canada.

Opponents of the Fugitive Slave Law in other Northern cities staged similar protests and rescues. In Christiana, Pennsylvania, in 1851, a riot broke out when slave catchers attempted to retrieve the fugitive slaves of Edward Gorsuch. Thirty-eight men were arrested for their role in aiding the fugitive slaves' escape. When the first trial ended in an acquittal, authorities dropped the charges against the other thirty-seven defendants. Later that year, in Syracuse, New York, Marshal Henry Allen arrested fugitive slave William Henry, also known as Jerry. An interracial crowd of armed men overwhelmed the marshals who were guarding Jerry. After his rescue, Jerry escaped to Canada. The event was later immortalized in an annual "Jerry Rescue" celebration.

The rendition of Anthony Burns, happening as it did amid debates about the Kansas-Nebraska bill, had a profound impact on city and state politics, the abolitionist movement, and the future of slavery in the territories. In Boston, buildings were draped in black and a coffin with the word "Liberty" on it was displayed as Burns was marched through the streets of Boston. Public sentiment had clearly changed. Opponents of the Fugitive Slave Law resolved to continue their resistance to the law. On July 4, 1854, Boston abolitionist William Lloyd Garrison burned a copy of the Constitution, the Fugitive Slave Law, and a copy of the court's decision that had ordered Burns's reenslavement. The Constitution, according to Garrison, was "a Covenant with Death, an Agreement with Hell." Significantly, many who had initially supported the law began to call for its repeal. Resentment of the "slave power" conspiracy continued to grow, with many opponents fusing the question of slavery in the territories with the question of the Fugitive Slave Law in the Northern states: "How clearly in the light of the Fugitive Act, the Nebraska Act, the still more astounding attempt to compel slavery in Kansas, does the slave power declare that the only issue it will accept is the legality of slavery anywhere and everywhere." Envisioned as a compromise measure, the Fugitive Slave Law of 1850 only deepened the sectional divide.[5]

"Honest Old Abe Is Bound to Win"

The Election of 1860

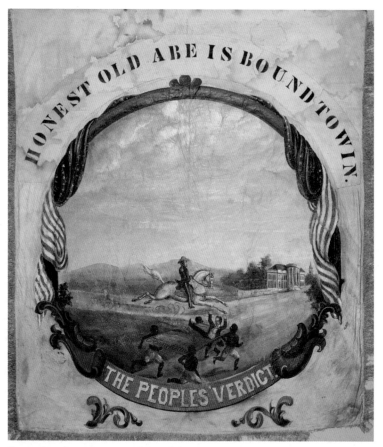

Campaign banner created by Edward L. Curtis for the supporters of Abraham Lincoln.

SOURCE: NEW HAMPSHIRE HISTORICAL SOCIETY.

New Hampshire artist Edward L. Custer created this banner during the 1860 presidential campaign, sometime between May 1860, when Abraham Lincoln received the Republican nomination, and November 1860, when Lincoln was elected president. In February 1860, in response to an invitation from Henry Ward Beecher's Plymouth Church in Brooklyn, New York, Lincoln gave his now-famous Cooper Union speech, setting forth an argument to limit the expansion of slavery. Afterward, in a triumphal tour of New England, including the New Hampshire cities of Concord, Manchester, and Nashua, Lincoln repeated his Cooper Union speech. During the tour, Lincoln was celebrated as the nation's next president or vice president. It is likely Custer heard Lincoln speak during his New England tour. Inspired by the politician from Illinois, Custer later offered his talents to Lincoln's supporters by creating this campaign banner.[1]

In the election of 1860, four men vied for the office of president: Abraham Lincoln (Republican), John C. Breckinridge (Southern Democratic), Stephen Douglas (Northern Democratic), and John Bell (Constitutional Union).

The Democrats met first, convening in Charleston, South Carolina, on April 23, 1860. Even before the convention began there were indications the party might break apart over the issue of slavery. Four months earlier, at the Alabama state convention, delegates resolved to demand a national platform that protected slave property in the territories. At the national convention, the platform committee produced two versions. The first endorsed the "Cincinnati Platform." Adopted at the national convention in 1856 in Cincinnati, Ohio, the "Cincinnati Platform" called on political leaders to adopt popular sovereignty as "the only sound and safe solution" to the slavery question. It also recognized the right of states to form a constitution *with or without* slavery and to be admitted into the Union on an equal basis with other states. The second version endorsed the Alabama platform, claiming Congress had no constitutional right to abolish slavery in the territories and that no "Territorial Legislature" could legally "destroy or impair the right of property in the states by any legislation whatever." Delegates voted to accept the "Cincinnati Platform" by a vote of 165 to 138, prompting about fifty Southern delegates to leave the convention. The remaining delegates attempted to nominate a presidential candidate. After fifty-seven failed ballots, Democrats adjourned, agreeing to reconvene in June in Baltimore, Maryland.

The Constitutional Union Party met next, holding their convention six days after the Democrats had adjourned. Formed in late 1859 and early 1860, the party's defining political ideology was compromise. Sweeping the issue of slavery under the rug, convention delegates claimed to recognize only three "political principles": "The Constitution of the Country, the Union of the States, and the Enforcement of the Laws." The platform was adopted unanimously. On the second ballot, candidate John Bell received enough votes to secure the nomination.

On May 16, the Republicans gathered in Chicago, Illinois. The Republican Party emerged from the discord surrounding the collapse of the Whig Party in the early 1850s. It was a distinctly Northern organization embracing the Wilmot Proviso and standing against the expansion of slavery into the Western territories. In 1856, the Republican Party ran its first presidential candidate, John C. Fremont. Although Fremont lost, the Republicans consolidated their Northern base, picking up strength in the congressional elections of 1858 and electing the party's first Speaker of the House in 1860. Influenced by the events in Charleston and Baltimore, Republicans sought a candidate who could carry the states taken by Fremont in 1856 and add other key Northern states, including Pennsylvania, Illinois, and Indiana. Leading candidates for the Republican nomination were William Seward, Salmon P. Chase, and Abraham Lincoln. Seward and Chase were considered extreme in their antislavery views, while Lincoln was viewed as a moderate. Although Seward was the favorite, delegates were unable to nominate him on the first ballot. Ultimately, Lincoln prevailed, gaining enough votes to secure the nomination on the third ballot.

When the Democrats reconvened in Baltimore in June, all Southern states except South Carolina sent delegates. This created a credentials issue because many of these state delegations had withdrawn from the Charleston gathering. After four days of debate, the decision was made not to seat several Southern delegations. Several other Southern delegations withdrew from the convention in protest, leading to an irreparable division in the party. The remaining delegates nominated Illinois senator Stephen Douglas, author of the Kansas-Nebraska Act and supporter of popular sovereignty, on the second ballot. Those delegates who left the Baltimore convention held a separate convention. Southern Democrats adopted a platform that included a slave code plank, protecting slavery in the Western territories, and quickly nominated Vice President John C. Breckenridge.[2]

In the election of 1860, as was the customary practice in the nineteenth century, presidential candidates did not personally campaign for office. (In 1860, Douglas was the glaring exception.) Instead the political parties managed the job of seeking votes. Campaign songs, banners (like that painted by

Custer), broadsides, and other print and visual media supported the efforts of the political parties.

Custer may have been inspired by the popular campaign song "Lincoln & Hamlin," published by the prolific music publisher H. De Masan. The song, like Custer's campaign banner, captured the character of the 1860 race for the presidency:

> Come, all ye friends of freedom,
>   And rally in each State,
> For Honest Old Abe Lincoln,
>   The people's candidate!
> With Lincoln as our champion,
>   We'll battle for the Right,
> And beat the foes of Freedom,
>   In next November's fight.
>
> The people want an honest man—
>   They're tired of fools and knaves;
> They're sick of imbecile "J.B.,"[3]
>   That in the White House raves.
> They want a man for President
>   Of firm, unyielding will,
> That is both honest, brave and true,
>   And Old Abe fills that bill!
>
> Old Fogies down at Baltimore[4]
>   In solemn conclave met,
> The "Union-Saving" farce to play,
>   With Bell and Everett.
> But the people, next November,
>   Will put them all to rout,
> And make them long remember
>   That the Fillmore game's "played out."
>
> The Democrats are in a "fix,"
>   No wonder that they shiver;
> For they all feel it in their bones,
>   That they're going up Salt River![5]

With their party split asunder,
   The truth is plain to all,
That though united once they stood,
   Divided, now, they fall!

Oh, Douglas, you can't win this race,
   You'd better clear the way—
Your humbug doctrines won't go down;
   At home you'll have to stay.
The Wide-Awakes are on the march[6]
   O'er all our hills and vales—
Our Giant-Killer's after you,[7]
   With one of those old rails!

And Breckenridge will soon find out
   The people he can't fool:
They've had enough, these last four years,
   Of Democratic rule.
But Lincoln is their favorite,
   And he is bound to win—
When Buck steps out, next Fourth of March,
   Old Abe will then step in!

The composer of this song dismisses each of Lincoln's opponents and celebrates the verdict of the people that "Honest Old Abe Lincoln," the champion of freedom, "is bound to win."[8]

In his campaign banner Custer, unlike the composer of "Lincoln & Hamlin," focused on only one of Lincoln's opponents, Breckinridge. Campaigning on a platform that called for the protection of slave property, the Southern Democratic candidate provided the sharpest contrast to Lincoln. The campaign banner is painted and stenciled on a cotton background and trimmed with silk fringe. It measures nearly four feet square. At the top of the banner, nail holes and ferrous staining (rust) suggest it was meant to be carried aloft on a staff. The central image shows Lincoln galloping toward the White House astride a white horse, clad in full military dress. In his hand, Lincoln clutches a copy of the U.S. Constitution. Running slightly behind Lincoln is Breckinridge, who is carried on a rickety wooden litter labeled "Cincinati [sic] Platform." The central image is framed by the words "Honest Old Abe Is Bound

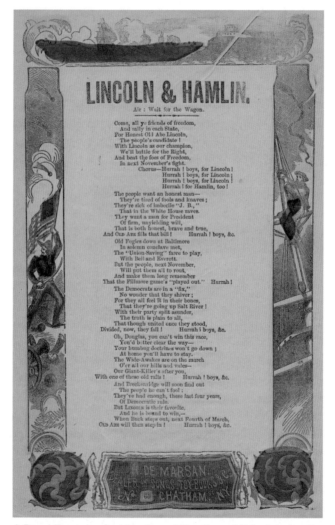

A Republican glee for Lincoln and Hamlin, published during the 1860 presidential campaign.

to Win" and "The People's Verdict." Stenciled on the reverse of the banner are the words, "Lincoln & Liberty Forever, Brekenridge [*sic*] & Slavery Never. Old Derry Is All Right."

It is possible to read Custer's banner, much like we would read a text, to understand the politics of the 1860 election. By depicting Lincoln in military dress astride a strong, white steed, Custer relied on a traditional association between martial costume and capable and strong leadership, an association that dated back to General George Washington. The Constitution placed strategically in Lincoln's hand evoked the candidate's belief that the Constitution was inviolable. For his Cooper Union speech, Lincoln had conducted weeks of painstaking research into the views of the Constitution's framers and concluded that not one of them denied the federal government's power to limit the expansion of slavery in the territories. Northerners were the conservative nationalists, according to Lincoln. In contrast to Lincoln, Breckinridge is carried on a litter held aloft by four enslaved men. The label "Cincinnati Platform" references both the Democratic platform and the argument made by Lincoln that Douglas's Kansas-Nebraska Act departed from the settled orthodoxy of the Constitution. Clad in a suit, Breckinridge is on the verge of falling through the litter (one leg is visible under the litter), suggesting the political weakness of the Democrats' position on slavery.[9]

On election day, Lincoln swept the Northern states. He carried no slave state; indeed, he was not on the ballot in many Southern states. Lincoln received nearly 40 percent of the popular vote but won a majority in the electoral college with 180 electoral votes. For Southerners—and for a significant number of Northern Democrats—Lincoln's election by a minority of people from a sectional political party was a dangerous accomplishment. By the time Lincoln was inaugurated in March 1861, seven Southern states had seceded.[10]

The Union Is Dissolved!

The Secession Crisis

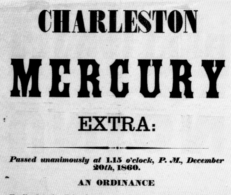

Charleston (South Carolina) *Mercury Extra*, December 20, 1860.

On November 10, 1860, just four days after Lincoln was elected, the South Carolina state legislature voted to hold a secession convention. This broadside, printed by the Charleston, South Carolina, *Mercury*, was printed on December 20, 1860, shortly after delegates signed the state's ordinance of secession. According to the editors, "Within a very few minutes after the announcement of the secession vote, our messengers arrived . . . in less than fifteen minutes Extras, containing the long looked for Ordinance, were being thrown off by fast presses and distributed among the eager multitude that thronged under the great banner of the 'Southern Confederacy.' As the brief and expressive words of the ordinance were read from our bulletin by the crowd, cheer after cheer went up in honor of the glorious event."[1]

It is fitting that what is thought to be the first Confederate imprint, by its timing, was printed by the *Mercury*. Founded in 1822, the *Mercury* was an extreme and vocal opponent of the abolition of slavery and a fierce advocate of nullification, or the constitutional theory that upheld the right of states to nullify federal acts within their boundaries. The *Mercury* was widely respected in the North despite its zealotry. Robert Barnwell Rhett Jr., son of the fiery secessionist legislator Robert Barnwell Rhett, assumed editorial control of the *Mercury* in 1857. He and his brother Edmund whipped the South's secession sentiment to a fever pitch.[2]

In the weeks following South Carolina's withdrawal from the Union, six other slaveholding states seceded: Mississippi (January 9), Florida (January 10), Alabama (January 11), Georgia (January 19), Louisiana (January 26), and Texas (February 1). Each state drafted an ordinance of secession, a formal and brief declaration that the state had severed from the Union. Only Texas submitted its ordinance of secession to the voters for ratification. The secession conventions of four states—South Carolina, Mississippi, Georgia, and Texas—also produced official statements, approved by the state's convention, justifying their vote for secession. For example, in the Mississippi statement, after emphasizing the importance of slavery to the state's economy and culture, the delegates listed a "few unquestionable facts" to demonstrate the necessity of secession:

> The hostility to this institution [slavery] commenced before the adoption of the Constitution, and was manifested in the wellknown [*sic*] Ordinance of 1787, in regard to the Northwestern Territory.

> The feeling increased, until, in 1819–1830, it deprived the South of more than half the vast territory acquired from France.

The same hostility dismembered Texas and seized upon all the territory acquired from Mexico.

It has grown until it denies the right of property in slaves, and refuses protection to that right on the high seas, in the Territories, and wherever the government of the United States had jurisdiction.

It refuses the admission of new slave States into the Union, and seeks to extinguish it by confining it within its present limits, denying the power of expansion.

It tramples the original equality of the south under foot.

It has nullified the Fugitive Slave Law in almost every free State in the Union, and has utterly broken the compact which our fathers pledged their faith to maintain.

It advocates negro equality, socially and politically, and promotes insurrection and incendiarism in our midst.

It has enlisted its press, its pulpit and its schools against us, until the whole popular mind of the North is excited and inflamed with prejudice.

After this series of grievances, the delegates concluded with a reference to colonists' separation from England nearly a hundred years earlier, "For far less cause than this, our fathers separated from the Crown of England. Our decision is made. We follow in their footsteps. . . . we resolve to maintain our rights with consciousness of the justice of our course, and the undoubting belief of our ability to maintain it."[3]

In other slaveholding states, including Virginia, Arkansas, North Carolina, Tennessee, Kentucky, Maryland, Delaware, and Missouri, the decision to remain in the Union or to separate was not so straightforward. Virginia, by population the largest Southern state, held a special legislative session, authorizing elections for a state secession convention. Staunch Unionists in western Virginia were unconditionally opposed to secession. When convention delegates met on February 13, delegates voted two to one against immediate secession. The Arkansas convention rejected secession by a narrow margin. In Maryland, secessionists were blocked by Unionists who refused to call the legislature into session, effectively preventing a convention vote. In Kentucky, the governor called a special session of the legislature, but the legislature refused to call a secession convention. And in Missouri legislators voted against secession while reserving the right to secede.

As Southern states seceded, they seized federal property, including post offices, forts, arsenals, and even the U.S. Mint in New Orleans. In Charleston, the federal forts in Charleston harbor, including Fort Sumter, were at the center of an intense series of negotiations between state and federal officials. South Carolina governor Frances Pickens faced immense pressure to do something about the fort and its federal commander Major Robert Anderson and his men. Outgoing president James Buchanan preferred to leave the situation to his successor. In the meantime, Anderson and his men faced the dual threat of dangerously low supplies and a growing local militia. Despite Confederate demands for his surrender, Anderson resolved to hold the fort. Early in the morning on April 12, Confederate forces opened fire on Fort Sumter. After thirty-three hours of bombardment, Anderson's garrison surrendered. On April 14, the American flag came down and the Confederate flag rose over Fort Sumter. The following day Lincoln called seventy-five thousand militia men into service for ninety days to suppress the rebellion.

Secession Exploded by William Wiswell. This strongly anti-Confederate print presents a fantastical vision of the Union defeat of the rebellion. June 1861.
SOURCE: LIBRARY OF CONGRESS PRINTS AND PHOTOGRAPHS DIVISION.

The events at Fort Sumter prompted four more states to secede: Virginia (April 17), Arkansas (May 6), North Carolina (May 20), and Tennessee (June 8). The Confederacy had set up a provisional government in Montgomery, Alabama, after the first seven states had seceded. After the surrender of Fort Sumter, the Confederate capital was moved to Richmond, Virginia.

The four other slaveholding states—Kentucky, Maryland, Delaware, and Missouri—remained in the Union but were deeply divided. In Virginia, Unionist delegates from western Virginia walked out of the secession convention in protest. Two years later, the western counties of Virginia became the separate state of West Virginia.

"Strike for Your Altars and Your Fires!"

The Fight for the Border States

KENTUCKIANS!

I come to liberate you from the despotism of a tyrannical faction and to rescue my native State from the hand of your oppressors. Everywhere the cowardly foe has fled from my avenging arms. My brave army is stigmatized as a band of guerrillas and marauders. Believe it not. I point with pride to their deeds as a refutation to this foul aspersion. We come not to molest peaceful individuals or to destroy private property, but guarantee absolute protection to all who are not in arms against us. We ask only to meet the hireling legions of Lincoln. The eyes of your brethren of the South are upon you. Your gallant fellow citizens are flocking to our standard. Our armies are rapidly advancing to your protection. Then greet them with the willing hands of fifty thousand of Kentucky's brave. Their advance is already with you. Then

"STRIKE FOR THE GREEN GRAVES OF YOUR SIRES!"
"STRIKE FOR YOUR ALTARS AND YOUR FIRES!!"
GOD, AND YOUR NATIVE LAND'

JOHN H. MORGAN,
Brig. Gen. C. S. A.
GEORGETOWN, Ky. July 15th 1862.

In this handbill, John Hunt Morgan defends his actions in Kentucky.
SOURCE: DAVID M. RUBENSTEIN RARE BOOK AND MANUSCRIPT LIBRARY, DUKE UNIVERSITY.

In July 1862, the Confederate 2nd Kentucky Cavalry, under the command of Brigadier General John Hunt Morgan, conducted a three-week campaign through Kentucky, disrupting Union efforts to secure the state and raising the hopes of secessionists that the state might be brought fully into the Confederacy. During the campaign, regimental adjutant Gordon E. Niles, a former newspaper editor from New York, printed and distributed recruiting posters for the regiment using print shops along the campaign route. On July 15, when the 2nd Kentucky stopped in Georgetown, located about ten miles north of Lexington, Niles used the opportunity to print the handbill pictured here. After the handbills were printed, several men from the 2nd Kentucky slipped through federal lines into Union-occupied Lexington. There the cavaliers placed recruiting posters in prominent locations around town. The next day enough men showed up in Georgetown to form a new Confederate cavalry company.[1]

When Lincoln requested troops to put down the rebellion, border state politicians refused. The governor of Kentucky stated flatly that his state would not provide "troops for the wicked purpose of subduing her sister Southern states." In Tennessee, politicians refused to "furnish a single man for the purpose of coercion" but promised to provide "fifty thousand if necessary for the defense of our rights and those of our Southern brothers."[2]

The four slaveholding states that did not secede—Maryland, Delaware, Kentucky, and Missouri—were tied to the South through a shared interest in the protection of slavery but also had significant economic interests in the North. Although Unionists had managed to prevent secession, Maryland, Kentucky, and Missouri had significant secessionist minorities who hoped to secure these states for the Confederate cause. Securing these three states would provide critical resources to the Confederate cause, adding 45 percent to its white population and military manpower, 80 percent to its manufacturing capacity, and nearly 40 percent to its supply of horses and mules.

For Lincoln it was critical to keep the border states in the Union, denying the Confederacy valuable resources and providing important benefits to the North. Maryland, for example, surrounded the District of Columbia on three sides. (Virginia occupied the fourth side.) Its importance for the fate of the capital became apparent when the 6th Massachusetts Infantry passed through Baltimore. A violent mob attacked the soldiers, forcing the soldiers to fight back. By the time the soldiers boarded the train for Washington, four soldiers and twelve Baltimore citizens were dead. Lincoln responded by suspending the writ of habeas corpus and establishing martial law in the state.

In Missouri, the war assumed the form of an internal civil war with the Unionist state convention that replaced the state's secessionist government with a provisional government. Pro-secessionists, in the meantime, called the pro-Southern legislature into session at Neosho. On November 3, 1861, this political body adopted an ordinance of secession. Although Missouri was admitted as a Confederate state on November 28, the Confederate state government was forced out of Missouri and spent the rest of the war in exile. Major campaigns throughout 1862 and 1863 brought victories for each side. However, it was the brutal guerrilla war that tore the state apart and depopulated large areas of the state. Missouri and Maryland provided troops for both sides of the cause.

Although Kentucky declared its neutrality in the spring of 1861, it too experienced division, though not on the scale of that experienced in Missouri. In the elections of the summer of 1861, Unionist politicians gained more than a two-thirds majority in both houses of the General Assembly. The following year the state's pro-Southern governor resigned. As in Missouri, Confederate and Union forces vied for military control of the state. After the Confederate occupation of Columbus in 1861, Kentucky abandoned its policy of neutrality and promised to support the Union war effort so long as the federal government left slavery alone. Still, Confederate leaders like John Hunt Morgan hoped to liberate Kentucky from the Union and secure it for the Confederacy.

Morgan had fought at the Battle of Shiloh in April 1862. However, he was best known for his raids into Union-occupied territory, where he disrupted Union efforts in Kentucky, Indiana, and Ohio and captured much-needed supplies for the Confederacy. With the help of his adjutant Niles, in the summer of 1862, Morgan printed handbills, including the one featured in this chapter, to encourage the people of Kentucky to join the Confederate cause.[3]

The July 15 handbill begins with a promise to rescue Kentuckians from the oppressive grip of Union political and military forces. Morgan then justifies the military actions of his troops, defending them and himself against charges that they were a marauding guerrilla force. Morgan had already gained a reputation as "the highwayman of Kentucky" for his lightning raids behind Union lines. In August 1862, the Northern publication *Harper's Weekly* reported on Morgan's raids, claiming that he and his "band of dare-devil vagabonds" had distinguished themselves "by burning bridges, tearing up railway tracks, robbing supply trains, and plundering and wasting the few remaining prosperous portions of Kentucky. . . . They have just completed a most successful raid through Kentucky, stealing their food, clothing, and other necessaries from the people they claimed to be [their] friends." Although said to possess chivalrous qualities, those qualities "will not . . . save him from being hanged if he falls into the hands of his fellow-citizens of Kentucky."[4] In his handbill, Morgan promised to injure only his foes and to protect loyal Kentucky citizens, who were flocking to the cause in great numbers. Morgan concluded his handbill with three lines from Fitz-Greene Halleck's patriotic poem, "Marco Bozzaris."[5]

Between July 1862 and July 1863, Morgan and his troops conducted four raids into Kentucky, Indiana, and Ohio. In late July 1863, Morgan and his men

Brigadier General John Hunt Morgan, circa 1864.
SOURCE: LIBRARY OF CONGRESS, PRINTS AND PHOTOGRAPHS DIVISION.

attempted to escape from the federal cavalry. The ensuing fight cost Morgan more than eight hundred men, including seven hundred captured. Morgan and his remaining men attempted to outrun the Federals but were forced to surrender on July 26, 1863. Morgan was imprisoned in the Ohio State Penitentiary in Columbus. He escaped on November 26, 1863. Morgan died in battle in 1864.[6]

Securing Alliances

The Confederate Government and the Five Tribes

Manuscript report written by James E. Harrison, James Bourland, and Charles A. Hamilton, Texas State Commissioners to the Choctaw, Chickasaw, Creek, Seminole, and Cherokee Nations, April 23, 1861.

SOURCE: THE TEXAS COLLECTION, BAYLOR UNIVERSITY, WACO, TEXAS.

On February 1, 1861, the Texas legislature voted to secede from the Union. Three weeks later, on February 27, the Texas Secession Convention sent a delegation of three men north of the Red River into Indian Territory (present day Oklahoma) on a mission to convince the Five Tribes to join the Confederate cause. This handwritten manuscript details the committee's activities with the Five Tribes. It was later published in *The War of the Rebellion: A Compilation of the Official Records of the Union and Confederate Armies.*[1]

The Texas delegation consisted of James E. Harrison, James G. Bourland, and Charles A. Hamilton. Harrison, who was born in South Carolina, was distantly related to President William Henry Harrison. The wealthy, well-connected Harrison family counted many elite members of Lower South society, including Confederate president Jefferson Davis, among their friends and acquaintances. Prior to the Civil War, Harrison had traded with American Indians in Indian Territory and served as a Mississippi state senator. He moved to Texas in 1857, settling in Waco.[2] Bourland, who was also born in South Carolina, lived in Kentucky and Tennessee before moving to Texas in 1837. He fought in the Mexican War. During the Civil War, Bourland served as provost marshal for Cooke County, Texas, and in that role directed the investigation that led to the deaths of more than forty Unionist sympathizers in Gainesville in 1862.[3] Hamilton fought in the Mexican War. In 1861, he urged Texas governor Edward Clark to form a regiment of Texans and Native Americans to protect the region.[4]

Indian Territory was home to several Indian cultures, including the group known as the "Five Civilized Tribes"—the Cherokees, Creeks, Choctaws, Chickasaws, and Seminoles—who in the 1830s and 1840s had been forced to relinquish their lands in the southeastern United States and remove to Oklahoma. The removal treaties created divisions within the tribes that lasted long after their arrival in the West. The Five Tribes included individuals who rejected further accommodation and those who believed their survival depended upon accommodation.[5]

Indian Territory occupied a critical geographical position between Arkansas and Texas, two strongly secessionist states whose political leaders wanted to secure a buffer between their states and possible Union invasions from Kansas or Colorado. Moreover, Indian Territory could provide provisions, troops, and a highway for Southern troops invading Union areas to the north or west. Significantly, the Five Tribes included among its members slaveholders who held a disproportionate influence on politics among the tribes. The Five Tribes were also economically, politically, and socially connected to the

Confederacy. On February 17, ten days before the Texas delegation departed for Indian Territory, the Choctaws resolved that if a breakup of the Union occurred, "we shall be left to follow the natural affections of our people, which indissolubly bind us in every way to the destiny of our neighbors and brethren of the Southern States."[6]

Harrison, Bourland, and Hamilton arrived in Boggy Depot in the Choctaw Nation on March 10 in time for a critical convention of Choctaws and Chickasaws. The council convened the next day and requested to hear from the Texas delegation. Harrison addressed the council, claiming the U.S. government "had ceased to protect us or regard our rights." Harrison "announced the severance of the old and the organization of a new Government of Confederate Sovereign States of the South, with a common kindred, common hopes, common interest, and a common destiny; discussed the power of the new Government, its influence, and wealth; the interest the civilized red man had in this organization; tendering them our warmest sympathy and regard, all of which met the cordial approbation of the convention." The Choctaw and Chickasaws received his speech with embarrassment, Harrison noted, for their delegates were currently in Washington, DC, "seeking a final settlement" with the federal government. At the end of the meeting, the council took no action.[7]

On March 13, having learned the Creeks and the Cherokees were holding similar meetings, Harrison, Bourland, and Hamilton departed Boggy Depot and hurried north hoping to take part in the convention. But they arrived too late. The next day Harrison attended a religious meeting in the Creek Nation where he was able to schedule a convention of the leaders of the Five Tribes for April 8. In the meantime, the delegation visited Cherokee chief John Ross. "We were not unexpected, and were received with courtesy, but not with cordiality," the delegation later explained. Ross told the Texans he was not ready to act: "His position is the same as that held by Mr. Lincoln in his inaugural; declares the Union not dissolved; ignores the Southern Government." However, not all Cherokees agreed with Ross, according to the delegation. "Four-fifths, at least, are against his views, as we learned from observation and good authority." Ross did express sympathy for the Southern cause and intimated that "if Virginia and the other Border States seceded from the Government of the United States, his people would declare for the Southern Government that might be formed."[8]

On April 8, the delegation joined representatives from the Five Tribes at North Fork. Heavy rains, which flooded the land after months of drought, made travel difficult. The Choctaw and Chickasaw leaders were unable to cross the Canadian River to attend the meeting. Representatives of the Creek, Cherokee, Seminole, Quapaw, and Sauk tribes met with Harrison, Bourland, and Hamilton. Harrison gave an impassioned two-hour speech: "Our views were cordially received by the convention. The Creeks are Southern and sound to a man, and when desired will show their devotion to our cause by acts."[9]

In their report to Governor Clark, the delegation described the Five Tribes as "in a rapid state of improvement." The tribes had built substantial houses, schools, and churches in an area abundant with natural resources. "All this they regard as inviting Northern aggression, and they are without arms, to any extent, or munitions of war. They declare themselves Southerners by geographical position, by a common interest, by their social system, and by blood, for they are rapidly becoming a nation of whites. They have written constitutions, laws, &c., modeled after those of the Southern States. We recommend them to the fostering care of the South, and that treaty arrangements be entered into with them as soon as possible," the Texas delegation concluded. The delegation's report was forwarded by Clark to Confederate president Jefferson Davis.[10]

On May 25, the Chickasaws passed a set of resolutions, similar to those passed by the Choctaws in February, declaring that "our geographic position, our social and domestic institutions, our feelings and sympathies all attach us to our Southern friends." The other three tribes were divided. Within each group were pro-Unionists and pro-secessionists. "With a vow to uphold the sovereignty of Native nations should they win the war and a cautionary reminder the Indian annuities were invested in bonds held by the southern states rather than by the federal government, the Confederacy secured the loyalty of four of the Five Tribes."[11] By August 1, only the Cherokee had not signed a treaty of alliance with the Confederacy. "An ideological civil war soon erupted in Cherokee country, between pro-Confederate Cherokees and proneutrality Cherokees, who would soon redefine themselves as pro-Unionists." Confederate military victories in late July, as well as political concerns among Cherokee leaders, helped sway Cherokee loyalty toward the South. On August 24, the Cherokee issued a declaration announcing their support of the Confederacy: "the Cherokee people had its origin in the south; its institutions are similar to those of the southern states, and our interests are identical with theirs."[12]

The Five Tribes alliance with the Confederacy proved disastrous. When the South lost so did the tribes who found themselves reconstructed on less land with reduced authority.[13]

John Bull Makes a Choice

Cotton and International Politics

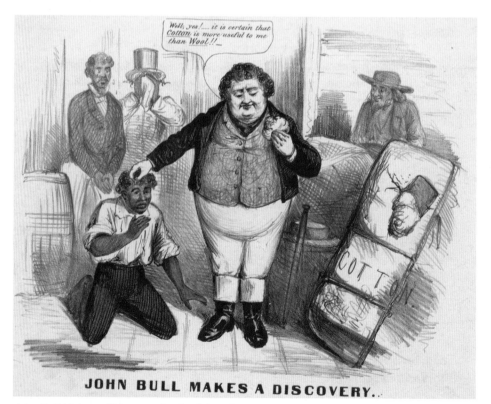

John Bull Makes a Discovery, Currier & Ives lithograph, 1862.

At the start of the Civil War, American-grown cotton dominated the global economy, constituting 61 percent of all U.S. exports and accounting for 77 percent of the eight hundred million pounds of cotton consumed in Great Britain. Moreover, the production of cotton supported an extensive network of goods and services that infiltrated economies far beyond the slaveholding South. Given cotton's importance "to the worldwide web of cotton production and global capitalism," it is not surprising that cotton stood at the center of both Southern and Northern political and diplomatic efforts.[1]

John Bull Makes a Discovery, a Currier & Ives lithograph from 1862, highlights the international politics of cotton. In the image, a stout John Bull, an imaginary literary and political character who is the personification of England, stands between a kneeling slave and a bale of cotton. Feeling the hair (that is, "wool") of the slave with one hand while holding a piece of raw cotton in the other, John Bull declares, "Well yes! . . . it is certain that *Cotton* is more useful to me than *Wool*!!" In the background, another Black man is visible standing alongside a gentleman wearing a tall hat, his face obscured by the handkerchief he is using to wipe away his tears. A planter in a broad-brimmed hat stands behind the bales of cotton. Printed at the height of the cotton famine, the lithograph reflected the conflict between the economics of cotton and the immorality of slavery. Although Britain had abolished slavery in the 1830s, British manufacturers remained heavily dependent on slave-grown cotton from the American South. Political leaders in the North worried economic interests might lead Britain to recognize the Confederacy and its slave labor economy.

In the spring of 1861, Confederate political leaders expressed confidence that European dependence on Southern cotton would make diplomatic recognition imminent. As Georgia delegate Thomas R. R. Cobb noted on February 19, 1861, there existed among Confederate leaders a "firm and universal conviction that Great Britain, France and Russia will acknowledge us at once in the family of nations." For Confederate political leaders, international recognition was their most important foreign policy goal. Shortly after Jefferson Davis was selected as provisional president of the Confederacy, he dispatched a three-man commission to London to request admission "into the family of independent nations." However, Confederate hopes for immediate recognition were quickly thwarted by Britain's desire to remain neutral in the conflict.[2]

For Britain, the decision to recognize, or to not recognize, the Confederacy was complex. As one historian notes, "Britain had to consider the fate of its Canadian provinces, and its growing dependence on wheat and corn imports from the northern United States." Moreover, although the Confederate Congress's new constitution provided safeguards for slavery, the United States had, at this early point in the war, refused to make slavery an issue in the war. Other factors were involved for the British: "reluctance to risk all-out involvement in war, mistrust of the French, and caution dictated by a fear of ending up on the losing side after all." Additionally, in 1861, Britain had ample supplies of cotton on hand. Cotton imports in the years immediately preceding the Civil War had been extremely high. Abundant supplies of cotton combined with expectations that the war would be short left many in Britain optimistic they could survive any short-term disruption in cotton imports.[3]

In the summer of 1861, in an attempt to force British diplomatic recognition, the Confederate government banned cotton exports. A Northern blockade of Southern ports also kept cotton supplies from reaching England. Initially, the export ban "meant rising prices for the stock at hand, which holders of cotton and cotton goods welcomed." However, by the second year of the war, as supplies dwindled and prices continued to rise, production slowed significantly. Between 1860 and 1862, cotton exports from the United States to Europe dropped from 3.8 million bales to virtually nothing.[4] As a result, unemployment in the British cotton industry soared, and unemployed workers rioted in the streets. In France, where imports of cotton fell from 600,000 bales in 1860 to just 4,169 bales in 1863, nearly a quarter million French textile workers were unemployed.[5]

Pro-Southern interests in British Parliament urged diplomatic recognition of the Confederacy, linking diplomatic recognition to an increase in cotton production. In Liverpool, at the time the world's largest cotton port, pro-Confederate supporters were so numerous that the city was considered "the most Confederate place in the world outside the Confederacy itself." Despite Britain's policy of neutrality, Liverpool merchants provided vital support to the Confederacy by helping bring cotton from ports blockaded by the Union navy, building warships for the Confederacy, and supplying the South with military equipment and credit. In Liverpool, groups like the Liverpool Southern Club and the Central Association for the Recognition of the Confederate States agitated for the Southern cause. Similar groups appeared in Manchester, another important site of the British cotton industry. In the streets of Manchester, thousands of participants from clubs like the Manchester Southern Club and the Manchester Southern Independence Association marched alongside textile workers demanding British recognition of Southern independence.[6]

Despite the efforts of Confederate political leaders and British pro-Southern supporters, King Cotton did not prevail. In January 1863, President Abraham Lincoln issued the Emancipation Proclamation. This shift in Union war aims combined with significant amounts of cotton arriving in Europe from sources other than the United States eased political pressure on European governments to recognize the Confederacy.

Part III

BATTLEFIELD

There were more than ten thousand military engagements during the Civil War. Of those, fifty are considered major battles with about one hundred other significant battles. There were three theaters of war: Eastern, Western, and Trans-Mississippi. Although the bloodiest battles of the war took place in the Eastern and Western theaters, the expansionist interests of the federal and Confederate governments assured the importance of the Trans-Mississippi, especially western states and territories, such as Colorado, Arizona, and New Mexico. Twice Confederate General Robert E. Lee invaded the North, at Antietam (1862) and at Gettysburg (1863), resulting in Union victory and devastating losses for both sides. During the Civil War, the number of men wounded and killed in battle occurred on a scale never experienced. The Union and Confederate governments struggled to care for the wounded and to identify and bury the dead. Many families never learned the fate of their soldier.

A Sacred Emblem of the Battle of Glorieta Pass

United States flag carried by the 1st Colorado Volunteers during the 1861–1862 New Mexico campaign.

SOURCE: ACCESSION NO. WR.1104.1, HISTORY COLORADO.

The 1st Colorado Volunteers carried this thirty-four-star United States flag during the 1861–1862 campaign along the Rio Grande in New Mexico Territory. The flag, which was sewn by the women of Denver, is made of cotton, wool, and brass and measures 48 by 105 inches. The tears in the field of stars and the stripes were made by Confederate grapeshot during the Battle of Glorieta Pass. The "riddled and torn battle flag" was saved "as a sacred emblem" of the Union's strategic victory that preserved Colorado and New Mexico for the Union and ended any hopes for a Confederate expansion into the West.[1]

In 1861, as the secession crisis unfolded, Union and Confederate military and political leaders fought for control of the American West. For Confederate president Jefferson Davis, New Mexico, Utah, and Colorado were important recruiting grounds for troops because these territories had populations that were loyal to the Confederacy. In March, southern New Mexico effectively seceded from the government at Santa Fe when a convention of Arizonians met at Mesilla and unanimously adopted a series of secessionist resolutions. As one Unionist observer wrote from Mesilla in June, "This country is now as much in the possession of the enemy as Charleston is." The Western territories also held extensive supplies of war material (that is, rifles and cannons) in federal forts that could be used to supply Confederate troops. Control of the West would also provide the Confederacy with access to the region's mineral riches and, perhaps most important, access to California's coastline with its many open, blockade-free ports.[2]

After Texas seceded, Texas authorities ousted the U.S. Army, insisting federal troops leave by way of the coast, thus preventing a military buildup in New Mexico and assuring that military stores would remain in their "rightful" location in Texas forts. Although federal military leaders like Colonel I. V. D. Reece, commander of Fort Bliss, complied with these demands, Texas forts were still vulnerable, especially those in west Texas. For example, Fort Bliss, near El Paso, was located just forty miles south of Fort Fillmore, which due to its location in New Mexico Territory remained under federal control. To secure these remote posts, the 2nd Texas Mounted Rifles was ordered to the area. Four companies of the regiment, under the command of Colonel John S. Ford, were dispatched to secure the region of the lower Rio Grande, while the other six companies, under the command of Colonel John R. Baylor, were ordered to secure Forts Lancaster, Davis, Stockton, Clark, and Bliss.

Baylor and his men arrived at Fort Bliss in mid-July. He soon moved his troops to Mesilla where he believed he could take a more offensive position.

On July 25, Major Isaac Lynde, commander of Fort Fillmore, ordered an attack on Baylor's troops. The stalwart defense of the Texans soon convinced Lynde to retreat to the safety of the fort. Although outnumbered, the Texas forces pursued the fleeing Federals. The faint-hearted major soon surrendered his command, an action that was described by one of his soldiers as the "most humiliating and disgraceful event that has ever blurred . . . the splendid record of the Regular Army."[3] Having secured the far western borders of Texas, Baylor turned his attention to Fort Craig, located on the Rio Grande just inside the northern boundary of the territory claimed by Confederate Arizona. Baylor requested his department commander send more men so that Baylor might more effectively fight both the Indians and the Federals.

Unknown to Baylor, Confederate Brigadier General Henry Sibley was in San Antonio organizing a brigade to engage in a campaign that would reinforce Baylor's troops and secure New Mexico for the Confederate cause. Sibley was familiar with New Mexico Territory, having served in the region before he resigned his commission to join the Confederacy. The brigade's first objective was Fort Craig, which controlled the Rio Grande corridor between Albuquerque and Santa Fe in the north and Mesilla and El Paso in the south. Capturing Fort Craig was critical for Sibley's plan to conquer New Mexico. The fort held the supplies and forage necessary for the success of Sibley's "live-off-the-land" strategy in the desert Southwest. Moreover, defeating the Union Army at Fort Craig would clear a path for Confederate forces to surge northward and secure Fort Union and the rest of northern New Mexico. By February 1862, three thousand Confederate troops were moving up the Rio Grande Valley.

Meanwhile, Colonel Edward R. S. Canby, Union commander of the Department of New Mexico, fearing an invasion, appealed to the governors of Colorado and New Mexico for more troops. By February 1862, Canby reported he had four thousand troops at the ready.

On February 16, 1862, Sibley attempted to draw Canby out of Fort Craig and into an open battle, but Canby and his troops remained near the fortification. Sibley was outnumbered and his howitzers were no match for the thick adobe walls of the fort. Realizing this, Sibley withdrew his forces, crossed the Rio Grande at Paraje, and moved upstream toward the ford at Valverde. On February 21, in the largest Civil War battle fought in the West, the Confederates waged a successful fight against Canby's forces in the Battle of Valverde. However, Fort Craig and its supplies remained under Union control. Rather than try to take Fort Craig, Sibley headed north toward Fort Union hoping to capture its stores and arsenal. The Confederates arrived in Albuquerque on

March 2. Major Charles Pyron's battalion of the 2nd Texas Mounted Rifles continued north toward Santa Fe, where on March 13, the Confederates hoisted their flag over the Palace of the Governors. Sibley, who had set up his headquarters in Albuquerque, used the opportunity to resupply and rest his men.

In the meantime, at Fort Craig, Canby decided to hold the fort and wait for reinforcements, while at Fort Union New Mexico troops cheered the arrival of the 1st Colorado soldiers, who had marched four hundred miles in just thirteen days. Assuming command of all the troops, Colonel John P. Slough, a Denver lawyer, led his troops out of Fort Union toward Glorieta Pass. The federal forces camped at Bernal Springs, which lay about forty miles southeast of Glorieta Pass. In Santa Fe, Major Pyron learned of Slough's movement and set out to meet the federal advance.

On March 26, troops under the command of Major John Chivington marched west, down into Apache Canyon toward the Confederate encampment at Johnson's Ranch. As they advanced, Union troops captured Confederate pickets, which gave the Federals the advantage and allowed them to surprise Major Pyron's Texas troops. Although the resulting skirmish resulted in minimal casualties on both sides, the Confederates lost about a quarter of their troops as prisoners. Still, the day's action was not decisive. Both sides fell back to gather reinforcements and renew the battle.

Having learned of Chivington's success in the Battle of Apache Canyon, Slough organized his troops into two units. The mounted troops, five companies of the 1st Colorado, and the two batteries of artillery formed the main column under Slough's direct control. The remainder of the command was placed under Chivington's control for use as a flanking force. The two units totaled nearly thirteen hundred troops. Meanwhile, Pyron's troops were reinforced by members of the 4th and 7th Texas. Colonel William R. Scurry assumed command of the Confederate force, which now numbered twelve hundred troops.

Slough sent Chivington's column south while he took the main column through Glorieta Pass, along the Santa Fe Trail. Federal cavalry met the advancing Confederate troops late on the morning of March 28. Unlike the skirmish in Apache Canyon, the Confederates seized the initiative and the Union troops assumed a defensive posture. Throughout the battle, Slough waited for word from Chivington's flanking force. Union troops were finally forced to retreat, and the Confederates won a tactical victory and held the field.

As Slough's forces met the Confederates in Glorieta Pass, Chivington's column advanced toward the southwest, arriving on high ground above

Johnson's Ranch where Scurry had left his supply train. Because it was so far behind Confederate lines, Scurry had left only two hundred men to guard it, most of them sick, wounded, or otherwise unable to join the main force in Glorieta Pass. Chivington's troops rapidly descended the steep cliffs, scattered the small force of Texans protecting the supply train, and, with only minor losses, captured Scurry's supply train. Concentrating the wagons, Chivington's forces burned the wagons along with their contents. Rather than risk an attack on the Confederate rear, Chivington's battalion instead reunited with Slough's main column. Exhausted, and with half their officers dead or wounded, the Confederates did not pursue the Union troops.

The Battle of Glorieta Pass was a tactical victory but a strategic loss for the Confederates. After the battle, the Texans retreated to Santa Fe without food or supplies. Confederate morale plummeted, and confidence in Sibley's leadership reached an all-time low. (Sibley was not present at the Battle of Glorieta Pass because he was rumored to be inebriated at his headquarters in Albuquerque.) Failing to receive reinforcements from Texas, Sibley's troops embarked on a long, dangerous march back to Texas. The failure of the New Mexico campaign marked the end of Confederate hopes for a western empire. For the duration of the Civil War, New Mexico Territory remained under Union control.

Sand Creek Massacre National Historic Site

The Indian Wars in the Civil War Era

Sand Creek Massacre by Andy Thomas. In this painting, Black Kettle and his wife Medicine Woman Later make a frantic dash to the creek bank during the Sand Creek attack by Colonel John Chivington's Colorado Volunteers. Medicine Woman Later was shot but survived her wounds. Black Kettle and Medicine Woman Later were killed four years later by troops under the command of George Armstrong Custer at the Washita River.
SOURCE: ANDY THOMAS.

The Sand Creek Massacre National Historic site is located nine miles north of the unincorporated community of Chivington, in the remote southeastern corner of Colorado. Covering more than twelve thousand acres of rolling prairie land, dotted with dry shrubs, cottonwoods, buffalo and grama grasses, and wildflowers, Sand Creek seems far removed from the more familiar Civil War battlefields of the East. Yet the massacre of more than one hundred Cheyennes and Arapahos at this site in November 1864 held great significance for Union military and political affairs. The Sand Creek Massacre is best understood as part of both the Civil War and the Indian Wars. It is, as historian Ari Kelman notes, "a bloody link between interrelated chapters of American history." The battle at Sand Creek underscores the ways in which the Civil War was "a war of empire, a contest to control expansion in the West"; it also marks the beginning of the Indian Wars, which culminated with the massacre of Native Americans at Wounded Knee in 1890.[1]

The root cause of the Sand Creek Massacre can be traced to the tens of thousands of white migrants who flowed into the Colorado Territory after gold strikes in 1858 and 1859. Aided by territorial officials and protected by federal troops, white migrants ignored tribal land claims, trampled crops and foliage, and demanded the federal government remove local tribes from the plains east of Denver. Cheyenne and Arapaho peace chiefs, including Black Kettle, attempted to secure their peoples' future. In 1861, the peace chiefs agreed to the Treaty of Fort Wise, which confined the tribes to a triangular reservation in eastern Colorado. Breakaway bands of military societies, especially the Cheyenne Dog Soldiers, refused to abide by the treaty or to be bound by lines on a map. Moreover, the reservation's proximity to white settlers, the scarcity of food caused by ongoing white migration, and the tribes' continued buffalo hunting resulted in escalating depredations.

John Evans, Territorial Governor of Colorado, worried that events in the East left white settlers in the West vulnerable to attack by Native Americans. In 1861, most of the U.S. Army's troops, some fifteen thousand soldiers, were stationed in the West, including the Colorado Territory. As Lincoln recalled these troops to fight the Confederacy in the East, Evans warned officials that without federal troops hostile tribes would wipe out the white population on the frontier. In Minnesota, in 1862, Dakotas killed hundreds of settlers after the federal government failed to deliver the annuities promised by treaty. Lincoln dispatched troops to Minnesota to restore peace. In December, thirty-eight Dakotas, allegedly the ringleaders, were hanged in Mankato, Minnesota, in the largest public execution in American history. The Dakota War of 1862 worried Evans, who feared an accord between Arapahos, Cheyennes, and other tribes.

Throughout 1863 and the early months of 1864, escalating violence convinced Evans, John Chivington, and others that Colorado's settlers were in grave danger, a fear that was confirmed by the brutal deaths of Nathan and Ellen Hungate and their two young daughters in June 1864. The traditional account of the Hungate murders places Nathan away from the family home, "working with a ranch hand named Miller, when the Indians surprised Ellen and the two girls. The Indians quickly killed the three female Hungates, looted the house and burned it. Nathan saw the smoke and raced toward the home but was overtaken and killed by Indians before he got there." Historian Jeff Broome challenges this account, claiming that when Nathan attempted to stop Indians' theft of livestock, he killed a member of the raiding party with tragic consequences for the entire Hungate family.[2]

Regardless of the sequence of events on that fateful day, the murder of the Hungates by Indians became a rallying cry for paranoid whites like Evans. The mutilated bodies of the Hungate family were transported to Denver where they were "placed in a box, side by side, the two children between their parents, and shown to the people. . . . Everybody saw the four, and anger and revenge mounted all day long as the people filed past or remained to talk over Indian outrages and means of protection and reprisal." The *Denver Commonwealth* reported details of the killings, knowingly encouraging "a reaction of disgust and fear from the public . . . help[ing] increase the vitriol of the Anglo citizens of the Territory against the American Indians regardless of the facts of the incident."[3]

Many settlers sought protection in Denver. Rumors of additional Indian attacks kept Denverites on edge. On June 15, 1864, "a man dashed into town, frightened almost out of his senses, and reported that a large company of hostile Indians were driving off stock and murdering the ranchmen. . . . Every bell in the city sounded the alarm. Men, women and children pushed through the streets . . . literally crazed with fear. In the general alarm, wells, cisterns, dark alleys and dry goods boxes became hiding places for the terror-stricken inhabitants." After a long night waiting for an attack that never arrived, residents learned "the army of hostile Indians had actually been drovers, their cattle kicking up dust on the way to market."[4]

Hostilities between white settlers and Native Americans escalated throughout 1864. Settlers continued to infringe on Arapaho and Cheyenne hunting grounds, Native Americans retaliated by raiding ranches and wagon trains and killing settlers, and newspapers continued "to stir up their readers with inflammatory reports." In the weeks before the Hungate murders, troops under the command of Lieutenant George Eayre killed Lean Bear and Star, peace chiefs who rode out to meet with federal troops. Once again, the tribes vowed revenge. Over the next month, Chivington and his troops had three major fights with the Cheyennes, burning four of their villages and killing a chief. On June 27, Evans issued a proclamation asking for help from "the friendly Indians of the plains." He promised to "protect and take care of" peaceful Indians "who remain[ed] friendly." Dividing Indians into "friendlies" and "hostiles," Evans asked "friendly Indians" to go to "places of safety" such as Fort Lyon. Calm settled on the eastern plains of Colorado. But it was short lived. In mid-July soldiers, without provocation, shot and killed Chief Left Hand, "a diehard proponent of peace." Again, tribes sought revenge. On August 7, Cheyenne, Arapaho, and Sioux warriors attacked several settlements, killing forty settlers and capturing at least six women and children. Days later Evans issued a second proclamation urging "all citizens of Colorado, either individually or in such parties as they may organize, to go in pursuit of all hostile Indians on the plains."[5]

Still hoping for peace, Chief Black Kettle attempted to reopen negotiations with white authorities. After meeting in Denver in September with Evans, Chivington, and Major Edward Wynkoop, commander of Fort Lyon, Black Kettle and the other peace chiefs moved to Fort Lyon to demonstrate their good intentions. Major Scott Anthony, who had replaced Wynkoop as commander of Fort Lyon, gave the Indians food and told them to camp at Sand Creek where they could hunt to feed their people.

On November 16, Chivington and the 3rd Colorado left Denver for Fort Lyon. Arriving at the fort on November 28, Chivington reinforced his troops with a group of soldiers from the 1st Colorado who had been stationed at Fort Lyon. The troops set out that evening for Sand Creek. Arriving at Black Kettle's camp just before dawn, on November 29, the troops were whipped into a fury by Chivington, who delivered a fiery speech about the need to avenge the Hungate family and other settlers who had suffered from Indian pillages. More than seven hundred soldiers attacked the Indian village without warning. Captain Silas Soule, who had been forced by Chivington to march with his men to Sand Creek, refused to commit the men under his command to the fight, believing the attack tantamount to murder. Black Kettle, who believed he had negotiated peace with white authorities, raised an American flag and a white surrender flag. Both were ignored. By the end of the day more than 150 Cheyennes and Arapahos were dead, most of them women, children, and the elderly. After the assault, the soldiers wandered over the battlefield gathering grim trophies, including scalps, fingers, and toes.[6]

A delegation of Arapaho and Cheyenne leaders met with the U.S. military on September 28, 1864, at Camp Weld, Colorado, to seek peace on the plains east of Denver. This meeting took place just two months before the Sand Creek Massacre. Chief Black Kettle sits in the middle with his face nearly obscured by the hat of Major Edward Wynkoop who kneels in front of Black Kettle.
SOURCE: WESTERN HISTORY COLLECTION, DENVER PUBLIC LIBRARY.

In the aftermath of Sand Creek, as word of the massacre spread, Chivington defended his actions. During the three federal investigations—one military and two congressional—into the massacre, Chivington insisted the Indians at Sand Creek were enemies not just of Colorado settlers but of the Union more broadly:

> Rebel emissaries were long since sent among the Indians to incite them against the whites, and afford a medium of communication between the rebels and the Indians; among whom was [George] Bent, a half-breed Cheyenne Indian, but educated, and to all appearances a white man, who, having served under [Confederate General Sterling] Price in Missouri, and afterwards becoming a bushwhacker, being taken prisoner, took the oath of allegiance, and was paroled, after which he immediately joined the Indians, and has ever since been one of their most prominent leaders in all depredations upon the whites. . . . Bent, in order to incite the Indians against the whites, told them that the Great Father at Washington having all he could do to fight his children at the south, they could now regain their country.[7]

Investigators disagreed. Chivington, they claimed, had engaged in a premeditated campaign, which resulted in the needless massacre of Arapahos and Cheyennes. The Joint Committee on the Conduct of War said Chivington had "deliberately planned and executed a foul and dastardly massacre which would have disgraced the veriest savages among those who were the victims of his cruelty." The committee also held Governor Evans accountable. By the time the investigation concluded, Chivington had left the service and could not be prosecuted. For the rest of his life, Chivington insisted that Sand Creek had been a glorious battle.[8]

Soule, who testified against Chivington during the federal investigation, was murdered on April 23, 1865, by a soldier from the 2nd Colorado Cavalry. Some believed Chivington had paid to have Soule silenced. As one observer noted, "The barbarism of slavery culminated in the assassination of Mr. Lincoln, the barbarism of Sand Creek has culminated in the assassination of Capt. Soule."[9]

Soldiers, survivors, and their descendants, as well as Coloradoans contested the meaning and even the location of the Sand Creek Massacre. Was it a glorious battle as Chivington asserted? Or was it a massacre as many others claimed? In the early 1900s, George Bent, who was wounded at Sand Creek but survived, published six articles in the magazine *The Frontier* debunking Chivington's account of the events at Sand Creek. Chivington's surviving men were outraged and sought to provide a counternarrative, an effort that culminated in the unveiling of a monument at the state capitol in 1909. The monument celebrated the Civil War battles in which Coloradoans fought. Sand Creek was among the battles listed. In 1950, the state erected two historic markers for Sand Creek both placing the event within the broader history of the conquest of the West and ignoring its connection to the Civil War. For their part, Native Americans, relying on the maps and writings of Bent, made pilgrimages to an area along Sand Creek, "a spot where they . . . performed sacred ceremonies and honored their ancestors." When the National Park Service sought to establish more exactly the location of the Sand Creek Massacre, descendants expressed outrage. After much back and forth between the NPS and descendants, a compromise was reached setting "boundaries capacious enough to encompass many different interpretations." On April 28, 2007, the Sand Creek Massacre National Historic Site opened to the public, the first site in the National Parks system to portray American soldiers as perpetrators of violence rather than heroes or victims.[10]

A Terrible Slaughter

The Battle of Gettysburg

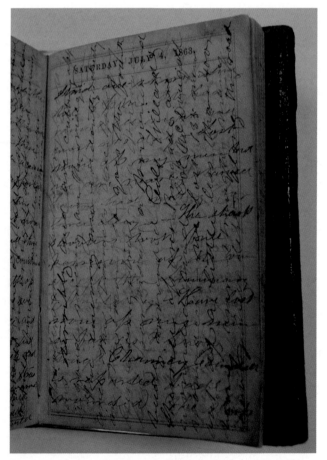

Diary of Lieutenant Lewis H. Crandell, 125th New York Infantry. The fighting on the third day of Gettysburg so overwhelmed Crandell that his diary entry is cross-hatched.

Lieutenant Lewis H. Crandell, 125th New York Infantry, carried this pocket-sized black leather diary throughout 1863. Most days Crandell's observations fit easily on the three-by-four-inch pages. For more than six months, through the spring and early summer of 1863, Crandell's regiment encamped near Centreville, Virginia. His entries for that period primarily document camp life. However, after fighting Confederate forces at Gettysburg and surviving Pickett's Charge, Crandell found the pages of his diary too small to contain all he had experienced. After filling the page, Crandell turned his diary ninety degrees and wrote across the lines he had just written, adopting a style of writing known as cross-hatching that allowed him to make the most of the diary's diminutive pages.[1]

The Battle of Gettysburg began on July 1 when soldiers from the 8th Illinois Cavalry engaged Confederate skirmishers under the command of Major General Henry Heth. The Union cavalrymen were part of two brigades, commanded by Brigadier General John Buford, who had arrived in Gettysburg the previous day. For three hours, Buford's dismounted cavalry slowed the Confederate advance west of Gettysburg. Even after Heth divided his forces, sending one brigade north of the Chambersburg Pike and another south of it, Buford held off the Confederates. "Thanks to the ease of reloading their single-shot, breech-loading carbines, the cavalrymen produced a volume of fire entirely disproportionate to their numbers." By mid-morning, Buford's men were reinforced by the lead division of the I Corps commanded by Major General John Reynolds. North of the Chambersburg Pike, Confederate Brigadier General Joseph R. Davis's brigade engaged Union Brigadier General Lysander Cutler's infantry brigade, while on the south side, Confederate Brigadier General James J. Archer engaged Brigadier General Solomon Meredith's famed Iron Brigade—consisting of troops from Wisconsin, Indiana, and Michigan.[2]

By afternoon both sides received reinforcements and the fighting extended from west of Gettysburg to north of town. South of the Chambersburg Pike, Heth sent his two remaining fresh brigades against the Iron Brigade. "Fate had thrown two of the largest regiments on the field—the 496-man 24th Michigan and the 800-man 26th North Carolina—against each other." Colonel Henry Morrow of the 24th Michigan considered his position "untenable," but he had received orders to hold the line. The 26th North Carolina lost eleven color bearers and their colonel, while the 24th Michigan reported 316 men killed and wounded, along with another eighty men listed as missing in action. On the Union right flank, north of town, the combined Confederate forces of

Major Generals Robert E. Rodes and Jubal A. Early forced the Union XI Corps to retreat through town to Cemetery Hill one-half mile to the south. "As the XI Corps' line disintegrated, the I Corps' line began to give way—but only after six hours of hard fighting."

On Cemetery Hill, Major General Winfield Scott Hancock, commander of the Army of the Potomac's II Corps, acting as General George Meade's personal representative, laid out a defensive line that curled around Culp's and Cemetery Hills extending two miles south along Cemetery Ridge to Little Round Top. Lieutenant General Richard S. Ewell had been ordered by General Robert E. Lee to attack Cemetery Hill "if practicable." Performing a perfunctory reconnaissance of the ground, Ewell decided not to launch an assault on the hill.[3]

Overnight, three more Union corps arrived, along with Meade, to reinforce the Union line. Among those reinforcements were the men of the Third Brigade, which consisted of four New York regiments—39th, 111th, 125th, and 126th—under the command of Colonel George L. Willard, who had led the 125th since its organization in the summer of 1862.[4]

On July 2, Lee assigned principal attack duty to Lieutenant General James Longstreet, who was ordered to attack the Union left on the southern end of Cemetery Ridge. Longstreet, however, delayed his attack until late in the afternoon. In the meantime, Major General Daniel E. Sickles, commander of the III Corps, had moved his two divisions one-half mile forward, seizing the high ground at the Peach Orchard. Finally, at 4:00 p.m. Longstreet ordered his brigades forward. For the next several hours a bloody battle was fought in the Peach Orchard, the Wheatfield, at Devil's Den, and on Little Round Top. When a gap opened in the Union line on Cemetery Ridge, the Third Brigade was ordered into position.[5] As Crandell later wrote,

> In line of Battle, the 126 on the left, the 111 on the right, 125 in the center, we deployed under a heavy fire of shot and shell and moved forward, the shell tearing our ranks fearfully. Into the bushes we went firing as we advanced and only two rods apart. Col. [Levin] Crandell ordered a charge and with a yell we sprung forward. We drove them at the point of the bayonet with an impetuosity that was irresistible . . . their guns pouring shrapnel, case shot, grape & cannister into us with a terrible precision. . . . When we were ordered to retreat . . . reluctantly the boys fell back and we found another Brigade there to relieve us and we moved to our post on the right. Color Sergeant [Lewis] Smith fell as the charge was ordered. Corpl [Harrison] Clark of E Co. caught up the Color and

sprang forward. Corpl [John] McGill on my left fell badly wounded. The man that took his place was torn in pieces with a shell. The ground we charged over was covered with killed and wounded, but we had done what old regiments had failed to do and not only drove them back but off their own ground and at the point of the bayonet.[6]

The regiment drove Confederate forces back, but Willard was killed in the assault. As regimental chaplain Ezra Simmons later recalled, Willard "was struck just after the brigade had by orders fallen back east of the wale through which it had just charged and driven the rebels. A piece of shell carried away a part of his face and head, and he fell from his horse instantly killed."[7]

By 10:00 p.m. the fighting subsided. Confederate forces had made some gains, but the Union had more men and a strong position.[8]

On July 3, "as soon as light enough the fight commenced again," Crandell wrote. Confederate forces having been rebuffed on both flanks the previous day, Lee reasoned the Union center might be weak. Meade, however, had anticipated such a move and prepared to meet the attack. Lee planned his assault around his only fresh division, which was under the command of Major

"Rifle Pits in the Woods," sketch by Alfred R. Waud, shows the position of the 125th New York Infantry during the Battle of Gettysburg.
SOURCE: LIBRARY OF CONGRESS, PRINTS AND PHOTOGRAPHS DIVISION.

General George E. Pickett. Lee added six brigades to Pickett's three, with another pair in support, all under the command of General Longstreet. At 1:00 p.m. Confederate cannons bombarded the Union center. "A continuous crash the whole length of the line," Crandell recalled. "Shell and shrapnel, case shot and railroad iron flew thick and fast around us. Limbs of trees, rails, stones and dirt blew around us and among us while the groans of the wounded were terrible & horses wild mangled and bleeding went dashing around . . . the dead and dying were lying thickly around." The Union artillery responded. The ninety-minute barrage was the largest of the Civil War. When the guns fell silent, the Union center on Cemetery Ridge still held.

"Fall in! Fall in! was yelled by a thousand throats," Crandell wrote. "The 125 was in line in an instant and moving to assigned position on a double quick. We lay behind a stone wall and now we saw what was the matter. The entire rebel force was in line of battle on the flats within 50 rods of our line. They were splendidly formed. One long line of battle with echelon supports six or eight deep and moving rapidly forward in splendid order."

Pickett's Charge had commenced.

"It looked rough for the center," Crandell wrote. General Alexander Hays ordered the 125th "across the field and in line of battle." As Crandell continued,

They moved rapidly forward and halted at the rail fence. . . . For two hours the Battle raged. We broke their lines. They formed again and rushed on but it was to certain death. Again they broke and again rallied standing with desperate bravery as rank after rank was mowed down and replaced. Now they wavered and then closed again. At last white flags waved along the line. . . . Cheer upon cheer rose from the victorious Third Brigade. The fields were filled with the confused rebels. . . . The slaughter was terrible. I was covered with blood, some of it dashing hot in my face.

Pickett lost roughly 60 percent of his men in the assault.[9]

On July 4, Meade congratulated his army for its victory and directed that the enemy's dead within their lines be buried. That evening, Lee withdrew Ewell's Second Corps from its position and consolidated his army along Seminary Ridge in preparation for the long march south to Virginia. On July 5, Union skirmishers entered Gettysburg and discovered that Lee's men had left town.[10]

The Battle of Gettysburg resulted in more than 50,000 casualties: 28,000 Confederates, more than one-third of Lee's army, and 23,000 Union soldiers killed, wounded, or missing, more than one-quarter of the Union soldiers engaged in the battle. Brigadier General Alexander Hays described the Third Brigade's operations as "written in blood." In addition to Willard's death on July 2, Colonel Eliakim Sherrill, his successor, died in the fighting on July 3. "The loss of this brigade," Hays reported, "amounts to one-half the casualties in the division." In the aftermath of the fighting, wounded soldiers outnumbered the local citizens of Gettysburg by more than twelve to one. Homes, churches, and farms became makeshift hospitals. In the short term, the dead were buried where they fell. Local citizens worked to rebury the Union dead in an organized cemetery.[11]

Gettysburg has been described as "the high water mark" of the rebellion, while others have pointed to it, along with the simultaneous Union victory at Vicksburg, Mississippi, as the war's "crucial turning point." After hearing of the fall of Vicksburg and the loss at Gettysburg, Confederate War Department clerk John Jones declared it "the darkest day of the war." On July 28, Josiah Gorgas, chief of Confederate ordnance, wrote, "The Confederacy totters to its destruction."[12]

The war continued for almost two more blood-soaked years. The 125th New York fought at the Battles of the Wilderness, Spotsylvania, and Cold Harbor, among others. After Cold Harbor, Lewis H. Crandell, who was promoted to first lieutenant after Gettysburg and to captain five months later, was discharged for disability. Lewis's cousin Levin Crandell, who was promoted to colonel after Willard's death on the second day of Gettysburg, resigned his commission and returned home in December 1864. Chauncey J. Crandell, an eighteen-year-old private in the regiment and likely a cousin to Lewis and Levin, was wounded at Gettysburg and died a week later. He was later buried in the Soldiers National Cemetery, which was dedicated on November 19, 1863. President Abraham Lincoln delivered "a few appropriate remarks" at the dedication: "We here highly resolve that these dead shall not have died in vain—that this nation, under God, shall have a new birth of freedom—and that government of the people, by the people, for the people, shall not perish from the earth."[13]

"We Will Prove Ourselves Men"

The United States Colored Troops

Eleven African American regiments were raised in Pennsylvania. Each had their own regimental flag. Of the eleven, this is the only one left. In 1906, the flags were moved to the museum of the U.S. Military Academy at West Point. In the early 1940s, most of the flags carried by the Colored Troops were discarded because of a lack of storage space. Prior to its acquisition by the Atlanta History Center, the regimental flag for the 127th U.S. Colored Troops had been displayed at the Grand Army of the Republic Civil War Museum and Library in Philadelphia.

The 127th Infantry Regiment, United States Colored Troops (USCT), was one of eleven USCTs trained at Camp William Penn, located eight miles north of Philadelphia in Montgomery County, Pennsylvania. African American artist David Bustill Bowser created regimental flags for each of the USCTs trained at Camp William Penn. Bowser's flags featured images of heroic Blacks while patriotic captions—"We will prove ourselves men" and "Rather Die Freemen Than Live to Be Slaves"—linked Black military service with Black manhood.[1]

On May 22, 1863, the War Department issued General Order Number 143, establishing the United States Colored Troops. The USCT was organized into three branches: cavalry, artillery, and infantry. To appease white skeptics, the USCT regiments were commanded by white commissioned officers, "a practice that angered many blacks, who were already displeased with the segregation of troops, inferior supplies and treatment, lower pay, and relegation to fatigue duty." In August, Frederick Douglass resigned as a recruiter over these inequalities.[2]

In Pennsylvania Black recruitment moved slowly. From the start of the war, Governor Andrew G. Curtin had spurned African American offers of military assistance. In April 1861, three companies of Blacks from Philadelphia had volunteered for service. Not surprisingly, the state refused to enlist the men. At that time no Northern state accepted Black soldiers. In February, Frederick Douglass appealed unsuccessfully to Curtin to enlist Black soldiers. Even as late as June, as Confederate forces threatened Pennsylvania, Black offers of military service were rejected. Instead Black Pennsylvanians enlisted in other states, most notably Massachusetts, where Black men from the Keystone state enlisted in the 54th and 55th Massachusetts Regiments, the first Black regiments in a Northern state. Nearly every company in each of these regiments included Pennsylvania Black soldiers. A Philadelphia newspaper claimed fifteen hundred Blacks from Pennsylvania had enlisted in Massachusetts regiments.[3]

The exodus of Black soldiers from Pennsylvania to other Northern states prompted action. A series of meetings held in Philadelphia in the spring and summer of 1863, in both the white community and the Black community, resulted in the establishment of the Supervisory Committee for Recruiting Colored Regiments. Thomas Webster, a Philadelphia businessman, was named chairman. On June 20, the committee received authorization from Secretary of War Edwin Stanton to recruit regiments of Black soldiers. Six days later Camp William Penn opened.

Located eight miles north of Philadelphia, near the home of Quaker abolitionists James and Lucretia Mott, Camp William Penn "encompassed an

88th Pennsylvania Regiment, Camp William Penn, Philadelphia, Pennsylvania, late 1863.
SOURCE: RANDOLPH LINSLY SIMPSON AFRICAN AMERICAN COLLECTION, JAMES WELDON JOHNSON MEMO-
RIAL COLLECTION, BEINECKE RARE BOOK AND MANUSCRIPT LIBRARY.

elevated piece of land commanding a splendid view of the cultivated, rolling countryside with nearby streams supplying the necessary water. In addition to the physical advantages, the camp rested only a half mile from Chelten Hills and the depot of the North Pennsylvania Railroad, thereby facilitating travel between the city and the installation." Camp William Penn was the first federal training site for Black soldiers. Initially, the camp used shelter tents for the recruits and wall tents for the officers. In September, Stanton named the camp a general training site for Blacks from Pennsylvania, New Jersey, and Delaware. "Within three months, barracks, officers' quarters, mess halls, guard houses, and a chapel replaced the shelter and wall tents."

Eleven USCTs—3rd, 6th, 8th, 22nd, 24th, 25th, 32nd, 41st, 43rd, 45th, and the 127th—received standard military training at Camp Penn under the direction of commander Colonel Louis Wagner, a former officer in the 88th Pennsylvania Volunteers.[4] Like white regiments, the USCTs each carried regimental colors, national colors, and guide markers. The Supervisory Committee hired African American artist David Bustill Bowser to paint flags for each of the eleven regiments trained at Camp Penn. Bowser had grown up in Philadelphia where he and his family were active in the antislavery movement. He had studied art under his cousin Robert Douglass Jr., who had studied with Philadelphia's leading portraitist Thomas Sully. The flags painted by Bowser featured patriotic images and phrases and portrayed the Black soldier as a citizen defending his country.[5]

For the Black soldiers who fought as part of the USCT, military service was a complex, ambiguous experience. The racism that had prevented Black enlistment in the North shaped Black military experience. Black soldiers were paid ten dollars a month, three dollars of which would be in clothing. In contrast, white privates were paid thirteen dollars a month and received their uniforms for free. After more than a year of protests by Black soldiers, Congress authorized equal pay but only for Black soldiers who were free at the beginning of the war. This pay distinction remained in place until May 3, 1865. Black soldiers were assigned a greater share of fatigue duty. Many Union generals believed USCTs should be used as labor and garrison battalions rather than as combat troops. African American soldiers who did see combat often received no coverage or even negative coverage in Northern newspapers. For example, after the Battle of the Crater, one the Civil War's bloodiest battles, African American soldiers received little notice in Northern newspapers. Moreover, at clashes like the Battle of the Crater, near Petersburg, Virginia, and the Battle of Fort Pillow, Tennessee, captured Black soldiers were subjected to violent abuse, the threat of being returned to slavery, and even death.[6]

The 127th USCT formed at Camp William Penn in August and September 1864. It was the last USCT organized at the camp, departing from Philadelphia in late September. Assigned primarily to fatigue duty, constructing fortifications, and performing guard duty, the 127th was assigned first to the X Corps, Army of the James, and later to the XXV Corps. After participating in the Appomattox Campaign, where they came under enemy fire, the 127th was transferred to Texas, where it remained on duty until the regiment was mustered out of service near the Rio Grande River on October 20, 1865.[7]

Nearly 180,000 Black soldiers served in the more than 160 regiments of the USCT, comprising approximately 10 percent of the Union Army's total manpower. Eighty percent of the enlisted men came from the Confederate states and were former slaves, while the remaining 20 percent came from Union states, representing nearly three-quarters of all Black men of military age in the North. Black soldiers "fought in every theater of the conflict, participated in over 400 engagements, and with almost 38,000 deaths, suffered an estimated 35 percent greater loss than white troops."[8]

Caring for the Wounded

Nurses in the Civil War

The Field Hospital by Eastman Johnson.
SOURCE: PHOTOGRAPH © MUSEUM OF FINE ARTS BOSTON.

The Field Hospital by American genre painter Eastman Johnson depicts an injured soldier lying on a cot dictating a letter to a young female nurse. The soldier is a good-looking youth, while the woman who tends to him is "appropriately attired in somber clothing" and appears to be "a suitable recruit according to Dorothea Dix's standards, except for her lack of plainness." The two figures are silhouetted against a sunny spot among a grove of trees. Nearby are a basin, a bottle of soap for bathing, and a crate labeled "U.S. Sanitary Com[mission]." The bucolic setting, the woman's attentive care, and the dappled sunshine "impart a healthful and optimistic air." Completed in 1867, the painting was inspired by Johnson's experience with Union troops after the Battle of Gettysburg.

By the beginning of the Civil War, Johnson had established himself as an American painter. He had sketched and painted George Washington's Mount Vernon, Blacks in Washington, Indians near Lake Superior, and farmers in New England. For Johnson, the Civil War was another source of uniquely American subject matter. In addition to *The Field Hospital*, Johnson captured the Civil War in several other sketches and paintings. *A Ride for Liberty—The Fugitive Slaves* (1862) and *The Wounded Drummer Boy* (1871) were based on Johnson's experience at the Battles of Bull Run and Antietam. Other works by Johnson, including *Knitting for Soldiers* (1861), *News from the Front* (1861), *Women Sewing—Work for the Fair* (1862), and *Writing to Father* (1863), focused on the connection between the home front and the battlefield. *The Field Hospital* also reminded viewers of this connection between home and battle by recognizing the nursing work performed by thousands of women during the Civil War.[1]

When the Civil War began, the Union and Confederate armies were ill prepared to care for wounded and sick soldiers. The Union army scarcely had a medical department; it had no general hospitals, few surgeons, and no established means for distributing food and medical supplies. Confederate medical service was nonexistent.

Dorothea Dix and the Blackwell sisters, Elizabeth and Emily, were among the first to develop plans for nursing services in the North. Dix, the daughter of an itinerant Methodist minister, began her reform career in 1841 when she agreed to lead a Sunday school class for women inmates at East Cambridge Jail in Massachusetts. Touring the jail, Dix was shocked by what she witnessed. For the next twenty years, Dix worked to change the care of the mentally ill in the United States by inspecting almshouses, workhouses, prisons, and jails; documenting her findings; and pressuring state legislators to institute reforms for the care of the mentally ill. By 1861, Dix was well known to most Americans. She used her connections in Congress and in the president's cabinet to secure an appointment from the Secretary of War. On June 10, Dix was commissioned as superintendent of nurses. Dix's nurses received a salary from the U.S. government and worked primarily in general hospitals far from the battle lines.

In 1857, Elizabeth Blackwell and her sister Emily, both medical doctors, founded the New York Infirmary for Women and Children, a hospital that "combined the training of female doctors and nurses with the care of indigent patients." In April 1861, the Blackwells helped established the Woman's Central Association of Relief (WCAR). The organization pledged to "'give organization and efficiency to the scattered efforts' already in progress; gather information on the wants of the army; establish relations with the Medical Staff of the army; create a central depot for hospital stores; and open a bureau for the examination and registration of nursing candidates." The WCAR appointed a board of managers composed of twelve men and twelve women. Although the men had final authority, the women held prominent positions. Unitarian minister Henry Bellows was appointed vice president.[2]

Blackwell and Dix held different views about how best to select and train nurses for service in military hospitals. Blackwell intended to consider all qualified applicants regardless of social class or age. She also insisted that nurses needed training, such as that offered by her hospital, to be effective. Dix, on the other hand, had no experience nursing but believed her knowledge of hospitals and Florence Nightingale's directives prepared her to select the best women to serve as nurses. Dix preferred "'persons of the highest respectability' who could afford to support themselves. . . . [N]urse candidates had to 'be between the ages of thirty and forty-five years,' had to be 'women of strong constitutions,' and were expected to 'present a written testimonial' of their moral character.'" Women who met these qualifications were expected to wear the "regulation dress" and "agree to adhere to the authority of 'the general superintendent.'" Blackwell and Dix managed to work together for a time, but relations began to sour after Dix was commissioned superintendent of nurses.[3]

The leadership of professional women like the Blackwells and Dix challenged male claims to expertise. In May 1861, Henry Bellows, along with three New York City physicians, traveled to Washington, DC, to evaluate the "government's management of military medical affairs." Traveling as representatives of the WCAR, the men transformed their mission into the creation of the

United States Sanitary Commission (USSC) with the WCAR as a branch and subordinate to the USSC. Justifying his actions, Bellows expressed concern that the "crude character" of women's benevolence would cause the WCAR to be overlooked by the government. Based in Washington, DC, the male-run USSC became a centralized, national relief agency coordinating donations, assisting in the management of military hospitals, and advising the government on recruitment, medical, and sanitary matters.[4]

Estimates vary as to the number of USSC-affiliated societies. Perhaps as many as thirty-two thousand societies served as auxiliaries of the USSC during the Civil War. These auxiliaries were managed by twelve regional branches in major Northern cities including New York, Boston, and Philadelphia. The USSC built and administered hospitals and soldiers' lodging houses; recruited nurses, doctors, and ambulance drivers; provided blankets, stationery, and stamps; delivered telegrams and letters; and helped soldiers apply for furloughs and disability pensions.

Once the USSC began operation, the Blackwells were removed from their places in the WCAR and the male leadership of the USSC abandoned Blackwell's plan to place women in hospitals for training as nurses. Dix too found herself on the outs with the male medical leadership. Although she maintained her position until 1863, Dix's "prickly personality" alienated many. In October 1863, U.S. Surgeon General William Hammond authorized surgeons assigned to hospitals to hire their own staff, including nurses, thus circumventing Dix's power. Still, Dix had a significant influence on nursing during the Civil War, having appointed more than three thousand nurses to work in military hospitals.[5]

Abolitionist and novelist Louisa May Alcott worked as a Dix nurse at the Union Hotel in Washington, DC, in the winter of 1862–1863. "My experiences had begun with a death," Alcott explained, "and owing to the defalcation [unanticipated leaving] of another nurse, a somewhat abrupt plunge into the superintendence of a ward containing forty beds, where I spent my shining hours washing faces, serving rations, giving medicine, and sitting in a very hard chair with pneumonia on one side, diphtheria on the other, two typhoids opposite, and a dozen dilapidated patriots, hopping, lying, and lounging about, all staring more or less at the new 'nuss,' who suffered untold agonies." Alcott contracted typhoid fever in her first month at the hospital and returned home unable to complete her three-month commitment to the nursing corps.[6]

Not all Northern nurses worked with the USSC or Dix. For example, Cornelia Hancock, who was rejected by Dix as being too young, nursed the wounded after the Battles of Gettysburg, Brandy Station, and the Wilderness, as well as the Siege of Petersburg. Similarly, Clara Barton appeared with wagonloads of supplies just after the Battles of Antietam and Fredericksburg. However, as the USSC improved its distribution of food and medical supplies, the need for the efforts of private individuals like Barton diminished.

In addition to the thousands of women who provided nursing services, thousands of men helped in military hospitals, including the poet Walt Whitman, who called himself "a regular self-appointed missionary to these thousands and tens of thousands of wounded and sick young men here, left upon government hands, many of them languishing, many of them dying." He worked in several Washington, DC, hospitals writing letters; dressing wounds; distributing gifts of money, food, and clothing; and reading aloud to wounded soldiers. At first Whitman was critical of the care wounded and sick soldiers received, describing certain doctors as "careless, rude, capricious, and needlessly strict" and ward masters as "tyrants and shysters." However, as Whitman spent more time volunteering in hospitals, his distress eased. In March 1863, Whitman told the *Brooklyn Eagle* "that the earnest and continued desire of the Government and much devoted labor are given to make the military hospitals here as good as they can be, considering all things. I find no expense spared and great anxiety manifested in the highest quarters to do well by the national sick."[7]

In the South, women like Juliet Opie Hopkins volunteered for nursing duties. Hopkins served as superintendent of hospitals for Alabama soldiers and officers in Richmond, Virginia, for the first three years of the war, wielding more power than most other Southern women in similar positions. Hopkins established three military hospitals in Richmond, known as the First, Second, and Third Alabama Hospitals. She was called upon to establish hospitals in Warrenton, Culpepper Court House, Yorktown, Bristow Station, and Monterrey, Virginia. Hopkins requisitioned supplies, inspected the wards, hired nurses, wrote letters for soldiers, distributed reading material, and recorded the names of the dead. Sallie Louisa Tompkins also operated a hospital in Richmond. Tompkins's success allowed her hospital to remain open even after Confederate president Jefferson Davis mandated that military hospitals be managed by military personnel. To allow Tompkins's hospital to remain open, Davis commissioned Tompkins as a captain in the Confederate cavalry, the only woman to hold a commission in the Confederate Army.[8]

Black women also provided vital nursing services. In the South, enslaved Black women aided their mistresses in nursing soldiers on their plantations when battles were far removed from Confederate hospitals. Among Northern

925 Penn. Ave.,
WASHINGTON, D. C.

Juliet Opie Hopkins helped organize, supply, and manage hospitals in Richmond, Virginia, for sick and wounded Alabama soldiers. Hopkins and her husband sold property and contributed as much as $500,000 for the care of sick and wounded Alabama Confederates. Neither Hopkins nor her husband accepted any payment for their efforts except for expenses.

SOURCE: ALABAMA DEPARTMENT OF ARCHIVES AND HISTORY.

troops, Black women, who were often runaway slaves, provided nursing duties in addition to their other duties such as laundry. For example, Susie King Taylor, a runaway from South Carolina, worked as a regimental laundress with the 33rd United States Colored Troops. In addition to washing clothes, taking care of livestock, and cleaning guns, Taylor nursed soldiers sick with typhoid and smallpox.[9]

Nurses provided important services for the dead as well the wounded and sick. In military hospitals, nurses served as substitute kin, "permitting delirious soldiers to think their mothers, wives, or sisters stood nearby." A popular Civil War–era song captured the plea of a dying soldier who asked his nurse to "Be My Mother till I Die." Nurses wrote letters home to families notifying them of their loved one's demise. When Juliet Opie Hopkins shipped the belongings of the dead home to their families, she included a lock of hair from the deceased soldier. In field hospitals, nurses "performed services over the dead when time and circumstances permitted." Confederate nurse Fannie Beers explained, "I insisted upon attending every dead soldier to the grave and reading over him a part of the burial service. But it had now [by the fall of 1862] become impossible. The dead were past help; the living *always* needed succor."[10]

"His name was Bidwell Pedley"

Caring for the Dead during the Civil War

Blood-stained Bible, diary, and prayer book of Bidwell Pedley.

SOURCE: PEARCE CIVIL WAR COLLECTION, NAVARRO COLLEGE, CORSICANA, TEXAS. PHOTO BY THE AUTHOR.

On May 3, 1863, Private Bidwell Pedley, 5th Wisconsin Infantry, died in the Second Battle of Fredericksburg, Virginia. Two weeks later, Pedley's widow Julia received a package containing her husband's diary, prayer book, and Bible. In Pedley's diary, penciled after his last entry, an unknown comrade wrote the following note for Julia: "The above was the last line poor Bidwell ever wrote. The next day 'May 3' he fell while charging on the Rebel fort at Fredericksburg. He died like a Man facing his country's foes. He was a loving husband, a brave soldier and a true friend. His comrades miss him from their ranks but their bayonets avenged his death by piercing the false heart of his murderer." Julia added her own note: "I [received] this with my Bidwell's other things today. Oh God to think they are bathed in his precious blood. My noble Husband fought and bled for his country."[1]

Julia Pedley was lucky; she knew her husband's fate. For much of the war, the Union and Confederate governments had no system for accounting for the

An unknown comrade added this note to Bidwell Pedley's diary after he died at Fredericksburg, Virginia, on May 3, 1863.
SOURCE: PEARCE CIVIL WAR COLLECTION, NAVARRO COLLEGE, CORSICANA, TEXAS. PHOTO BY THE AUTHOR.

dead or notifying their families, no burial details, no ambulance corps, and no means for shipping bodies home. Instead the work of caring for the dead was "an act of improvisation, one that called upon the particular resources of the moment and circumstance: available troops to be detailed, prisoners of war to be deployed, civilians to be enlisted." The Civil War changed Americans' relationship with death and redefined the government's responsibility toward the dead and their families.

In the spring of 1861, as young men on both sides of the conflict rushed to enlist, Northerners and Southerners alike believed the war would be a short-lived event with minimal causalities. That changed on July 21, 1861, at the First Battle of Bull Run. The Union defeat at Bull Run resulted in 900 killed and 2,700 wounded, nearly one-half the number killed during the entire Mexican American War (1846–1848).[2]

The scale of the Civil War exceeded all expectations. About 750,000 soldiers died during the war, which is approximately equal to the total of American fatalities in the Revolutionary War, the War of 1812, the Mexican American War, the Spanish American War, World War I, World War II, and the Korean War combined. The rate of death during the Civil War was six times that of World War II. About 2 percent of the U.S. population died during the war, an incidence rate that today would mean more than six million casualties.[3]

In the North and the South, armies and civilians attempted to care for the dead—naming and burying the deceased, notifying the families of the deceased, and, at war's end, accounting for and honoring the dead. The armies, however, were not prepared for the challenge, especially after major battles such as Antietam and Gettysburg, which left thousands of bodies scattered across the battlefield. In September 1862, at the battle of Antietam, 23,000 men were killed. Their bodies lay on the battlefield alongside an untold number of horses and mules who had been killed or wounded during the battle. One week after the battle ended, "the dead [of Antietam] were almost wholly unburied, and the stench arising from it was such as to breed a pestilence," a Union surgeon reported. "[S]tretched along, in one straight line, ready for interment, at least a thousand blackened bloated corpses with blood and gas protruding from every orifice, and maggots holding high carnival over their heads." The Battle of Gettysburg proved even more challenging. The fighting stretched over three days, delaying attention to the dead. By July 4, after the fighting had ceased, an estimated six million pounds of human and animal carcasses lay strewn across the field in the summer heat. The 2,400 citizens of Gettysburg struggled to deal with the 22,000 wounded and 51,000 dead.

Residents in the area complained of a stench that lingered from the time of the battle in July until the first frost in October. A young boy remembered that everyone "went about with a bottle of pennyroyal or peppermint oil" to counteract the smell.

Naming the dead proved as difficult as burying the dead. As historian Drew Gilpin Faust notes,

Men thrown by the hundreds into burial trenches; soldiers stripped of every identifying object before being abandoned on the field; bloated corpses hurried

"Civilians gawking at the dead and wounded soldiers strewn across the battlefield," *Frank Leslie's Illustrated Newspaper*, October 18, 1862.

into hastily dug graves; nameless victims of dysentery or typhoid interred beside military hospitals; men blown to pieces by artillery shells; bodies hidden by woods or ravines, left to the depredations of hogs or wolves or time: the disposition of the Civil War dead made an accurate accounting of the fallen impossible.

Tens of thousands of soldiers died without names, identified only, as the poet Walt Whitman wrote, by the "significant word Unknown." As the war intensified, merchants created identification disks for soldiers and soldiers themselves scribbled their names on pieces of paper pinned to their clothes. Still, more than 40 percent of Union soldiers and a far greater number of Confederates died without names, leaving behind families without any knowledge of their loved ones' fates.[4]

The U.S. and Confederate governments took steps to care for the dead. After the First Battle of Bull Run, the Union army issued General Orders no. 75, which made commanding officers responsible for burying soldiers who died within their jurisdiction. Deaths were to be recorded on a form, which was then submitted to the office of the adjutant general. A second order, General Orders no. 33, issued a little more than six months later, provided even more direction:

> In order to secure, as far, as possible, the decent interment of those who have fallen, or may fall, in battle, it is made the duty of Commanding Generals to lay off plots of ground in some suitable spot near every battlefield, so soon as it may be in their power, and to cause the remains of those killed to be interred, with headboards to the graves bearing numbers, and, when practicable, the names of the persons buried in them. A register of each burialground will be preserved, in which will be noted the marks corresponding to the headboards.[5]

Although procedures developed in the North and the South to maintain records of deceased soldiers, procedures were not established for notification of the family of the dead. Instead families relied on newspapers—who published reports of the dead and wounded—and letters from comrades or immediate military superiors or volunteers from organizations like the U.S. Christian Commission. Hundreds of families traveled to battlefields to search for their missing kin. Tens of thousands of families never learned the fate of their loved ones.

In early 1863, Virginia mother Fanny Scott contacted Confederate general Robert E. Lee asking for help in locating her son Benjamin I. Scott. Mrs. Scott had not heard from her son Benjamin since the Battle of Antietam the previous

September. Lee forwarded her letter across lines to Union general Joseph Hooker. Two months later, Lee forwarded to Mrs. Scott Hooker's response: "Diligent and careful inquiry has been made concerning the man referred to in the enclosure and no trace of him can be discovered in any hospital or among the records of the rebel prisoners." Mrs. Scott sent a request to Lee asking for a pass through Union lines to herself search for the missing Benjamin. Her search failed to provide any additional information. Still, Mrs. Scott continued to search for Benjamin. In July 1865, after hostilities had ceased, Mrs. Scott contacted Union general E. A. Hitchcock, who was responsible for war-end exchanges of prisoners. Responding to Scott, Hitchcock wrote, "From the length of time since the battle of Antietam and you not having heard from your son during all this time, I am very sorry to say that the presumption is that he fell a victim to that battle. If he were still living I cannot understand why he should not have found means of making the fact known to you."[6]

In the months and years after the war, Americans worked in official and unofficial ways to locate, bury, and honor the Civil War dead. Clara Barton founded the Office of Correspondence with the Friends of the Missing Men of the United States Army in the spring of 1865. Barton's office served as an information clearinghouse of the missing. By the time she closed her office in 1868, Barton had received 68,182 letters and provided families information about 22,000 missing soldiers. Quartermaster General Montgomery Meigs, using reports submitted by Union commanders, compiled the *Roll of Honor*, an eight-volume report of the names and burial places of "soldiers who died in defence of the American Union." In 1866, Congress authorized the establishment of a national cemetery association. These efforts focused on the Union dead. In the South, outraged whites mobilized private efforts to care for Confederate dead. As the *Richmond Examiner* told its readers in 1866, if the Confederate soldier "does not fall into the category of the 'Nation's Dead' he is *ours*—and shame be to us if we do not care for his ashes."[7]

In Wisconsin, Julia Pedley and her son Nathan continued without Bidwell, who died one week before his son's birthday. Two years later, in 1865, Julia married Simon Marugg and had three more children. The Maruggs moved to California, likely in the late 1880s. Nathan married Caroline E. Dexter in 1888. Their daughter Florence (born 1890) inherited her grandfather's diary, prayer book, and Bible. Sometime after 1913, Florence added her own note to the small archive: "These books, the Bible, Prayer book and diary were carried by my grandfather in the Civil War. The blood stains are his when he fell for his country. His name was Bidwell Pedley."[8]

Part IV

OFFICERS

One-third of the general staff on both sides of the conflict were graduates of West Point Military Academy: 220 of 560 Union generals and 140 of 400 Confederate generals. Nevertheless, the officers who served in the Union and Confederate armies were unprepared for the challenges of the Civil War. The curriculum at West Point focused on math and engineering rather than military strategy and tactics. Moreover, Civil War leaders were inexperienced in large-scale military engagements. No wartime army had exceeded fourteen thousand men. Union general Irvin McDowell fielded an army of thirty thousand at the First Battle of Bull Run. In the early years of the war, Lincoln struggled to find a general who would lead, who would move his forces and engage the enemy. Union General George B. McClellan, who took command of the Union's eastern forces in July 1861, had excelled at West Point, but once in command refused to move his army. Two years into the war, when General Ulysses S. Grant captured Vicksburg, Mississippi, in July 1863, Lincoln finally found a general who would fight.

"Let them surrender and go home"

Ulysses S. Grant and Robert E. Lee at Appomattox Court House

Let Us Have Peace, 1865, by Jean-Leon Gerome Ferris.

SOURCE: VIRGINIA MUSEUM OF HISTORY AND CULTURE.

On April 9, 1865, at Appomattox Court House, Virginia, General Robert E. Lee, commander of the Army of Northern Virginia, surrendered to General Ulysses S. Grant, commander of the Union army, effectively ending the Civil War. The surrender came after two weeks of hard fighting that had resulted in the Union seizure of Petersburg and Richmond, Virginia. In the 1880s Grant, writing his *Personal Memoirs*, reflected on that day at Appomattox: "I felt like anything rather than rejoicing at the downfall of a foe who had fought so long and valiantly, and had suffered so much for a cause, though that cause was, I believe, one of the worst for which a people ever fought, and one for which there was the least excuse."[1]

Much has been made of the contrast between Lee and Grant when they met in the parlor of Wilmer McLean's two-story brick farmhouse.[2] Attired in his full dress uniform, including a sash and jeweled sword, Lee had dressed for the occasion. Grant had not. The wagon carrying his dress uniform and equipment had been unable to keep up with the fast-moving Union army, so Grant wore his casual field uniform, his boots muddy from the journey. "Grant was the typical Western man," the poet Walt Whitman wrote about Grant at Appomattox, "the plainest, the most efficient; was the least imposed upon by appearances." Grant's careless appearance, according to Whitman, showed his democratic simplicity and aversion to "every form of ostentation, in war and peace," an attitude Whitman believed "amounted to genius." Grant later explained his appearance to Lee, saying that he "had not expected so soon the result that was then taking place [at Appomattox], and consequently was in rough garb."[3]

In the 1920s, American historical painter Jean-Leon Gerome Ferris painted *Let Us Have Peace, 1865*, his depiction of the surrender at Appomattox. The title of the painting came from Grant's 1868 presidential campaign, while the composition of the painting reflected contemporary views of Grant and Lee. By the 1920s, Lee had become the embodiment of the Lost Cause. In contrast, by this period Grant was believed by many to have been a drunk, a butcher of his own men, and a scandal-ridden president. In *Let Us Have Peace*, Ferris placed the Confederate general in the center of the painting, while Grant appears from the shadows on the left side. Dressed in muddy boots, Grant is a sharp contrast to the regal and confident Lee. In their handshake, Lee appears self-assured, while Grant appears to acquiesce. "If you didn't know better," one modern art critic notes, "you would think Lee had won."[4]

Robert E. Lee was born January 19, 1807, in Stratford, Virginia. He was the fourth child of Colonel Henry "Light-horse Harry" Lee and Ann Hill Carter.

The Lees and the Carters were prominent Virginia families. Henry gained renown during the American Revolution, fighting under the command of George Washington. In 1810, after a series of poor business decisions, Henry spent a year in jail for debt. In 1813, badly beaten by a political mob, Henry left the country never to return.

Robert E. Lee secured an appointment to the U.S. Military Academy at West Point where he graduated second in his class in 1829. He joined the Corps of Engineers and for the next fifteen years, Lee designed coastal fortifications, including Fort Monroe, Virginia, and surveyed newly acquired territory. In 1831, Lee married Mary Anne Randolph Custis, the great-granddaughter of Martha Washington.

During the Mexican War, Lee served with General Winfield Scott, fighting with distinction at the Battles of Vera Cruz, Cerro Gordo, and Chapultepec, earning three brevet promotions. After the war, he was appointed superintendent of West Point. While at West Point, Lee trained J. E. B. Stuart, Philip Henry Sheridan, and Joseph Wheeler, cavalry officers who would serve with distinction during the Civil War. In 1855, Lee accepted a post with the 2nd Cavalry in Texas where he remained until 1857 when he took an extended leave to settle his father-in-law's estate. Two years later, Lee was placed in command of a detachment of marines ordered to suppress an abolitionist insurrection led by John Brown at Harpers Ferry. Lee's men—including Second Lieutenant Stuart—captured Brown and his followers. In the spring of 1861, Lee turned down an offer from Lincoln to command all Union forces. Instead he resigned his commission and joined the Confederate military. On April 23, 1861, Lee assumed command of all armed forces in Virginia.

Ulysses S. Grant was fifteen years younger than Lee. Born on April 27, 1822, in Point Pleasant, Ohio, Grant was the eldest child of Jesse and Hannah Simpson Grant. Grant struggled to meet his father's high expectations. Grant attended West Point (1839–1843) where he was an average student but an excellent horseman. Like Lee, Grant fought in the Mexican War. He served with distinction at the Battles of Monterrey and Chapultepec, showing great courage and skill. Grant married Julia Dent in 1848. After the war, Grant served at remote forts in Oregon and California. Bored and lonely, Grant resigned from the army on April 11, 1854. For a time, Grant lived on his father-in-law's land outside St. Louis, Missouri, before moving to Galena, Illinois, in 1859 to work as a clerk in his father's store. When the Civil War broke out, Grant reenlisted, serving as a colonel in the 21st Illinois Infantry. "I have but one sentiment now," Grant stated at the beginning of the war. "That is, we have a

Government, and laws and a flag, and they must all be sustained. There are but two parties now, traitors and patriots and I want to be ranked hereafter with the latter."[5]

For the first year of the war, Lee served as a military advisor to Confederate president Jefferson Davis. When General Joseph E. Johnston was wounded at the Battle of Seven Pines on May 31, 1862, Lee took command of what would become the Army of Northern Virginia. Lee halted the Union offensive into Virginia in the Seven Days' Battles. After a decisive triumph at the Second Battle of Manassas (Bull Run) in August 1862, Lee decided to attempt an invasion of the North. That invasion ended in September at the battle of Antietam, Maryland. It would be six months before Lee would attempt another invasion of the North when he led his forces into Pennsylvania. The three-day battle at Gettysburg ended in a disastrous loss for the Confederates, who retreated to Virginia.

Grant served in Kentucky and Missouri during the first few months of the war. In February 1862, when Grant's forces captured Fort Donelson and Fort Henry, Tennessee, Grant became a national hero and earned the nickname "Unconditional Surrender" Grant. When the Confederate commander at Fort Donelson asked to negotiate the terms of surrender, Grant replied, "The only terms I can offer are immediate and unconditional surrender."[6] Two months later, at the Battle of Shiloh, Grant rallied his men to hold their ground until reinforcements arrived. Grant then ordered a full-scale Union attack that forced Confederate troops to retreat. In early 1863, Grant launched a plan to capture the Confederate stronghold at Vicksburg, Mississippi. By mid-May, after several weeks advancing on Vicksburg, Grant's troops completely encircled Vicksburg. On July 4—as Lee's troops retreated into Virginia—Confederate forces at Vicksburg surrendered to Grant. In the spring of 1864, Lincoln, having finally found a general who would fight, placed Grant in command of the entire Union Army.

Lee and Grant fought their way across the state of Virginia, including the Battle of the Wilderness in May and June and the Siege of Petersburg from July 1864 until April 1865. As Lee's forces assumed defensive positions around Petersburg, Grant ordered other Union armies in a march across the South, seizing Atlanta, Savannah, Columbia, and Wilmington. In late March, Grant launched what would be his final offensive. He recognized the desperate situation faced by Lee's army, including scarce supplies and an increase in troop desertions. For nearly two weeks, Grant pursued Lee. Grant's forces captured Richmond on April 3 and pinned down Lee's forces at Appomattox Court House on April 8. The following day Lee surrendered his army.

Grant outlined generous terms of surrender: "Men and officers who surrendered were to be paroled and could not take up arms again until exchanged properly. The arms and supplies were to be turned over as captured property." Grant (and Lincoln too) desired leniency. Grant allowed Confederates to keep their horses and other personal effects, including their side arms. "This done," Grant concluded, "each officer and man will be allowed to return to their homes not to be disturbed by United States authority so long as they observe their parole and the laws in force where they may reside." This sentence, described by Civil War historian Bruce Catton as "one of the greatest sentences of American history," set the tone for the peace to follow.[7]

The following day Confederate troops listened as Lee's farewell address was read aloud. In his address, Lee praised the "unsurpassed courage and fortitude" of the "brave survivors of so many hard fought battles who have remained steadfast to the last." Lee also reassured his men that the surrender was not their fault: "the Army of No. Va. has been compelled to yield to overwhelming numbers & resources."[8] As historian Caroline Janney points out, in his address Lee—"the foremost Confederate hero"—"set forth two of the central tenets of the Lost Cause: Confederate soldiers had been devoted, honorable, and chivalric; and the Confederacy had not been defeated on the field of battle but had been overwhelmed by the Union's forces and material." Lee's order overlooked the high rate of desertion among Confederate forces in the last few months of the war. Moreover, by emphasizing the North's superior resources, Lee suggested that it was not Grant's military skill that had led to Southern defeat, a claim that would be repeated after the Civil War. Beginning in the postwar period and continuing well into the twentieth century, Lee's farewell order held "relic-like status" and helped sustain a particular memory of the Confederate cause.[9]

In the decades after the war, Lee and Grant's reputations rose and fell in relationship to each other. Lee—the "patron saint of the Lost Cause," according to historian Joan Waugh—was revered for his "brilliant generalship, his stainless character, his old-fashioned and gentlemanly style of warfare, and his noble acceptance of defeat." Former Confederate general Jubal Early and other early historians of the Civil War promoted the Confederate version of the war, idolizing Lee and destroying Grant. According to Early, Grant was not even remotely Lee's equal when it came to military strategy or tactics. Southern journalist and Lost Cause historian Edward A. Pollard claimed Grant was "a man without any marked ability, certainly without genius, without fortune, without influence." Although the Lost Cause ideology has been discredited by scholars, it still holds, as Waugh notes, "a powerful grip on popular imagination, albeit in a less racist form than it took during the last decades of the nineteenth century."

Grant served two terms as president (1869–1877), almost the entire period of Reconstruction. Historians sympathetic to Lee and the Lost Cause have pointed to Grant's shortcomings as president as further proof of his poor leadership. Accusations of corruption in the Grant administration have overshadowed Grant's accomplishments, including his support for laws that upheld civil rights and his skill in ensuring the passage of the Fifteenth Amendment. For much of the twentieth century, historians portrayed Grant as a cold-blooded killer during the war and a dictator during Reconstruction. In the past thirty years historians have begun to reinterpret Grant's military and political career recognizing his strengths as well as his weaknesses.[10]

Lee's Right Arm

"Stonewall" Jackson

Women mourning at the grave of Stonewall Jackson, ca. 1866.

SOURCE: VIRGINIA MILITARY INSTITUTE ARCHIVES.

Just after dark on May 2, 1863, in Chancellorsville, Virginia, a North Carolina regiment, unable to see the troops approaching their location, opened fire, striking Confederate general Thomas "Stonewall" Jackson. Jackson's left arm was shattered just below the shoulder. He was evacuated from the area. A surgeon later amputated his left arm. "He has lost his left arm," Robert E. Lee said of Jackson's wound, "but I have lost my right." Pneumonia set in. Jackson died on Sunday, May 10, 1863. His death triggered a wave of mourning across the South. A grief-stricken Lee declared, "I know not how to replace him."[1]

In this photograph, dated to around 1866, a group of young women from a local girls' school mourn at Jackson's grave. The women encircle the gravesite, eyes cast down as if in prayer. Two women can be seen touching the stone in an attitude of reverence. Although the occasion and the exact date of the photograph are unknown, it is likely this photograph was taken on the anniversary of Jackson's death, the young women honoring the Confederate hero by decorating his grave.

Thomas J. Jackson was born in January 1824 in northwestern Virginia (now West Virginia). Orphaned as a child, Jackson was raised by an uncle. In 1842, Jackson secured an appointment to the U.S. Military Academy at West Point. Because of his lack of formal education, Jackson began at West Point at the bottom of his class. With perseverance and hard work, Jackson graduated four years later, in 1846, ranking seventeenth out of fifty-nine cadets. The class of 1846 became famous having provided twenty-one Civil War generals. After graduation, Jackson was sent to Mexico where he served as a lieutenant in the 3rd U.S. Artillery, serving under General Winfield Scott. In the Mexican War, Jackson took part in the Siege of Veracruz and distinguished himself in several battles, earning the rank of brevet major. In Mexico, Jackson learned valuable lessons that would serve him well in the Civil War, including the advantages of swift movements and flank attacks and the importance of drill and discipline in handling volunteer soldiers.

After the Mexican War, Jackson was assigned to Fort Hamilton, New York. It was during this period that Jackson gave increasing attention to religion. Unsure whether he had been baptized as a child, he was baptized. He read the Bible and attended Methodist, Baptist, Episcopal, and Catholic churches seeking a church home. In this same period, Jackson also became obsessed with his health, adopting a rigid diet and seeking out "water-cure" establishments. He also deepened his devotion to his "heavenly Father."

In 1851, Jackson accepted a position as instructor at the Virginia Military Institute (VMI), which had been founded at Lexington twelve years earlier on the model of West Point. Jackson had little classroom experience. For the next ten years, he served as professor of natural philosophy (that is, physics, astronomy, magnetism, and light and vision). Not an inspiring teacher, and often regarded as somewhat of an eccentric for his rigid ways and odd mannerisms, Jackson did earn the grudging respect of his students. In 1859, Jackson and the VMI corps of cadets served as gallows guard at the hanging of John Brown, who had been convicted of murder and treason for leading the insurrection at Harpers Ferry, Virginia.

Jackson found his church home—the Lexington Presbyterian Church—while at VMI. He served as deacon of his church and maintained a Sunday school for slaves. Jackson attended church regularly, prayed habitually, and tithed faithfully. As one fellow worshipper noted, "It would be difficult to find in the entire Presbyterian Church any other member who disciplined himself so strictly, obeyed what he believed to be the will of God so absolutely, prayed so fervently, or found so much happiness in his religion."

In 1853, Jackson married Eleanor Junkin, the daughter of a Presbyterian minister. Unfortunately, she died in childbirth a year later. Jackson married again in 1857, this time to Anna Morrison, the daughter of another Presbyterian minister. Jackson and his wife had one daughter, born in 1862.[2]

In April 1861, Jackson was commissioned a colonel in the newly formed Confederate army. He was placed in charge of the rendezvous camp at Harpers Ferry, where he molded recruits into soldiers. Receiving a promotion to brigadier general and appointment to command the First Brigade of Virginia, Jackson's first engagement came at the First Battle of Manassas on the banks of Bull Run Creek in July 1861. It was in this opening battle of the Civil War that Jackson earned his nickname "Stonewall." As the Confederate line broke under pressure from Union forces, Confederate general Barnard Bee rallied his troops, shouting, "Look men! There stands Jackson like a stone wall! Rally behind the Virginians!" Jackson's brigade broke the Union line. As fresh Confederate units attacked the Union flank, the federal retreat turned into a rout.[3]

Throughout 1862, Jackson continued to inspire the South, clearing the Shenandoah Valley of Union threats and achieving victories in the Battles of Second Manassas and Fredericksburg. The Seven Days' Campaign brought Jackson and Lee together in what would come to be regarded as the greatest military partnership in modern warfare. Although a strange alliance, Lee and Jackson shared three things in common: love of Virginia, faith in God, and aggressiveness in combat. In 1863, at the Battle of Chancellorsville, the partnership of Lee and Jackson simultaneously reached its highest and lowest points.

Facing the larger Union force under command of General Joseph Hooker, Lee made the decision to split his force, sending Jackson's army around Hooker's right flank. The move worked, resulting in a stunning Union defeat. When darkness brought an end to the fighting, Jackson and a small staff reconnoitered the battlefield to determine a route for another Confederate advance. However, as Jackson's scouting party returned to its own lines, the group was mistaken for a Union cavalry patrol and fired upon.

Jackson's death dealt a significant blow to the Confederacy. The absence of his leadership was missed by the Confederates in the Eastern Theater. Lee once remarked that if he had had Jackson at Gettysburg, he would have won that crucial battle. Regardless of such speculation, Jackson was by far the most popular commander on either side of the war.[4]

"The Beast"

Benjamin Butler and the Occupation of New Orleans

Chamber pots with the image of Major General Benjamin Butler on the bottom were produced to protest Butler's General Order Number 28, also known as the "Woman Order."

SOURCE: ALABAMA DEPARTMENT OF ARCHIVES AND HISTORY.

Major General Benjamin Butler's seven-month tenure as military governor of New Orleans, Louisiana, transformed the city and the general, who would become one of the most hated Union officers of the Civil War. As one historian notes, when Butler arrived in the city on May 1, 1862, "an incorrigible citizenry met the most stubborn military governor who could have been chosen to rule over them." It was Butler's tough attitude toward the secessionist women of New Orleans, promulgated through his General Order No. 28, that earned Butler lasting infamy and the nickname "Beast Butler."[1] In the weeks after Butler issued his infamous order that threatened to treat ill-behaved secessionist women as prostitutes, entrepreneurs made the most of the "twaddle" about Butler's order by manufacturing chamber pots, including the one pictured here, with Butler's image on the bottom, "perfect for target practice."[2]

Before he became the South's most despised officer, Butler had supported Jefferson Davis for the presidential nomination at the Democratic National Convention in Charleston, South Carolina, in 1860. After the Democratic Party split, Butler supported Southern Democratic candidate John C. Breckenridge for president. When the Civil War broke out, however, Butler supported the Union. Using his political connections in Massachusetts and

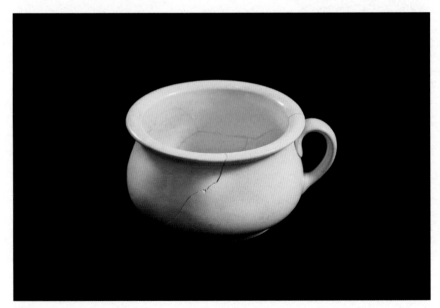

Profile view of chamber pot.
SOURCE: ALABAMA DEPARTMENT OF ARCHIVES AND HISTORY.

Washington, Butler secured a political appointment as brigadier general of the Massachusetts state militia.[3]

Butler was in Philadelphia with the 8th Massachusetts Infantry when he learned the 6th Massachusetts had been mobbed by secessionists in Baltimore, Maryland. A "nominally neutral but dangerously pro-South state," Maryland surrounded Washington on three sides, and most northern rail traffic headed to the capital traveled through Baltimore. Cut off from Washington, Butler moved his troops by rail ferry from Philadelphia to Annapolis, Maryland, where he seized control of the railroad terminus. Butler's troops repaired the tracks and a locomotive and successfully transported the 8th Massachusetts, the 7th New York, and the 1st Rhode Island to Washington.

Major General Winfield Scott, commander in chief of the army, ordered Butler to make his headquarters in Annapolis. Butler, having learned the secessionists in Baltimore were poorly armed, decided to seize the city—without informing Scott. On May 13, Butler loaded a thousand troops on a train and sent them into Baltimore. Once the city was secured, Butler issued a proclamation "enforcing respect and obedience to the laws" of Maryland and the United States. He also arrested several prominent men, confiscated arms, and threatened to hang an elderly man who had advocated secession. Butler's actions horrified Scott and President Abraham Lincoln, who worried Maryland might secede. An angry General Scott relieved Butler of his command and transferred him to Fort Monroe, Virginia.[4]

Located in Hampton at Old Point Comfort, on the southern tip of the Virginia peninsula, Fort Monroe remained a Union stronghold, even after the state seceded. On May 23, three enslaved men, who had been working on Confederate fortifications at Sewall's Point, fled to Fort Monroe where they sought asylum. An agent for the slaves' owner Charles K. Mallory arrived at the fort on May 24 demanding the return of the three fugitives under the provisions of the Fugitive Slave Act. Butler refused, claiming the confiscated slaves were "contraband of war."

Butler's actions were motivated by military necessity not antislavery ideals. Although Butler doubted "there may be property in human beings," he did believe it was legitimate to deprive the enemy of their slaves' labor under the laws of war. "[P]roperty of whatever nature, used or capable of being used for warlike purposes, and especially when being so used, may be captured and held either on sea or on shore, as property contraband of war," Butler noted. He sent a report of his actions to Washington asking for approval of his plan to retain the fugitives. Butler told his superiors the Confederates were using slaves to build fortifications at Sewall's Point and elsewhere. On May 30, Secretary of War Simon Cameron informed Butler that his contraband policy had been approved. By July more than nine hundred fugitive slaves had made their way to Fort Monroe. In August, Congress passed the First Confiscation Act allowing for the seizure of all Confederate property, including slaves used to aid the war effort.[5]

While Washington dealt with Butler's contraband policy, Butler set his sights on the Confederate capital at Richmond. Once again, Butler did not share his plans with Scott. Having secured Hampton and Newport News, Butler made plans to attack the small Confederate garrison at Big Bethel. Capturing Big Bethel, Butler believed, would clear the way for Union forces to attack Richmond. On June 10, Butler sent two militia units toward Big Bethel. Instead of attacking the enemy, the inexperienced troops mistook each other for the enemy and opened fire. The skirmish sent Union troops rushing back to Fort Monroe.

After the failure at Big Bethel, Lincoln directed Scott to relieve Butler of his command. A series of fortuitous events (and a little political lobbying by Butler) created an opportunity for Butler to redeem himself. In a joint operation of the navy and the army against Cape Hatteras, North Carolina, naval forces under the command of Flag Officer Silas H. Stringham and army forces under Butler captured Forts Clark and Hatteras. On August 29, Butler entered Fort Hatteras and ordered a salute fired in honor of his victory. Butler then rushed back to Washington to give his report. A naval officer later wrote of the operation, "We have a joke down here on the two late commanders of the 'Hatteras' expedition—That after the fight they had a foot race North to see who should get there first and get the most credit. Butler beat Stringham.—Had they both remained, we might have had the whole coast in our possession."[6]

Butler's success at Cape Hatteras and in Washington helped the general expunge "the infamy of Big Bethel and reestablish his image as the hero of the public." Butler proposed going home to Massachusetts to raise a new command. Lincoln agreed. For the next few months, Butler recruited troops. However, by early 1862, Lincoln had decided to send Butler to New Orleans, Louisiana.[7]

On April 25, 1862, the city of New Orleans—"the jewel of the South"—fell to Union naval forces under the command of Admiral David G. Farragut. Six days later, fifteen thousand Union troops under Butler's command marched into the city.

From the start, the Confederate women of the city made known their dislike of Union officers and soldiers. When walking through the city, women took "great pains to hold [their] skirts aside as if [they] feared they might be contaminated if they touched the soldier." One woman who fell refused the assistance offered by two officers, claiming "she would rather lie in the gutter." When "an officer would get into a street car," the women "would immediately jump from the car with every sign of disgust, abhorrence and aversion." Butler, on one ride through the city, recalled "five or six women leaning over a balcony" who called out with "something between a shriek and a sneer," whirled on their heels, and presented Butler with a full view of their backsides. One of Butler's officers, on his way to church, "met two very well dressed and respectable looking women, and as a gentleman should, he withdrew to the outer side of the sidewalk to let them pass by. As he did so, one deliberately stepped across in front of the other and spit in his face." The most egregious incident involved Farragut. As Farragut and another officer walked along one of the city's streets, "there fell upon them what at first they took to be a sudden and heavy shower; but it proved to be the emptying of a vessel of water upon them from the balcony above, and not very clean water at that."[8]

On May 15, 1862, Butler issued General Order No. 28, "an ingenious order that simultaneously diminished the acts of recalcitrance and demeaned the perpetrators," as historian Jacqueline Campbell notes. Butler's order read:

As the officers and soldiers of the United States have been subject to repeated insults from the women (calling themselves ladies) of New Orleans, in return for the most scrupulous non-interference and courtesy on our part, it is ordered that hereafter when any female shall, by word, gesture, or movement, insult or show contempt for any officer or soldier of the United States, she shall be regarded and held liable to be treated as a woman of the town plying her avocation.

Butler's order transformed "a political act of resistance into a misdemeanor," as Campbell notes. "Rather than arrest unruly women, thereby creating martyrs and risking popular insurrections, Order No. 28 rendered them insignificant."[9]

Not surprisingly, Butler's order sent shock waves through the South and across the Atlantic in England. The governor of Louisiana declared, "the annals of warfare . . . afford[ed] no similar instance of infamy than this order." Confederate general P. G. T. Beauregard asked his troops whether they would allow their female kin "to be thus outraged by the ruffianly soldiers of the

North to whom is given the right to treat at their pleasure the ladies of the South as common harlots." Writing to Charles Adams, British prime minister Palmerston claimed, "I venture to say that no example can be found in the history of civilized nation . . . of so infamous an act as deliberately to hand over the female inhabitants of a conquered city to the unbridled license of an unrestrained soldiery."[10]

Yet for all the uproar over Butler's "Woman Order," it was not his coup de grâce. General Order No. 76, enacted four months later, required men *and* women take the Oath of Allegiance to the United States or face confiscation of their property and expulsion from New Orleans. Marion Southwood, a Confederate woman living in New Orleans, called Order No. 76 the "most detestable" of Butler's acts. She dismissed Order No. 28 as "unmeaning twaddle." Being forced to take the oath made one's "brain burn with indignation." Butler, according to Southwood, was "Satan himself."

Butler's critics described the Confederate women of New Orleans as victims. Butler, however, recognized and respected the political and economic power wielded by Confederate women. He held them accountable for their behavior on the streets and in their homes. By forcing Confederate women to police their own behavior, Butler blunted the impact of their protests of Union authority. Unable to openly defy Butler, Confederate women resorted instead to lampooning Butler with their words. Butler paid little attention. Claiming the last word, he dismissed one such letter as the "ridiculous attempt of a she adder to wound with her poisonous venom the greatest snake tamer now alive."[11]

"Father of Black Nationalism"

Martin Delany

Martin Delany helped recruit troops for the 54th Massachusetts Infantry. In 1865, he was promoted to major, the first Black man to receive a regular army commission.

In early 1863, Martin Delany working alongside other prominent Black abolitionists, including Frederick Douglass, Henry Highland Garnet, and John Mercer Langston, actively recruited African Americans for the 54th Massachusetts Infantry, the Black regiment that gained fame for its fighting prowess and for the courage of its men. Delany's son Toussaint L'Ouverture Delany was one of the earliest volunteers in the regiment. In 1865, the elder Delany was commissioned a major in the Union army, the first African American field officer.[1]

Delany was born in May 1812 in Charles Town, Virginia (now West Virginia). His father Samuel was an enslaved carpenter and his mother Pati a free seamstress. After Pati Delany was found guilty of teaching her children to read and write, she moved with her children to Chambersburg, Pennsylvania. Eventually, Samuel purchased his freedom and joined his family in Chambersburg. In 1831, at the age of nineteen, Delany moved to Pittsburgh. Working on the waterfront at night, Delany studied Latin, Greek, the classics, and other subjects at the school operated by Black activist Lewis Woodson in the basement of the African Methodist Episcopal Church. Delany boarded with African American barber John Vashon, a friend of William Lloyd Garrison. Vashon introduced Delany to the local Black community.

Throughout the 1830s, Delany was involved in a variety of reform movements, including antislavery, moral reform, and temperance. He served as secretary for the Temperance Society of the People of Color and manager of the Moral Reform Society. However, it was the antislavery movement that captured much of Delany's reform efforts. Like most Black abolitionists he opposed the American Colonization Society (ACS). Yet as Delany observed the discrimination and violence directed toward the Black community in Pittsburgh and elsewhere, he could not help but wonder whether Blacks and whites could ever live in harmony. In 1839, Delany toured Texas, Mississippi, Louisiana, and Arkansas to learn more about slaves and slavery and to explore the possibility of Black emigration to Texas, which had recently become an independent republic.

In addition to his reform work, Delany apprenticed with local white doctor Andrew McDowell. By 1837, Delany was listed in the *Pittsburgh Business Directory* offering services such as "Cupping, Leeching and bleeding."

In 1843, Delany married Catherine Richards. The couple had seven children, whom he named after famous Blacks. His son, Toussaint L'Ouverture, for example, was named after the leader of the Haitian Revolution.

That same year Delany founded the short-lived abolitionist newspaper *Mystery*, which he used as a platform to attack racial prejudice. In the late 1840s, Delany was coeditor of Frederick Douglass's *North Star* and traveled the abolitionist lecture circuit. However, by 1850, Delany decided to pursue formal medical studies. Rejected by the University of Pennsylvania and Jefferson Medical College, both located in Philadelphia, Delany accepted an offer of admission to Harvard Medical School, one of the first Blacks to be admitted. His time at Harvard was cut short when white students protested his admission.

Outraged by his treatment at Harvard and by the Compromise of 1850, Delany published his influential emigration manifesto *The Condition, Elevation, Emigration, and Destiny of the Colored People of the United States*. "I . . . would as willingly live among white men as black, if I had an equal possession and enjoyment of privileges," Delany told Garrison, who had given notice of Delany's book in *The Liberator*. "I should be willing to remain in this country, fighting and struggling on, the good fight of faith. But I must admit, that I have not hopes in this country—no confidence in the American people . . . Heathenism and Liberty, before Christianity and Slavery."[2] Delany broke with mainstream abolitionism, and Douglass, by becoming the foremost proponent of Black emigration, a movement with parallels to the colonization movement Delany had rejected in the 1830s. Delany, however, made a clear distinction between colonization, as advocated by the ACS, and the emigration he advocated.

In 1854, Delany led the National Emigration Convention meeting in Cleveland, Ohio, where he delivered a powerful speech on "The Political Destiny of the Colored Race on the American Continent." Outlining the worsening lives of American Blacks, Delany called for emigration to Africa. Although Delany chose flight as the means to resist oppression, he did not rule out violence: "If he [slave catcher] crosses the threshold of my door, and I do not lay him a lifeless corpse at my feet, I hope the grave may refuse my body a resting place, and the righteous Heaven my spirit a home." Delany organized subsequent emigration conferences in 1856 and 1858. In 1859, Delany traveled to Africa where he visited African American minister Alexander Crummell. While in Africa, Delany made arrangements to establish a community of educated African Americans who would settle in West Africa and lead the development of commercial production of cotton using free West African labor. With the outbreak of the Civil War, the plan was placed on hold.[3]

It was in this same period that Martin, Catherine, and their children emigrated to Canada. The move was in part to provide more opportunities for their children. Delany had written about the "pernicious and degrading" effect racism had on Black children. "How could it otherwise be when they see . . . every situation of respectability, honor, profit or trust filled by white men, and [Blacks] existing among them merely as a thing of convenience? . . . They cannot be raised in this country without being stoop shouldered."[4]

In 1859, Delany published a fictional account of his travels in the South in the 1830s. *Blake; or, the Huts of America*, which would become one of the most important African American works of fiction in the nineteenth century, tells the story of Henry Blake's escape from a Southern plantation and his subsequent travels across the United States, Canada, Africa, and Cuba on a mission to create a transnational Black revolt against slavery. *Blake* was serialized in the *Anglo-African Magazine* in 1859 and the *Weekly Anglo-African* in 1861 and 1862. Given the timing of *Blake*'s publication, Delany may have also been influenced by Harriet Beecher Stowe's novel *Uncle Tom's Cabin* published in 1852 and the case of *Dred Scott v. John F. A. Sandford*, the Supreme Court's 1857 decision that African Americans were not and could never be citizens of the United States.

Delany returned to the United States in 1861 to enlist Black volunteers to fight for the Union. As historian Kellie Carter Jackson notes, "Fleeing was practical, but fighting was powerful."[5] In 1863, the enactment of the Emancipation Proclamation reversed the Union War Department's refusal to enlist Black soldiers. In 1864, Delany and his family moved to Wilberforce, Ohio, where he continued to recruit African Americans for the Union army. In early 1865, Delany met with Lincoln at the White House to discuss the possibility of using African American officers to lead Black troops. Lincoln commissioned Delany a major in the 104th United States Colored Troops.

Delany's postwar life was as complex and busy as it had been before the war. Delany served with the Freedmen's Bureau in South Carolina, where he continued to promote Black self-sufficiency and just treatment for ex-slaves. He received his military discharge in 1868 but remained in South Carolina where he became involved in politics and continued his efforts to assist freedmen. In 1879, Delany published *Principal of Ethnology: The Origin of Races and Color*, in which he praised the accomplishments of African civilization. Delany also edited the Charleston *Independent*, served as minor court official in Charleston, and became involved in a Liberian emigration scheme.[6]

In 1880, he returned to Wilberforce. After his death in 1885, the African Methodist Episcopal priest James T. Holly proclaimed Delany "one of the greatest men of this age," a person whose life was "filled with noble purposes, high resolves, and ceaseless activities for the welfare of the race with which he was identified," and who "has given us the standard of measurement of all the men of our race, pact, present, and to come, in the work of negro elevation in the United States of America."[7]

Part V

SOLDIERS

Estimates of the total number of Union and Confederate soldiers vary. About three million men fought: two million for the Union and one million for the Confederacy. In his pioneering studies of the common soldier, Bell I. Wiley described the average soldier as a "white, native-born, farmer, protestant, single, between 18 and 29." Although most Union soldiers were native born, a significant percentage, about 25 percent, were immigrants, including Germans, Irish, English, Canadians, and Mexicans, among others. Likely, there were a substantial number of immigrants in the Confederate ranks. About 10 percent of the Union army was made up of African American soldiers. In the Union army, 80 percent of the men were in the infantry, 14 percent in the cavalry, and 6 percent in the artillery. In the Confederate army, 75 percent of men served in the infantry, 20 percent in the cavalry, and 5 percent in the artillery. Exact numbers of captured soldiers are unknown, but estimates suggest about two hundred thousand Union soldiers and four hundred thousand Confederates were captured. Most of those were paroled in the field. Of those who were sent to prisoner of war camps, about 12 to 15 percent died in captivity.

"Those d—d black hatted fellows"

The Iron Brigade of the West

Philander B. Wright, a color bearer and a first sergeant in the 2nd Wisconsin, wore this hat into the battle at Gettysburg, Pennsylvania. The upper crown of the hat was punctured by a bullet while the regiment pursued Confederates across Willoughby Run.

SOURCE: WISCONSIN VETERANS MUSEUM, MADISON, WISCONSIN.

On July 1, 1863, First Sergeant Philander B. Wright, a color bearer for the 2nd Wisconsin Infantry, wore this Model 1858 Hardee hat into battle at Gettysburg, Pennsylvania. The hat is embellished with a black grosgrain ribbon, a light blue cord, a red disk, and brass ornamentation: the number "2," the letter "C," and two ventilation grommets. The crown, which is more than five inches tall, is torn at the top where the hat was punctured by two bullets while the regiment pursued Confederates across Willoughby Run on the first day of fighting at Gettysburg. A third bullet pierced the flagstaff and passed through Wright's side. Wright continued the charge until a bullet struck his left thigh and another his arm. The young Wisconsin soldier survived his wounds and was discharged in June 1864.[1]

The Battle of Gettysburg cemented the reputation of the 2nd Wisconsin and the other members of the Iron Brigade, a storied group of men who saw action in every major military engagement of the war. An all-western brigade noted for fighting with an iron disposition, the Iron Brigade was also known as the "Black Hats" because of the black Hardee hats the men wore instead of the standard-issue blue kepis.

The Iron Brigade and Gettysburg were part of an unknowable future when Philander B. Wright enlisted in April 1861, ten days after the fall of Fort Sumter. He was enrolled as a private in Company C. The 2nd Wisconsin Infantry, one of the first Union regiments sworn in for a three-year term of service, mustered into service on June 11 under the command of Colonel S. Park Coon, a native of New York and Wisconsin's attorney general. The regiment's officers wore traditional blue dress coats, while the enlisted men were outfitted in state-issued gray uniforms. The men of the 2nd Wisconsin traveled east to Washington, DC, by train. In Chicago, where they stopped briefly, the residents turned out to cheer the new regiment. A writer for the *Chicago Tribune* described the men as "hard-fisted lumbermen" who "say they will fight if ordered, and if not ordered will fight any way." Once in Washington, the 2nd Wisconsin was brigaded with three New York Regiments under the command of Colonel William T. Sherman.[2]

In July 1861, the men of the 2nd Wisconsin saw their first combat when they engaged the enemy at Blackburn's Ford, near Centreville, Virginia. It was there the regiment had its first casualty: Myron Gardner, a nineteen-year-old farmer from La Crosse County who had his leg blown off just above the knee. He died the next day.[3] Two days later, on July 21, the 2nd Wisconsin was in the advance in the assault on Henry House Hill during the First Battle of Bull Run. After exchanging fire with Confederate forces under the command of

Colonel Thomas J. (Stonewall) Jackson, the 2nd Wisconsin was forced to fall back. As they did so, the men of the 79th New York fired on them, believing the gray-clad Wisconsin men were the enemy. Although the 2nd Wisconsin rallied and advanced a second time, the battle was lost and ended in an ignominious retreat to Washington.

After Bull Run, the 2nd Wisconsin was reorganized into a brigade with the 6th and 7th Wisconsin and the 19th Indiana under the command of Brigadier General Rufus King, creating the army's only all-western brigade. In the winter of 1861–1862, Battery B of the 4th U.S. Artillery was also assigned to the brigade.

Late in the summer of 1861, the 2nd Wisconsin received new uniforms: dark blue wool trousers; blue wool, nine-button frock coat; and the Model 1858 black felt hat, all like that worn by the Regular Army. The state uniforms were ordered packed and shipped home to Wisconsin. Although the 2nd Wisconsin now had matching uniforms, there was at the brigade level a great unevenness in appearance. Hats ranged from caps to the tall black felt dress hats, while trousers ranged from dark blue to sky blue. In May 1862, after General John Gibbon assumed command of the brigade, he required all soldiers in his command be issued the Model 1858 felt hat, a dark blue, nine-button frock coat, white linen leggings, and white cotton gloves. Soldiers were also supplied with trousers and shirts.

In addition to regularizing the uniform of the western brigade, Gibbon tightened its discipline. A West Point graduate, Gibbon established a strict routine, including weekly baths, a daily review, and a regimen of drills. "There were early morning drills, before breakfast, forenoon drills, afternoon drills, evening and night drills, beside guard mounting and dress parades," recalled one member of the brigade. Tents were arrayed in neat lines, sentries had to walk their posts (rather than sit there), and enlisted men had to salute officers.[4]

The discipline instilled in the brigade by Gibbon would prove important in August 1862 when the brigade was engaged in battle at Gainesville. On August 28, while marching quietly along the Warrenton Turnpike, the brigade was attacked by Confederate General Stonewall Jackson's brigade, a unit of highly regarded, combat-hardened veterans. The Battle of Gainesville, now more commonly known as the Battle of Brawner's Farm, was a stand-up battle at ranges of seventy to one hundred yards as both sides stood in an open field. The battle ended when it became too dark to see. The losses to the Iron Brigade were staggering. The 6th Wisconsin had 72 killed, wounded, or missing, while the 7th Wisconsin lost 164 of its 580 men. Losses in the 19th Indiana and the 2nd Wisconsin were even higher: 210 and 276 respectively. More than one-third of the brigade were casualties.[5]

During the fighting at Gainesville, Private Philander B. Wright was shot. Wounded for the first time since in his enlistment one year earlier, Wright described how he had been changed by the battle: "Lie upon the battlefield bleeding—see your faithful line grow thinner and thinner & your best friends weltering in their own blood—see them, unharmed cowards straggle to the rear—and the few firm brave ones in front, outnumbered & over-powered—beaten & forced back—all for the want of help that might & should be had—then lie on the field a prisoner and think not of home, but tax your soul to conjure a Curse on Cowards!!!!"[6]

The brigade was engaged at the Battles of Second Bull Run, South Mountain, and Antietam. It was at South Mountain that the brigade earned their famous sobriquet, "Iron Brigade." As General George McClellan recalled in 1900,

> McClellan: "What troops are those fighting on the pike?"
>
> Joseph Hooker: "General Gibbon's Brigade of Western men."
>
> McClellan: "They must be made of iron."
>
> Hooker: "By the Eternal they are iron. If you had seen them at Second Bull Run as I did, you would know them to be iron."
>
> McClellan: "Why General Hooker, they fight equal to the best troops in the world."

After the battle, according to McClellan, Hooker rode up to headquarters and called out to McClellan, "General, what do you think of the Iron Brigade?"[7]

As historian Lance Herdegen points out, it was an exchange that may or may not have happened. What is known for certain is that a reporter from the *Cincinnati Daily Commercial* overheard an exchange similar to the one later recalled by McClellan. Published eight days after South Mountain and five days after Antietam, the reporter described the brigade: "The last terrible battle has reduced this brigade to a mere skeleton; there being scarcely enough members to form half a regiment. The 2nd Wisconsin, which but a few weeks since, numbered over nine hundred men, can now muster but fifty nine. This brigade has done some of the hardest fighting in the service. It has been justly termed the Iron Brigade of the West."[8]

The Iron Brigade led the initial assault against Confederate General Robert E. Lee's Army of Northern Virginia along the banks of Antietam Creek, Maryland, in September 1862. Emerging from a cornfield, the 2nd and the 6th Wisconsin were greeted with a hail of gunfire. The cornfield changed hands six times over the course of the day. The Iron Brigade played an important part in the fighting at Antietam, but the engagement decimated the brigade. After Antietam, the remaining men of the Iron Brigade were reinforced by another western regiment, the 24th Michigan. Organized in Detroit in the

In February 1864, Timothy O. Webster, a soldier in the 24th Michigan, sent home a piece of his regiment's badly damaged flag.

SOURCE: TOM BREAKEY AND RUTGER BREAKEY.

summer of 1862, it would take time for the 24th Michigan to earn the respect
of the battle-hardened members of the Iron Brigade. That respect would come
at Gettysburg.

Regimental Percentages Killed during Entire Term of Service

Ranking	Regiment	Enrolled	Killed	Percent
1	**2nd Wisconsin**	**1,203**	**238**	**19.7**
2	1st Maine Heavy Artillery	2,202	423	19.2
3	57th Massachusetts	1,052	201	19.1
4	140th Pennsylvania	1,132	198	17.4
5	**7th Wisconsin**	**1,630**	**281**	**17.2**
	26th Wisconsin	1,089	188	17.2
6	69th New York	1,513	259	17.1
7	11th Pennsylvania Reserves	1,179	196	16.6
8	142nd Pennsylvania	935	155	16.5
9	141st Pennsylvania	1,037	167	16.1
10	**19th Indiana**	**1,246**	**199**	**15.9**
41	**6th Wisconsin**	**1,940**	**244**	**12.5**
51	**24th Michigan**	**1,654**	**189**	**11.4**

Of the 7,673 men enrolled in the five regiments of the Iron Brigade, 1,151 were
killed or died of wounds, a 15 percent loss. *Source*: William F. Fox, *Regimental Losses in the American Civil* War (Albany, New York, 1889), 8–15.

On the morning of July 1, 1863, the Iron Brigade marched north into
Pennsylvania in pursuit of Lee's Army of Northern Virginia. The brigade arrived in time to reinforce the Union cavalry line northwest of town. The 2nd
Wisconsin was sent forward into a wooded lot on McPherson's Ridge. The 2nd
and 7th Wisconsin drove the Confederate brigade from the field, while the
6th Wisconsin attacked the Confederate line at an old railroad cut. The losses
were staggering: the 2nd Wisconsin lost 233 men, while the 24th Michigan
lost 363 of its 496 men, 73 percent of its ranks. After Gettysburg, the 2nd
Wisconsin, the oldest of the Iron Brigade regiments, could not muster fifty
men. As at Antietam, the Iron Brigade had, at great cost, outfought some of
the Confederacy's best units.

Less than two weeks after the battle, much to the anger and disappointment
of the hard-fighting survivors, the Iron Brigade was reinforced by nine-month
troops from the 167th Pennsylvania. Within weeks, however, the Pennsylvania troops were replaced by the 1st Battalion of New York Sharpshooters,
three-year men who would stay with the brigade through most of 1864. Although the New Yorkers were generally accepted by the old members of the
Iron Brigade, the addition of the eastern troops forever altered the character
of the famed western brigade.

Lee's Shock Troops

Hood's Texas Brigade

Nine Texas Gold Stars were awarded to the "bravest soldiers" of Hood's Texas Brigade by their old commander, Senator Louis T. Wigfall. This is the only one left.

SOURCE: TEXAS HERITAGE MUSEUM, HILL COLLEGE, HILLSBORO, TEXAS.

In February 1865, the remnants of Hood's Texas Brigade assembled for an inspection and review by their old commander, Senator Louis T. Wigfall. A few days earlier General Robert E. Lee had received a package from a "young lady in Texas" that contained stars made of gold "too precious for ordinary use." The young woman asked that they be awarded to the nine bravest soldiers of the brigade. Neither Lee nor Colonel Frederick W. Bass, the brigade's commander, selected the nine recipients. Instead the men of the Texas Brigade voted on the recipients, selecting two each from the 1st Texas, the 5th Texas, and the 3rd Arkansas, and three from the 4th Texas. Historian Susannah Ural describes the event as "a fascinating demonstration of democracy" that captures the ideological devotion of Texas Brigade soldiers.[1]

Often described as "Lee's favorite shock troops," Hood's Texas Brigade was one of a handful of Civil War units to earn an elite reputation.[2] In 1862, as he trained North Carolina troops, Major General Dorsey Pender observed, "If any effort of mine can do it, this Brigade shall be second to none but Hood's Texas Boys. He has the best material on the continent without a doubt."[3] At the Battle of the Wilderness, when the Confederate position began to collapse, General Robert E. Lee celebrated the brigade's arrival on the field waving his hat and yelling, "Hurrah for Texas! Hurrah for Texas!" As the Texans advanced against the Federals along the Orange Plank Road, Lee said, "Texans always move them."[4] Writing after the war, Private Alexander Hunter of the 1st Virginia Infantry referred to the Texas Brigade as "the pride and glory of the Army of Northern Virginia."[5]

Organized on October 22, 1861, the brigade was initially composed of the 1st Texas, the 4th Texas, the 5th Texas, and the 18th Georgia regiments. The three Texas regiments, which were formed in the spring and summer of 1861, became the core of the brigade and were the only Texas units to fight in the Eastern Theater. In February 1862, Wigfall resigned command of the brigade to serve in the Confederate Senate and John Bell Hood, commander of the 4th Texas, was promoted to Brigadier General and placed in command of the brigade. After the battle of Seven Pines, Hampton's Legion from South Carolina joined the brigade. Four months later, after the Battle of Antietam, the Georgians and the South Carolinians were reassigned to brigades from their respective states. The 3rd Arkansas, the only trans-Mississippi regiment serving in the Army of Northern Virginia, was added to the Texas Brigade in November 1862. Still, the brigade was best known for its Texans and their commander who led them through the defining battles of 1862, earning the brigade its reputation and its name, "Hood's Texas Brigade."

The men of Hood's Texas Brigade were proud of their state and its reputation for producing hard-fighting men. In a letter to his sweetheart, James H. Manahan, of the 4th Texas, expressed faith in his regiment's ability to fight: "We have got a great reputation to sustain." Confident in his abilities even though he had yet to see combat, he wrote, "I will not disgrace myself nor the Lone Star Guards." The Texans "have a great reputation here as fighters," noted 4th Texan Robert Gaston. "The people here look upon a Texian ranger . . . as a person who don't care for anything. They say that they had as soon as fight devils at once as Texians." Gaston continued, "We will have enough to do, if we do get into a fight, to sustain our reputation." John Marquis "Mark" Smither, of the 5th Texas, noticed the "Texas boys" were "a perfect curiosity" to the other Southerners. "The people come from every direction to see the boys from Texas . . . they had great ideas of the Texans," Smither told his mother.[6]

The pride exhibited by the Texans was "both a cause and effect of their faith in their leaders," according to Ural. The majority of the men shared a powerful devotion to Hood, who was described by James Murray of the 4th Texas as "one of the best generals we have in this army. If he could have had his way at the Battle of Sharpsburg [Antietam], we would have routed the entire Yankee army in 3 hours." Joe Polley of the Mustang Greys claimed Hood

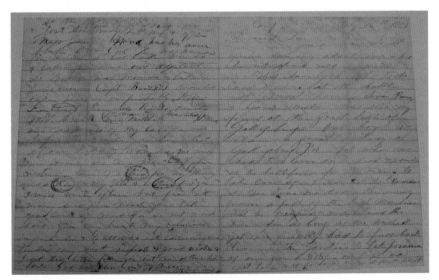

J. R. Loughridge drew "kiss" symbols in his wartime letters home to his wife, Felicia, and daughters, Mary and Ella. Taken from a July 25, 1863, letter.
SOURCE: PEARCE CIVIL WAR COLLECTION, NAVARRO COLLEGE, CORSICANA, TEXAS.

succeeded where others failed because he knew how to lead volunteers rather than regulars. "Never did I see or know a man to rise higher and more quickly in the estimation of others than did Col. Hood. Well versed in human nature and thoroughly understanding the peculiarities of Texans character." According to Polley, Hood "tempered his conduct . . . as to win our favor at once." The men of the brigade praised their other leaders, including regimental and brigade commander Colonel Jerome B. Robertson, who was described by one 5th Texas soldier as "a brave man" and an "entrepid [*sic*] leader." Regimental commander John C. Upton, of the 5th Texas, was described by one soldier as "a daredevil—[an] open hearted and brave Texan."[7]

The Texans also held great faith in their comrades in the rank and file. H. W. Berryman, of the 1st Texas, wrote his mother of the brigade's desperate fight at Gettysburg. His brother Newt, he wrote, "was wounded in the head. He was right by my side. It knocked him down. I thought he was killed, but he jumped up, and kept to fighting harder than ever." Berryman tried to persuade him to leave, but Newt refused, saying, "if every man left for a single wound we would never gain a battle." A frustrated 1st Texas soldier complained of being denied a furlough: "If I was mean enough I could slip away and go home." To do so, however, would mark him a deserter. "I would rather die," he resolved. In February 1864, in a letter home, Manahan wrote, "the men are still in fine spirits and as sanguine of success as they were when war began."[8]

Hood's Texas Brigade also experienced considerable support from the home front. In the hundreds of letters Texas Brigade soldiers sent home and the dozens the soldiers received from home, only a few encouraged their loved ones to quit the fight and return home to Texas. "There are complaints to be sure," Ural notes, "But of the wealth of southern letters from home that encourage men to desert or beg them to come home to save the farm, these do not exist for Texas Brigade soldiers." The families of Texas Brigade soldiers were as motivated as their men to support the Confederacy's bid for independence.[9]

The brigade's pride in their unit, their region, and their reputation, as well as the support from home, sustained them through some of the hardest fighting of the war. The Texas Brigade engaged in all the battles fought by the Army of Northern Virginia except Chancellorsville. In June 1862, at the Battle of Gaines' Mill, the brigade distinguished itself by capturing a battery of guns and repulsing a cavalry counterattack. The brigade suffered over five hundred casualties. At the Second Battle of Bull Run (Manassas) a month later, the brigade overran two Union regiments, nearly annihilated the 5th New York Zouaves, and captured a battery of guns. However, it was at the Battle of Antietam that the brigade secured its reputation for hard fighting. The repeated charges through the cornfield cost the brigade dearly and began a long decline. Having suffered a 64 percent casualty rate across the brigade, including 86 percent in the 1st Texas, the brigade was in reserve at Fredericksburg and Chancellorsville. At the Battle of Gettysburg, they charged through the Devil's Den toward Little Round Top. Again, the brigade suffered heavy losses, including Hood and three of the four regimental commanders, as well as 54 percent losses among the rank and file. By the 1864 Overland Campaign in Virginia, the brigade rarely mustered an average of two hundred effectives per regiment. During the Wilderness Campaign, the brigade suffered mightily, an estimated 66 percent casualty rate. Throughout the winter of 1864–1865, rumors abounded the brigade might be disbanded or consolidated. Only 617 men were left to surrender at Appomattox in April 1865.

The success of Hood's Texas Brigade, as Ural points out, "was grounded in the men's strong self-identity as Confederates, in the mutual respect between the brigade's junior officers and their men, and in their constant desire to maintain their reputation not just as Texans but also as the best soldiers in Robert E. Lee's army and all of the Confederacy." The men of Hood's Texas Brigade shared a strong sense of themselves as white Southern men, more specifically as Texans, an identity that included the assumption "the men were natural born scouts and sharpshooters." Significantly, the families of the men of the Texas Brigade were instrumental in sustaining troop morale. As a result, Hood's Texas Brigade experienced desertion rates that were less than half the rate for Lee's army overall. In the postwar era, the men of Hood's Texas Brigade maintained close connections and led efforts in the state to establish their veteran's organization.[10]

"What is to be done with the prisoners?"

Union and Confederate Prisons

Confederate Soldiers at Camp Douglas, Chicago, Illinois, circa 1863.
SOURCE: CHICAGO HISTORY MUSEUM, IMAGE ID ICHI-001800.

Neither the federal nor the Confederate government was prepared to deal with military prisoners. Northern and Southern officials did not expect the war to last four years; they also did not anticipate the scale of imprisonment that would occur after major battles such as Gettysburg. During the Civil War, more than four hundred thousand soldiers were held prisoner. Nearly fifty-six thousand of those prisoners died in confinement, accounting for nearly 8 percent of the war's seven hundred fifty thousand casualties. For comparison, during the American Revolution, the British held as many thirty-two thousand Americans prisoner. Numbers, however, "only at hint at the depth of the catastrophe," according to historian Benjamin Cloyd. "Both the Lincoln and Davis administrations consistently emphasized the pragmatic needs of the war effort over humanitarian concerns for prisoner welfare." The soldiers who were imprisoned in Union and Confederate camps, such as Camp Douglas (Illinois) and Andersonville (Georgia) pictured here, suffered greatly because their respective governments were ill prepared to deal with the task of managing a large prisoner of war population. Unfortunately for the prisoners, both the Union and the Confederacy used the suffering of prisoners to further their war aims. Prisoners were, as Cloyd argues, "placeholders for the fundamental issues of the war—racial equality, Confederate sovereignty, moral superiority."[1]

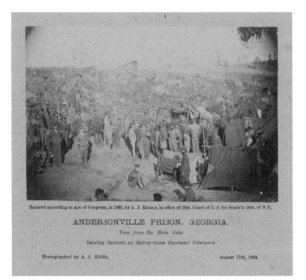

Entered according to Act of Congress, in 1865, by A. J. Riddle, in office of Dist. Court of U. S. for South'n Dist. of N.Y.

ANDERSONVILLE PRISON. GEORGIA.

View from the Main Gate.

Issuing Rations to thirty-three thousand Prisoners

Photographed by A. J. Riddle,   August 17th, 1864.

Andersonville Prison, Georgia.
SOURCE: LIBRARY OF CONGRESS, PRINTS AND PHOTOGRAPHS DIVISION.

General Montgomery Meigs, the Union's quartermaster general, was one of the first to express concerns the war would result in the United States caring for "large numbers of prisoners of war." In July 1861, Meigs made two recommendations to Secretary of War Simon Cameron. First, he recommended the appointment of a commissary general of prisoners, an officer who would oversee prison policies and supervise prisons. He also recommended the selection of a "depot and place of confinement for prisoners of war." Cameron approved the plan. In October, Lieutenant Colonel William Hoffman was appointed. He set out a few days later for Lake Erie to visit four islands as possible prison sites. After visiting several islands, Hoffman informed Meigs that Johnson's Island was the best site. Work on the prison continued through the winter of 1861–1862.[2]

In the meantime, the few prisoners of war held by the Union were housed in existing facilities, such as the Old Capitol Jail in Washington, DC, Fort McHenry in Baltimore, and Fort Lafayette located in "the Narrows" between Staten Island and Long Island. Many of the Union's earliest captives were political prisoners: civilians from the border regions of Maryland, western Virginia, Kentucky, and Missouri. These individuals posed little to no threat but had nonetheless been "caught in a rather wide net cast by an administration facing an unprecedented challenge to the nation's existence." In the West, during the summer of 1861, Confederate military and political prisoners also trickled into Camp Chase, four miles west of Columbus, Ohio, which was adapted from a training camp to a prison for Confederate captives.

By February 1862, despite bad weather, Hoffman declared the camp on Johnson's Island ready to receive a limited number of prisoners, perhaps five to six hundred. However, the military situation had changed. That same month, Union forces under Grant had captured Fort Donelson, Tennessee, and seized fifteen thousand Confederates. Grant proposed paroling all the prisoners, but Union policy precluded such an action. Instead Grant's superior Major General Henry Halleck sent a flurry of telegrams to various governors seeking facilities to house the prisoners. A few captives were sent to prisons in Missouri and Illinois, while others were sent to Union training camps, such as Camp Douglas in Chicago, Illinois. Occupying about three hundred acres of land, Camp Douglas housed more than four thousand Union recruits who lived in one-story wooden barracks that offered little protection from Chicago's harsh winters. Prisoners from Fort Donelson began to arrive at Camp Douglas soon after the battle ended. By March 1862, the camp held more than five thousand Confederate prisoners.

From the beginning, there were problems managing the camps. Most of the Union army's most competent, best trained officers were in the field supporting the war effort. Thus officers who were responsible for commanding prison camps were far less capable and experienced. In Ohio, at Camp Chase, the commander Colonel Charles W. B. Allison received his appointment because he was the son-in-law of Ohio's lieutenant governor. An officer inspecting the camp declared Allison "utterly ignorant of the most common requirements of Army Regulations" and "not in any degree a soldier." The first prisoners to arrive at Camp Chase were housed in tents with insufficient wood to keep them warm. Poor drainage meant the tents were always surrounded by mud. Construction of more permanent structures did not always result in better conditions. Even after barracks were constructed at Camp Chase, Hoffman's inspecting officer noted, "The spaces between the [buildings] are heaped with the vilest accumulations of filth which has remained there for months, breeding sickness and pestilence."

When Hoffman visited Camp Douglas in June 1862, he reported, "There has been the greatest carelessness and willful neglect in the management of affairs of the camp." The recently departed commander, Colonel James Mulligan, had left things in "a shameful state of confusion." Moreover, "standing water, unpoliced grounds, foul sinks, [and] unventilated and crowded barracks" led him to recommend either relocating the camp or burning it down.[3]

The Confederacy also struggled to house prisoners of war. After the First Battle of Bull Run, Confederates seized nearly fifty officers, a thousand enlisted men, and a few Union civilians who had ridden out from Washington, DC, to watch the battle. These prisoners were jailed at makeshift facilities in Richmond. However, the influx of prisoners presented a serious logistical problem. As the *Richmond Whig* observed on August 5, "Everybody is asking, 'What is to be done with the prisoners?'" By the fall of 1861, Confederate officials were looking for sites further south. Sites were established in Charleston, South Carolina, and as far away as New Orleans, Louisiana. Still, these efforts did little to relieve the overcrowding in Virginia.[4]

As Northern prisoners by the thousands poured into inadequate Southern prisons, the Confederate government struggled to care for them. After the Battle of Shiloh in April 1862, the Confederates sent their prisoners to the former fairgrounds in Macon, Georgia, renamed Camp Ogelthorpe. Although one prisoner termed it "a splendid place," Confederate officials were short on resources. The arrival of hundreds of prisoners at the camp prompted the *Macon Telegraph* to exclaim, "At a time when it is difficult to feed our own population, we are to be blessed with the presence and custody of 900 prisoners of war!" The camp surgeon appealed to the public for donations of mattresses, quilts, and other supplies for the hospital.[5]

As the war entered its second year, the press and the public pressured their respective governments to enter into an exchange agreement for prisoners of war. Some Northerners believed poor prison conditions and federal prisoner mortality was part of a Confederate conspiracy to abuse Union soldiers. Lincoln was reluctant to enter into an exchange agreement to avoid recognizing the Confederacy as an independent nation. Finally, Lincoln relented. In July 1862, Union general John A. Dix and his Confederate counterpart General Daniel Harvey Hill agreed to a cartel exchange for prisoners of war modeled on the agreement between the Americans and the British during the War of 1812. The Dix-Hill cartel regulated exchanges on a national basis for the next several months, effectively emptying prisoner of war sites in the North and the South. Between July 1862 and March 1863, the number of prisoners at Camp Douglas went from nearly eight thousand to about three hundred.

Unfortunately, by early 1863, the cartel began to break down. Agents on both sides of the agreement accused each other of cheating on numbers. There were also debates about the validity and the terms of the paroles issued. Soldiers who were paroled resisted a return to the front lines, insisting their paroles exempted them from service until their exchange had been completed. Instead of sending paroled prisoners home, Union and Confederate military officials sent them to parole camps. But parole camps further strained limited resources as the military had to feed and house paroled soldiers awaiting exchange.

The most significant challenge to the exchange agreement centered on the treatment of captured Black soldiers. The Emancipation Proclamation had transformed Union war aims and led to the enlistment of thousands of Black soldiers. An outraged Confederacy adopted a "black flag" policy toward African American soldiers. The Confederates' no-quarter policy toward Black soldiers and their white commanders resulted in the deaths of thousands of Blacks. At battles such as Fort Pillow, Saltville, and the Crater, Black soldiers died in numbers and under circumstances that suggest African American soldiers were much more likely than their white comrades to die if overrun or captured. The few Blacks who survived capture were reenslaved, even if the soldier had been free before the war. Cloyd estimates that only about twelve hundred African American soldiers ever made it to a Confederate prison camp.[6]

By mid-1863, the exchange had collapsed, just as both sides faced unprecedented numbers of prisoners after the Battles of Chancellorsville and Gettysburg. In the North and the South officials expanded existing facilities and opened new camps. In 1863 and 1864, Hoffman established prisons at Point Lookout, Maryland, and Elmira, New York. Hoffman's counterpart in the South General John Winder established facilities throughout the South, including Richmond (Libby Prison and Belle Isle); Salisbury, North Carolina; Macon, Georgia; Andersonville, Georgia; and Tyler, Texas.

Conditions in the camps deteriorated even further. Disease was a common problem. In some camps, prisoners created makeshift shelters out of blankets and poles or simply burrowed into the ground. One prisoner at Andersonville wrote, "Many of the poor prisoners are standing like horses and cattle, with their backs to the storm, and no shelter." Another prisoner complained of rotten meat. "We took it back to the Quarter master and showed it to him," he wrote. "He said he did not care a damn if it was all rotten he could not help it." One medical inspector at Andersonville reported that virtually every prisoner in the camp suffered from either diarrhea or dysentery, a result of exposure; the dust, smoke, and filth of the camp; and a diet of cornbread made from unbolted cornmeal. In April 1864, Union and Confederate forces agreed to a special exchange of the sickest prisoners. The "living skeletons" of Northern troops returned by the Confederacy confirmed for Northerners the suffering Union soldiers were enduring in Confederate prisons. The Secretary of War ordered the rations of Confederate prisoners cut in half in retaliation.[7]

Andersonville, according to Cloyd, "represented the nadir of the Confederate treatment of their captives." By May 1864, Andersonville housed more than twelve thousand prisoners; one month later that number had ballooned to eighteen thousand. Thirteen thousand Unionists, or more than one in three prisoners, died while confined at Andersonville. After the war, Andersonville's commander, Swiss-born Henry Wirz, became the target of Union vengeance. He was arrested in May 1865 and taken to Washington, DC, where Wirz faced trial for "maliciously, willfully, and traitorously" conspiring to "injure the health and destroy the lives" of prisoners. Wirz was found guilty; he was hanged on November 10, 1865, becoming the only ex-Confederate officer executed for conspiracy against Union prisoners of war.[8]

Days of Infamy and Disgrace

The New York City Draft Riots

"The Riots in New York: Destruction of the Coloured Orphan Asylum"
SOURCE: NEW YORK PUBLIC LIBRARY.

The New York City Draft Riots of 1863 lasted four days, caused an estimated $1.5 million in damage (about $30.5 million today), and killed nearly one hundred New Yorkers, many of them African Americans. What began as opposition to the draft for the Union army escalated into a riot that targeted African Americans, including the children at the Colored Orphan Asylum. Quick action by orphanage staff spared the more than two hundred children from injury or death. For many, the destruction of the asylum, pictured here, was one of the worst offenses of the riot. "Men have been killed and houses burned," noted the editor of *Harper's Weekly*, "worst of all, an orphan asylum—a noble monument of charity for the reception of colored orphans—has been ruthlessly destroyed, and children and nurses have lost every thing they had in the world." In a subsequent issue, *Harper's* featured seven images from the riots: six images shared a two-page spread, while the seventh, an image of the burning of the asylum, filled an entire page.[1]

The violence that spilled onto the streets of New York in the summer of 1863 resulted from old grievances and new pressures. For the first time in American history, compulsory military service was imposed nationally, and many men and their families felt the government was infringing on individual liberties. The perceived unfairness of the draft, longstanding ethnic and racial tensions, and Northerners' frustration with the progress of the war came together in an explosive protest that revealed deep fractures in the Union war effort.

Between 1845 and 1860, three million immigrants arrived in the United States, most from Ireland and Germany, where crop failure, economic crises, and political upheaval had sparked a massive exodus. The migration of primarily poor (Irish) and non-English-speaking (German) immigrants, many of them Catholic, triggered an increase in nativist sentiment in the United States. The Order of the Star-Spangled Banner, also known as the American party or the Know Nothings, reached prominence in the 1850s as a movement of native-born white Protestants. The Know Nothings sought limits on immigration, exclusion of the foreign-born from voting, and lengthy residency requirements for citizenship. Although the Know Nothing party broke apart in the sectional tensions of the 1850s, nativist sentiment remained strong. The Irish were seen as violent and disorderly, while the Germans, particularly those known as the "Forty-Eighters," were viewed as potentially dangerous political radicals. Their shared cultural affection for alcohol and their Catholicism placed Irish and German immigrants outside the American Protestant mainstream with its emphasis on temperate behavior. In eastern cities like New York, unskilled Irish immigrants often competed with free Blacks for jobs as domestics, waiters, and laborers. Employers often pitted the two groups against one another. When Irish workers struck for higher wages, Blacks were brought in as strikebreakers.

In the fall of 1860, Irish Catholics voted overwhelmingly Democratic. The Republican Party held little appeal for the Irish. The Republicans included abolitionists, who seemed more concerned with the plight of Southern slaves than the plight of poor Irish laborers. The party also included nativists, the "scattered and broken forces of the Know Nothing party" that represented "hatred and prejudice and injustice to the Irish," according to Boston's Irish newspaper the *Pilot*. That changed when the Confederates fired on Fort Sumter. "Duty and patriotism prompt me to [support the Union]," claimed Irishman Thomas Francis Meagher. "The Republic that gave us an asylum and an honorable career,—that is the mainstay of human freedom, the world over—is threatened with disruption. It is the duty of every liberty-loving citizen to prevent such a calamity at all hazards."[2]

Between 1861 and 1865, an estimated one hundred fifty thousand Irish and two hundred thousand German-born men volunteered for military service. The Irish Brigade was organized by Meagher, who served as the brigade's commanding general. Three regiments—the 63rd, 69th, and 88th New York—formed the core of the brigade, along with the 28th Massachusetts and the 114th Pennsylvania. The Irish Brigade fought in every major battle in the Eastern Theater from the Peninsula Campaign to Appomattox. At the Battle of Antietam, the brigade suffered a 60 percent casualty rate. In December 1862, the 69th New York lost all sixteen of its officers at the Battle of Fredericksburg. "It was not a battle," brigade historian Henry Heisler said, "it was a wholesale slaughter of human beings." Fredericksburg broke the Irish Brigade. Only 340 men were present for duty in February 1863. In July, the Irish Brigade mustered just over five hundred men for the Battle of Gettysburg, where the brigade was ordered into the thick of the fight at the Wheatfield and Devil's Den.[3]

By June 1863, the Union war effort was not going well. In the West, Grant's forces had waged a months-long campaign against Confederate forces at Vicksburg, the "Gibraltar of the West." In the East, Union forces had suffered defeat at Fredericksburg, where the postbattle fiasco known as the "Mud March" led Lincoln to replace General Ambrose Burnside with General Joseph Hooker. In May 1863, at the Battle of Chancellorsville, Virginia, the Union army lost more than seventeen thousand men wounded or killed. The Confederate success at Chancellorsville led General Robert E. Lee to march his army into southern Pennsylvania in late June. Three days of fighting at Gettysburg resulted in fifty thousand casualties (twenty-three thousand Union and twenty-eight thousand Confederate). Although the Union prevailed at Gettysburg and Vicksburg, the high casualty rate stunned Northerners, including the survivors of the Irish brigade, who lost another two hundred men at Gettysburg.

The enactment of the Emancipation Proclamation on January 1, 1863, marked a significant shift in Union war aims, a shift many Irish did not support. Irish newspapers referenced the labor competition emancipation would bring to Northern cities. Others noted "the irredeemable malignity of the Abolition hatred of [the Irish] race." Abolitionists, Irish Americans claimed, were hypocritical, showing prejudice toward the Irish while simultaneously denouncing Southerners' treatment of slaves. "We Catholics, and a vast majority of our troops in the field, have not the slightest idea of carrying on a war that cost so much blood and treasure just to gratify a clique of Abolitionists," warned New York Archbishop John Hughes.[4]

For many Irish, the passage of the Enrollment Act in March 1863, combined with the Emancipation Proclamation, "revealed a war that held nothing for them but prejudice, sacrifice, and death," as one historian notes. The Irish community claimed the new law targeted aliens. The Enrollment Act made all single male citizens between twenty and forty-five and married men between twenty and thirty-five subject to military service. However, if selected, citizens could pay $300 to avoid service, or they could provide a substitute to fight in their places. For the working poor, $300 was more than half a year's wages. Many Irish Americans believed the law was unjust. John England, an Irish American soldier, spoke for many when he claimed the law "was framed for the benefit of the rich and the disadvantage of the poor." The "conscription law, no matter how constructed," England noted, "can never become popular, for it is the last alternative of an unpopular cause."[5]

On Saturday, July 11, in New York City, the first lottery of the conscription law was held. That weekend dissent spread throughout the city. On Monday morning, July 13, as officials pulled the second round of names at the draft offices, a crowd gathered outside grew unruly. They smashed windows, destroyed the draft wheel, and set fire to the building. By noon, the crowd had forced the draft office to close and the crowds took to the streets. Estimates suggest there were as many as fifty thousand rioters, including women and children. The eight hundred police officers who were on duty were unable to stop the destruction that followed.

Initially, the mob focused on military officials and government buildings. However, by Monday afternoon, the mob turned their anger on African Americans and the draft riot became a race riot. According to the *New-York Tribune*, "An attack was made upon colored men and boys in every part of the city during the day, crowds of 100 to 500 persons hunting them like blood-hounds." Although abolitionists and prominent Republicans were also targeted, African Americans and their property bore the brunt of the attacks. Black men were singled out for the most brutal violence: torture, hanging, and burning. The violence continued until July 15, when soldiers fresh from the Battle of Gettysburg arrived in the city to assist the police. By Wednesday, July 17, law and order had been restored. Nearly one hundred people died and more than fifty buildings, including the Colored Orphan Asylum, had been destroyed by fire. Although *Harper's Weekly* called for "sharp and extreme" punishment," none of the rioters was ever brought to justice.[6]

The Evolution of
the Union Cavalry

Friedrich Holdmann of the 2nd Wisconsin Cavalry on his horse.

SOURCE: WISCONSIN HISTORICAL SOCIETY, WHS-7819.

On December 30, 1861, German immigrant Friedrich Holdmann enlisted in the 2nd Wisconsin Cavalry, one of four cavalry units from Wisconsin. The regiment was recruited and organized under the command of Colonel Cadwallader C. Washburn, a three-term congressman and one of the best-known Republicans in the state. In this undated photograph, Holdmann sits in what may be a McClellan saddle with hooded stirrups, saddlebags to the rear, and a regulation horse blanket. He is wearing a black felt hat and a regulation cavalry uniform jacket. Holdmann fought in Missouri, Arkansas, Mississippi, Louisiana, and Texas before mustering out on February 4, 1865, and returning to Milwaukee.[1]

Civil War armies consisted of three major components: infantry, artillery, and cavalry. At the start of the war, the role of the infantry and the artillery, as well as the training of new recruits for those branches, was clearly defined. The cavalry, however, had been neglected before 1861. When the war began it was unclear what role the cavalry would play in military strategy, what tactics would be needed to carry out those tasks, and how the cavalry related to the infantry and the artillery in support and in combat. Additionally, secession resulted in some of the most experienced cavalry officers resigning their positions to join the Confederacy. In general, Southern cavalry troops were from a culture and a class of society where riding was natural and expected. "The typical recruit from New England and the Middle Atlantic states . . . knew a horse only as a farm animal or as the motive power for a streetcar," notes one historian. As a result, for the first two years of the war, Southern cavalry forces outperformed Northern cavalry troops.[2]

At the start of the war, the United States had just five mounted regiments all scattered at western posts. A sixth cavalry regiment was organized in May 1861, and the six regiments were renumbered by the date of their organization as the 1st to 6th U.S. Cavalry. Despite these efforts, it was "nearly like having no cavalry at all," especially as Southern cavalry troops resigned their positions and joined the Confederacy. For General Winfield Scott, commander of the federal forces, the lack of cavalry was not a problem. He saw no use for mounted troops in the conflict. Scott was focused on Virginia, where the landscape prevented the use of cavalry tactics. Moreover, Scott believed the war would be a short-lived conflict. Cavalry was expensive to outfit and time consuming to train. By the time cavalry regiments could be trained and outfitted, the war would be over. The First Battle of Bull Run in July 1861 put to rest any hopes for a brief war. Lincoln overruled Scott and by December fifty regiments of cavalry, including the 2nd Wisconsin, were being raised.[3]

The cavalry regiments that were sent off to the front had limited experience with dismounted and mounted drills and were poorly equipped. Typical is the experience of one member of the 7th Pennsylvania Cavalry, which shipped west to Louisville with three Pennsylvania infantry regiments in January 1862:

> The work of packing had to be done in a hurry. Most of our company (The Independent Dragoons) were excellent horsemen, accustomed to the saddle; but how to pack bed and board, household goods and three days provender on horseback, was a mystery yet to be solved. To leave anything behind was not once thought of; the castaway clothing of other regiments had to be gathered and lugged, that nothing be lost.

> Two woolen blankets and a coverlet brought from home were hurriedly rolled into a bundle two feet long and a foot thick, which was strapped on the saddle behind; the rubber dolman overcoat, carpet sack with several suits of under-clothing, shaving-tools, shoe-brush and blacking, and perhaps a sheep-skin, had to be packed in front. The side-pockets or saddle-bags, were filled with crackers and forty rounds of ammunition.

> The dragoon then girded himself with a heavy cavalry sword: on one shoulder hung a monstrous shooting-iron, . . . and on the other a haversack holding three days' rations. Thus equipped, the horses were led into a line, each with a nose-bag dangling on his neck containing a feed of oats, and a weight of one hundred and fifty pounds on his back. The command is given. "Attention: Prepare to mount: Mount!"

> Each trooper was expected to obey the command with his accustomed agility. The scrambling to get into the saddle was highly amusing to a disinterested spectator. Some sat astride the stern of the ship, but how to get over the rear bundle was the difficulty. Short-legged men had to lead their horses to the nearest fence, and from the top rail drop down amidships. When once mounted, it was only a question of time as to how we should dismount. . . . As soon as the horses began to gallop, the rigging of the ship and the passenger on the upper deck began to slide backward, notwithstanding the pilot held on to rein and mane for dear life. The sight was indeed ludicrous . . .

> Now and then a saddle would turn earthward toward the centre of gravity, leaving the rider and his bundles, mud-splashed, in the middle of the road. . . .

This first bloodless charge will never be forgotten by those of our boys who were under the painful necessity of casting anchor in the middle of the street for repairs, at high noon on that memorable Sunday.[4]

Friedrich Holdmann participated in the transformation of the Union cavalry from a poorly organized, ineffectively used branch of the military into a powerful combat arm that provided valuable aid to the Northern war effort. During McClellan's Peninsula Campaign, eastern cavalry units gained experience handling their weapons, and using dismounted and mounted tactics effectively. By 1863, the federal cavalry demonstrated technical and tactical expertise and "their ability to be an integral striking force of the army." In 1863, the cavalry began to carve out a larger role for their branch of the military at the Battles of Brandy Station, Gettysburg, and Chickamauga, where they showed "they showed they could delay and pursue infantry as well as cavalry, demonstrating a striking power that had not been anticipated."

In the West, Union cavalry suffered from similar problems with organization and leadership as mounted troops had in the East. Attacks by Confederate cavalry leaders like John H. Morgan, Nathan B. Forrest, and Joseph Wheeler harassed Union forces. However, by 1863, western cavalry regiments like the 2nd Wisconsin were coming into their own, providing valuable support to Grant in his Vicksburg campaign and General William Rosecrans's Tullahoma campaign.

During the second half of the Civil War, Union cavalry troops were as comfortable completing both mounted and dismounted attacks as they were standing behind a stone wall breaking the charge of the enemy. The mission of the cavalry was as clear as that of the infantry and artillery. Armed with better firepower and appropriate tactics, the Union cavalry had by the end of 1863 become an effective fighting force capable of acting with newfound autonomy that bolstered their success.[5]

Part VI

HOME FRONT

There was no single experience of the home front during the Civil War. Factors, such as class, race, family size, and geographic location, affected women's experience of the wartime home front. Some women thrived in the absence of their husbands, while others fought for survival. For example, Boston writer Caroline McKendry continued to publish regularly throughout the war, supporting herself and her son while her husband William served in the Union Navy. In contrast, Harriet Webster, a working-class woman from Detroit, struggled to support herself and her two children after her husband enlisted in the 24th Michigan. His death in 1864 forced her back onto the mercies of her abusive extended family. Women in borderland areas like Arkansas, Missouri, and Texas achieved greater autonomy despite being isolated and subject to the depredations of guerrilla fighters. For these women, the conditions of the home front often meant husbands, fathers, and sons were unavailable for aid. For Black women and children, race defined available aid, including jobs and pensions.

"The Last Thought of a Dying Father"

The Northern Home Front

"The Children of the Battlefield," a reproduction of the original ambrotype portrait of Franklin, Frederick, and Alice Humiston, children of Sergeant Amos Humiston, Company C, 154th New York Infantry.

SOURCE: LIBRARY OF CONGRESS PRINTS AND PHOTOGRAPHS DIVISION.

This carte-de-visite, or calling card–size photograph, is one of dozens reproduced from an ambrotype found on a dead soldier after the Battle of Gettysburg. Philadelphia physician John Francis Bourns had traveled to Gettysburg via Chambersburg to treat the wounded in the days after the battle. During a stop at a tavern in Graeffenburg, Bourns heard the story of the fallen soldier and saw the ambrotype. He convinced the innkeeper to give him the photograph so he might attempt to locate the dead man's family. When Bourns returned to Philadelphia, he had duplicates made of the image and had the Philadelphia *Inquirer* run an article about the unknown soldier. The article was later reprinted in the *American Presbyterian*:

The Dead Soldier and the Daguerreotype

An interesting and touching relic from the battle-field of Gettysburg, is in possession of J. F. Bourns. . . . It is [an] . . . Ambrotype . . . of three children, two boys and a girl, and was taken from the hands of a dead soldier belonging to the Union army. He had been mortally wounded, and crawled to a sheltered spot, where his body was found with the picture of his children so placed within his folded hands that it met his dying gaze. There was no clue to his name or regiment, or his former place of residence, but his grave is marked, and it is hoped that he may be identified by the picture of his children.

The little ones have all interesting faces, and would seem to be nine, seven, and five years of age. The youngest is seated on a high chair, with his brother on his right hand, and his sister on his left. The little girl has a plaid dress, and the oldest boy a jacket of the same material. The miniature has a flat gilt frame, and may have been sent from home in a letter. On the frame, faint but traceable, is the inscription: "*Holmes, Booth & Haydens. Superfine.*" Our exchanges, by copying this notice, may bring some comfort to a widow and orphans, by giving them intelligence of the hero's last resting place. Dr. Bourns will give further information to those who desire it.

In the fall of 1863, the soldier was identified as Amos Humiston of the 154th New York Infantry. His widow Philinda lived with her three children in Portville, New York. Bourns later traveled to meet Philinda and to present her and her children with gifts and the profits of the sale of copies of the picture.[1]

The story of Philinda Humiston is the story of many Northern women during the war. Although their experiences varied by age, class, race and ethnicity, and geographic location, Northern women confronted the disruption brought by the absence of husbands, fathers, sons, and brothers. Women like Philinda struggled to hold their families together economically and emotionally. They did what they could to support Northern soldiers on the battlefield by collecting blankets, sewing shirts and flags, nursing sick and wounded soldiers, managing family finances, and writing letters and sending photographs.

At the beginning of the war, Amos Humiston owned a harness shop in Portville, New York. Married and the father of three young children—six-year-old Franklin, four-year-old Alice, and two-year-old Frederick—Humiston did not volunteer in 1861. "When the rebellion first took the form of open war upon the country, [Amos] was anxious to enlist," Portville minister Isaac Ogden later recalled, "but his duty to his family seemed then to be paramount to his duty to his country." For the first year of the war, Amos, like many on the home front, followed the progress of the war through news accounts, celebrating Grant's success at Fort Henry, Tennessee, and mourning the devastating losses of the Seven Days' Battles.

On July 1, 1862, as the Union army soundly defeated the Confederate army in the Battle of Malvern Hill—the last of the Seven Days' Battles—Lincoln issued a call for more volunteers. One can imagine Philinda's anxiety when Amos told her of his decision to enlist. Although he loved his family very much, Amos felt it wrong to stay home. Desperate to keep Amos home, Philinda reminded him of his promise to repair their run-down home and pleaded with him to think of the children. Amos assured Philinda that Reverend Ogden had promised him the town would care for his family in his absence. Amos would not be dissuaded from his decision to enlist. By August 22, Amos and the rest of his company had arrived at the regimental rendezvous in Jamestown, New York. On September 24, 1862, Amos mustered in for service. With the stroke of his pen on the enlistment form, Amos consigned Philinda to sustain their family in his absence.

On September 26, Amos sent $40 to Philinda and told her he had allotted $10 of his monthly pay directly to her, "so that if I am taken prisoner or aney thing else should happen," she would have a steady source of income. "You must use your own judgement about this money that I have sent you," he told Philinda, suggesting she should not pay all the money they owed to local real estate agent and grocer Mark Comstock, who expected the money to be sent directly to him. "I made up my mind to send it to you," Amos told Philinda, "then you can do with it as you like."[2]

After Amos's departure, Philinda and the children waited anxiously for each letter he sent home. On May 9, 1863, after the Battle of Chancellorsville, Amos wrote Philinda a letter thanking her for a recent gift:

I got the likeness of the children and it pleased me more than eney thing that you could have sent me how I want to se them and their mother is more than I can tell I hope that we may all live to see each other again if this war dose not last to long.[3]

After the Battle of Gettysburg, no word came from Amos. One local paper published an erroneous report that the 154th New York had been detached from the Army of the Potomac before the battle and, as a result, had not been at Gettysburg. A week later, the paper admitted the 154th had indeed been at Gettysburg, but "probably did not participate in the engagement." The details that came out in the following weeks were sketchy, but it was clear that most of the regiment was missing. A list of the regiment's casualties was never published: "The survivors were too few and too uncertain to notify the homefolk adequately of the fate of their comrades."

In January 1864, the story of Amos Humiston, along with a fanciful wood-cut titled "The Last Thought of a Dying Father," ran in the popular weekly *Frank Leslie's Illustrated* in January 1864. Referring to Humiston only as "a volunteer from New York," the article described the story as "one of the most touching scenes of the battlefield of Gettysburg." By 1864, the story of Amos, Philinda, and their three children was widely known, making celebrities of the family. Still, Philinda struggled to keep body and soul together. In June 1864, Philinda applied for a widow's pension. It would take nearly two years for her application to be approved. In the meantime, the cartes-de-visite made by Bourns continued to sell and poems and songs recounted the story of Amos. However, it is unlikely the family received any benefit from the fundraising efforts that were launched on their behalf. "It is believed that my mother received a portion of the money raised by the sale of the pictures," Alice Humiston told a reporter in 1914. "This is not so." Alice claimed Bourns had taken advantage of Philinda. "If Mother had been older and a little more used to the ways of the world Dr. Bourns would not have sit at his ease all his life and she living the way she had to. I boil every time I think of it."[4]

Philinda remarried twice and was widowed twice. She died in 1913. Franklin Humiston became a successful physician in New Hampshire, while his brother Frederick became a prosperous grain merchant in Massachusetts. Alice Humiston never married and lived a somewhat nomadic life, working a variety of jobs in the New England area.[5]

In 1993, a monument was erected near the spot where Amos was found. It is the only monument to an individual enlisted man on the battlefield of Gettysburg.[6]

"Bread or Blood!"

The Southern Home Front during the Civil War

"Sowing and Reaping," *Frank Leslie's Illustrated*, May 23, 1863. In this telling image of the Southern bread riots that broke out in 1863, the artist makes clear who he believes is to blame for food shortages in the South. The left image depicts beautiful Southern belles "hounding" their men to join the rebellion. On the right, two years into the war, unattractive, starving women feel the "effects of the rebellion."

SOURCE: LIBRARY OF CONGRESS PRINTS AND PHOTOGRAPHS DIVISION.

In the spring of 1863, more than a dozen food riots broke out across the South as women took to the streets shouting, "Bread or Blood!" Wartime inflation, a shortage of fairly priced food supplies for civilians, and the impressment of provisions by the Confederate government for the military created conditions in which demand outstripped supply. On May 23, the Northern publication *Frank Leslie's Illustrated* ran this unsympathetic image of the riot in Richmond, Virginia. Titled "Sowing and Reaping," the illustration placed the blame on Southern women, who had "hound[ed] their men to rebellion" and were now "suffering the effects of the rebellion, and creating bread riots."

The food riots occurred at a critical moment in the Confederate war effort. In the spring of 1863, the Confederacy was two years into a war many had believed would end quickly. The government struggled to field, feed, and equip an army "adequate to the size and extent of the conflict." Because 40 percent of the population was enslaved and unavailable for military service, the Confederacy mobilized an ever-higher percentage of its adult white male population. In 1862, the Confederate government adopted a draft of all white men aged eighteen to thirty-five years. As a result, husbands as well as sons, brothers, and sweethearts were drafted into the military. The Confederate War Department's conscription policy exempted virtually no one. The Confederacy mobilized 75 to 85 percent of its adult white male population, significantly higher than the Union's 50 percent. Confederate women "who described a rural landscape literally stripped of men did not exaggerate," notes historian Stephanie McCurry.[1]

The loss of the labor and wages of husbands, sons, and brothers, however, was but one aspect of a larger problem as Confederate officials also moved to regularize the practice of impressing slave labor and provisions to support the war effort. In April 1863, the War Department imposed the tax-in-kind. Although the tax was meant to be assessed against surpluses, the tax was in practice yet another burden on the poor. As McCurry notes, "To poor soldiers' wives, the 10 percent tax was, quite literally, an insupportable burden, the very difference between an eked-out subsistence and starvation."[2]

Confederate women protested. "We hav seen the time when we could call our Little children and our Husbun to our tables and hav a plenty and now wee have Becom Beggars and starvers an now way to help ourselves," wrote Margaret Smith to North Carolina governor Zebulon Vance. "You our govner of north carlina has promust the soldier that thare families shod sher of the Last," she reminded the governor, "and wee think it is hie time for us to get help in our time of need." In February 1863, a group of women—"our company will be calld Reglators"—informed Vance "we the common people has to hav bread or blood and we are bound boath men and women to hav it or die in the attempt." The women outlined the crisis Confederate soldiers' wives faced and the conspiracy they believed existed:

> Our people is drove of in the ware to fight for the big mans negro and he at home making nearly all the corn that is made and then because he has the play in his own fingers he puts the price on his corn so as to take all the solders wage for a fiew bushels and then them has worked hard was . . . in living circumstances with perhaps a good little homestid and other thing convenient for there well being perhaps will be credited until the debt will take there land and every thing they have . . . and then they will have to rent thure land of them lords.[3]

The first riot broke out in Atlanta, Georgia, on March 18 when a group of women held up a shop owner at gunpoint. In the following days, riots occurred in Salisbury, North Carolina; Mobile, Alabama; Petersburg, Virginia; and Macon, Georgia. In each street action the rioters, who self-described as "soldiers' wives" or "soldiers' mothers," led carefully organized attacks against merchants they regarded as speculators. So similar were the riots that rumors of conspiracy abounded by the time the largest riot occurred in Richmond, Virginia, on April 2.

Richmond was, as one historian notes, "a powder keg awaiting only a spark to explode." The city's population had increased nearly fivefold since 1860. In the early years of the war, the government bureaucrats, laborers, spies, soldiers, prostitutes, gamblers, speculators, and refugees who flocked to the Confederate capital overwhelmed existing resources. Housing was limited and expensive, forcing families to share cramped quarters. The crowded conditions contributed to epidemics of smallpox and other diseases. Crime was common as the small local police force struggled to maintain control. Food and fuel were scarce, further adding to the misery.[4]

Between August 1862 and March 1863, the prices of most foodstuffs tripled. Confederate war clerk John B. Jones tracked rising prices in his diary. Noting the near disappearance of meat from the market and the increased prices for meal and potatoes, Jones noted soberly, "the gaunt form of wretched famine . . . approaches with rapid strides." Flour that had sold for $7.50 per barrel in 1860 rose to $30 a barrel in 1863. A late spring snowfall exacerbated food shortages. "All who made no provision for such a contingency are subsisting on very short-commons," Jones noted. "There are some pale faces seen in the streets from the deficiency of food; but no beggars, no complaints. . . . This for liberty!" On March 27, Confederate president Jefferson Davis declared a day of fasting and prayer. "Fasting in the midst of famine!" Jones noted in his diary. "May God save this people!"[5]

On April 1, three hundred women met at the Belvidere Baptist Church in Richmond to plan the riot. "The object of the meeting," according to a Mrs. Jamison, "was to organize to demand goods of the merchants at government prices; and if they were not given, the stores were to be broken open and goods taken by force." On April 2, 1863, one thousand women gathered at Capitol Square before heading to the governor's mansion to demand an interview with Governor John Letcher. Dissatisfied with Letcher's response, the women left the square and started down Ninth Street, passing the War Department, where Jones watched the procession. "Not knowing the meaning of such a procession," Jones stopped someone and asked. "A young woman, seemingly emaciated . . . answered that they were going to find something to eat," to which Jones responded, "they were going in the right direction to find plenty in the hands of the extortioners." Although Jones did not follow the crowd, he later learned the crowd had emptied the "diverse stores of the speculators." Armed with pistols, bowie knives, and hatchets, the crowd "impressed all the carts and drays in the street, which were speedily laden with meal, flour, shoes, etc." The looting continued, according to Jones, until the governor read them the riot act and "threatened to fire on the mob." Davis appeared on the scene and urged the mob to return to their homes. Several rioters were arrested. By afternoon, quiet had been restored, and, according to Jones, "the government is issuing rice to the people."[6]

Confederate political officials tried and failed to prevent news coverage of the riot. Southern newspapers dismissed the rioters as criminal agents for the North. Calling the riot "outrageous," the *Staunton Spectator* (Virginia) claimed it "did not proceed from want, but from crime." The riot had been "instigated by the enemies of the South, with the view of encouraging the North to prosecute the war by making the impression that the South is approaching a starving condition." Quoting from the *Richmond Examiner*, the reporter described the riot and its participants as "a handful of prostitutes, professional thieves, Irish and Yankee hags, gallows-birds from all lands but our own congregated in Richmond, with a woman huckster at their head, who buys veal at the toll gate for a hundred and sells the same for two hundred and fifty in the morning market."[7]

In the North, the *New York Times* printed a statement from a Colonel Stewart of the 2nd Indiana, who had just been released by Confederate officials in Richmond. Under a headline proclaiming "Three Thousand Hungry Women Raging in the Streets," Stewart described the "great bread riot." Calm was restored once Davis and other government officials told the crowd "they should have what they needed." The *New York Daily Herald* predicted the end of the war was "at hand" as the Confederacy found itself "threatened with the more formidable dangers arising from the sufferings of the starving populations of their cities, and which recently found vent in bread riots, that most significant and menacing of all the evidences of popular discontent." The *New York Times* connected Southern women's patriotism and Southern suffering. "Every one remembers how the Southern women stimulated the war fever in its early stages," noted the *New York Times*, "how, at the bombardment of Sumter, two short years ago, the fashionable belles of Charleston crowded in thousands on the Battery, on the streets, on the housetops, and on every spot on which they could catch a glimpse of the battle." "Secession was an exhilarating draught" that had become a "draught of despair, a hungry and sorrowful fury for them now."[8]

Although prices remained high and often out of reach for poor Confederates even after the bread riots, the bread riots brought some change. In Richmond, city officials adopted an ordinance for the "Relief of Poor persons not in the Poor House." This and other similar efforts in other Confederate cities attempted to ease the suffering of the poor. Confederate officials also tightened security in the capital as further disincentive for rioting.[9]

"Pounding on the Rock"

African American Families in the Civil War North

Unknown African American soldier with his wife and two daughters, circa 1863–1865.

The unidentified African American family pictured in this quarter-plate ambrotype had their picture taken some time between 1863 and 1865.[1] It was an important moment for the family. The father wore his Union uniform, pinning an 1864 Abraham Lincoln campaign button to the lapel of his jacket. The mother selected a dark-colored dress and hat, while the twin daughters were carefully outfitted in matching dresses, jackets, and hats. Father and mother sat erect, while the two girls leaned against their parents; all four gazed directly into the camera. After the photographer had recorded the negative image on the glass plate, he placed a dark background behind the plate to create a positive image. The plate and the background were then secured in an ornate case and presented to the family.[2]

Portraiture was an important form of photography during the Civil War. Photographs had been available for more than twenty years, but new technology made ambrotypes and other forms of photography more affordable. As young men enlisted and families faced the likelihood of separation, sitting for a photograph became an important occasion. Soldiers wanted to document their new identity and to celebrate their bravery, while women, children, and families sat for portraits so that the soldiers who carried those images remembered what they were fighting for.[3] Photographs commemorated special events, connected distant loved ones, and comforted wounded and dying soldiers on the battlefield. For this unidentified African American family, their portrait captured a significant moment. For two years, African American men had sought enlistment in the Union army to prove their loyalty to the Union and demonstrate their worthiness for full citizenship. By 1863, with the enactment of the Emancipation Proclamation, that hope had become a reality.

In 1860, nearly one-half million free Blacks lived in the United States, divided almost evenly between the North and the South. Of the 225,000 free Blacks living in the North at the start of the Civil War, some had been born free in the North, descended from families who had been free for a generation or more, men, women, and children who had been freed by the gradual emancipation laws that were passed in the Northern states beginning after the American Revolution. Still others had been born free or manumitted in the South. These free Blacks emigrated north in search of greater freedom and economic opportunity. Other free Blacks in the North were former slaves who had escaped from the South either alone or with their families. Although their lives were closely circumscribed by racism and segregation, free Blacks in the North enjoyed greater freedom and more economic opportunities and, in a few states, even had the right to vote.

Despite the persistent racism that defined their lives, African American men and women in the North supported the Union war effort from the start. Former slave and abolitionist Frederick Douglass recognized both the promise and the importance of Black participation in the Union military effort: "Let the black man get upon his person the brass letters 'U.S.'; let him get an eagle on his button, and a musket on his shoulder and bullets in his pocket, and there is no power on earth which can deny that he has earned the right to citizenship in the United States." Lincoln, however, refused to make abolition a Union war aim, believing such a policy would have little public support in the North. The disappointment of being excluded from military service frustrated free Blacks. "What a spectacle of blind, unreasoning prejudice and pusillanimity is this!" Douglass fumed. "The national edifice is on fire. Every man who can carry a bucket of water, or remove a brick, is wanted; but those who have the care of the building, having a profound respect for the feeling of the national burglars who set the building on fire, are determined that the flames shall only be extinguished" with white hands. "Keep pounding on the rock," Douglass advised, and listen for the thunder.[4]

African American women in the North were also excluded from the Union war effort. Because African American women were not always welcome in relief efforts to support Union soldiers in 1861 and 1862, many focused their efforts on helping other African Americans by sending aid to former slaves in the South, using their skills to create societies for benevolent and charitable work. Former slave Elizabeth Keckley, for example, helped found the Contraband Relief Association in Washington, DC, in 1862 to care for recently freed slaves. In Philadelphia, Black women organized the Colored Women's Sanitary Committee and the Ladies Sanitary Association of St. Thomas African Episcopal Church. Philadelphia abolitionists and educator Charlotte Forten traveled to Port Royal, South Carolina, as a representative of the Philadelphia Port Royal Relief Association (later renamed the Pennsylvania Freemen's Relief Association). In addition to teaching freedmen, Forten worked as a nurse.

On January 1, 1863, Lincoln issued the Emancipation Proclamation. In addition to changing the Union war aim from the preservation of the Union to the abolition of slavery, the Emancipation Proclamation included a provision for the enlistment of African American men. African Americans volunteered in large numbers motivated by a desire to hasten their own liberation and that of their people. Nearly 200,000 Black soldiers served in the Civil War: 178,975 in the army and the rest in the navy. Of those soldiers, 32,723 were from the North. Seventy percent of all Black men of military age in the North served in the Civil War. By war's end, African Americans made up 12 percent of the Union army, had participated in 41 major battles and 449 smaller actions, and had earned 16 Medals of Honor.

African American men were subject to the persistent racism of the period. Black soldiers, including noncommissioned officers, were paid $10 a month, $3 less than white privates. Additionally, Black soldiers had to pay for their uniforms, while white soldiers were given their uniforms. Black soldiers protested the inequitable pay. For example, the Black soldiers of the 54th Massachusetts refused their pay for over a year until the pay inequity was addressed. On June 15, 1864, Congress voted for equal pay for USCT troops, but only for men who were free at the start of the war, further depressing morale and driving a deeper wedge between Northern and Southern Blacks. This pay distinction remained in place until March 3, 1865.

Black soldiers performed a greater share of fatigue duty compared to white soldiers. This reflected a view common among Civil War generals that USCTs should be used as labor and garrison battalions and not for combat. Fatigue duty impaired morale, contributed to an increase in disease among Black soldiers, and wore out soldiers as well as their supplies. As a result, one in five African American soldiers died of disease compared with one in twelve white soldiers. Ten Black soldiers died of disease for each one who died in battle compared to white soldiers who had a ratio that was two to one.

On the home front, Black families struggled. African American women faced harsh economic conditions. A lack of well-paying jobs as well as the absence of male wage earners destabilized Northern Black families. On November 21, 1864, Jane Welcome asked Lincoln to release her son Martin from the army: "H is all the suleport I have notice his father is dead and his brother that wase all the help that I had he has bean wonded twice he has not had nothing to send me yet notice." Julia Rouser, wife of William, a soldier in the 10th USCT, told Lincoln she lacked the options available to other women: "I can find no person who will give me employment, and no relative or firend to whom I can look for aid or assistance." In a letter to Secretary of War Edwin Stanton, Mrs. John Davis asked for a furlough for her husband, a member of the 102nd USCT: "I have no support except what I can earn by my own labor." This problem resulted from the fact that her husband had received no pay, and it ensured that she was "completely distitute." Rosanne Henson explained to Lincoln that "being a colored woman [I] do not get any state pay." The federal government made some initial steps in relieving the economic plight of African American women, especially after the massacre of Black soldiers at Fort

Pillow on April 12, 1864, by amending pension laws so that wives of Black soldiers could receive pensions. With greater economic opportunity came greater government oversight, however, as the federal government investigated "proper" and "improper" marriages among a people who were often denied the right to legally marry.[5]

For Northern Black families, like their white counterparts, a man's decision to enlist brought great sacrifice. However, racism and segregation made the decision much more difficult for African American men and their families. Still, Black men like Alfred Green recognized the importance of their decision. "God will help no one that refuses to help himself," Green wrote the *Anglo-African*, a metropolitan weekly. He continued, "The prejudiced white man North or South never will respect us until they are forced to by deeds of our own." Of the nearly two hundred thousand Black men who served in the Union army and navy, more than thirty-seven thousand never returned home. Thousands more returned severely wounded or disabled. For their families, the extreme hardships of the war continued as they dealt with both emotional and economic loss. Even those men who were restored to their families faced the challenge of securing their civil and political rights. Working-class Black women continued to work to support their families. And Black men and women struggled to secure pensions. Still, as historian James Mendez notes, after the Civil War, "Northern black families moved forward better prepared to achieve greater gains and accomplishments as Americans."[6]

"I Wanted to Be My Own General"

Guerrilla Warfare and the Home Front

Howell "Doc" Rayburn, circa the 1860s.

SOURCE: LAWRENCE T. JONES III TEXAS PHOTOGRAPHY COLLECTION, DEGOLYER LIBRARY, SOUTHERN METHODIST UNIVERSITY.

Although Confederate guerrilla Howell "Doc" Rayburn, pictured here, did not gain the notoriety of John S. Mosby in Virginia or William Quantrill in Kansas and Missouri, Rayburn was a hero to Southern sympathizers in Arkansas. Born around 1841 in Tennessee, Rayburn and his family moved to Texas sometime before the Civil War. In October 1861, Rayburn joined the 12th Texas Cavalry. In mid-1862, the 12th Texas was sent to Arkansas to fortify Confederate defenses there. While in Arkansas, Rayburn contracted a persistent fever, and he was left with a sympathetic family when his regiment left the state for Louisiana. In 1863, recovered from his illness and unable to join his regiment, Rayburn recruited volunteers for an independent command in Des Arc in central Arkansas. For the remainder of the war, Rayburn led an irregular company of partisan rangers on lightning-quick raids in Union-occupied Arkansas between Des Arc and West Point.

Rayburn's story is a mix of fact and legend. One of the more colorful stories about Rayburn describes how he played Santa Claus to his men. In 1864, "one evening preceding Christmas," the young soldiers "jested of what good old St. Nicholas had in store for them." Rayburn in his droll way interrupted with, "Boys, I am going to be Santa. I will go within the Federal lines tomorrow night . . . and bring each of you one of Uncle Sam's best cavalry horses." Disguising himself as a woman, Rayburn slipped through Union lines where he joined a dance hosted by Union officers. After an evening of dancing, Rayburn "bade good night to his newly-made acquaintances, with the assurance to them of attending later social functions; then he stole quietly under cover of darkness, to the corral. Mounting what he judged to be the fleetest horse, he easily stampeded a score of others and was in full flight before the astonished soldiers were fully aroused. His promise of a Christmas gift to his men fulfilled."[1]

Historian T. Lindsey Baker describes the Civil War in Arkansas as "a gruesome, ugly conflict in which throat slitting became commonplace; defenseless old people, women, and children routinely were robbed and burned out of their homes; and bands of armed men mostly wearing civilian clothing roamed the countryside fighting with each other and executing prisoners who might fall into their hands." Arkansas was bordered on the north by Missouri, a state whose residents had contributed to irregular warfare in Kansas in the 1850s. In early 1861, a state convention removed Missouri's pro-secessionist governor Claiborne Jackson from office. Governing in exile, Jackson worked with members of the Missouri General Assembly, also in exile, to pass an ordinance of secession for the state in late 1861. For the remainder of the war,

Missouri was at once a Confederate and a Union state. The military fight for Missouri mirrored the political struggle. Arkansas and Missouri experienced the most sustained guerrilla combat of any borderlands area. In Arkansas, irregular warfare caused most of the terror and suffering and devastated the land and the people.[2]

During the Civil War, civilians organized guerrilla bands to resist occupation, to protect themselves against the enemy, or to take advantage of the chaos of war. Several different kinds of guerrillas emerged in this period, including bushwhackers, who were so named because of their tendency to hide in foliage and "whack" their enemies from the brush. Ununiformed and therefore difficult to distinguish from peaceful Southern civilians, bushwhackers had no affiliation with the Confederate army. Partisan rangers were sanctioned by the Confederate government after the passage of the Partisan Ranger Act of 1862. Under the act Confederate men could enlist for service in a partisan corps rather than the regular army. Bushwhackers and partisans used irregular tactics. Partisans, however, had leaders who held Confederate commissions, reported to a superior in the Confederate army, and wore Confederate uniforms. The term jayhawker, as well as the terms Red Legs and buffaloes, described Unionist sympathizers. All these guerrilla groups shared two characteristics. First, guerrillas, whether bushwhackers or jayhawkers, used irregular tactics, using methods unlike those used by regular soldiers in conventional armies. Second, guerrilla groups organized for local defense, "protection of their families or communities against both internal and external foes."[3]

After the Battle of Pea Ridge, Arkansas, in March 1862, ended in Confederate defeat, hundreds of soldiers deserted the Confederate army to fight in isolated bands, many of them in northwest Arkansas. In June, Confederate General Thomas Hindman issued General Order No. 17, approving the formal organization of guerrilla groups that would harass Union soldiers and their supply lines. Hindman also used existing guerrilla bands. Hindman's order, however, had the opposite effect, giving sanction to outlaws who preyed upon Arkansas civilians. By 1863, guerrilla bands disregarded attempts by the Confederate government to control them.

For many Arkansans, the Partisan Ranger Act and Hindman's directive legitimized their preferred style of military operations. George T. Maddox of Madison County found that regular military service did not suit him. "I wanted to get out where I could have it more lively," he explained, "I wanted to be my own general." Joseph M. Bailey said of his fellow partisans, "Most of these men preferred the free but more hazardous life of independent soldier and scout to the more irksome duties of the regularly organized forces of the Confederate Army." For many Arkansas guerrillas, irregular warfare allowed them to fight where it mattered most, near their homes. When Federals attacked homes in the vicinity of Petit Jean—stealing horses, bridles, guns, and ammunition—residents acted, hiding out in the bushes and guarding their homes against further deprivations.[4]

Guerrilla warfare in the border states and Union-occupied areas of the Confederacy upended gendered distinctions between combatants and non-combatants and altered ideas about war and combat. "To fight guerillas you had to go after people—often networks of kinfolk—who aided and abetted them," notes historian Stephanie McCurry. "When you did, you ended up fighting not just the men but the women as well."[5]

In northwest Arkansas, Union occupation and Confederate guerrilla warfare made dependents of white men and granted greater autonomy to Black men and white women. On the border, women rather than men held things together in the community. Women relied "on patriarchal ethos to protect them when challenging soldiers in ways that would have brought great harm to men, at the same time as they did 'men's' work—hunting, loading wagons, and trading in town." Confederate men like Robert W. Mecklin of Washington County relied on the women in the area, who nursed both neighbors and soldiers, bartered for goods, hid resources from soldiers, and, at times, protected themselves and their homes. Mecklin, who wished to avoid taking the loyalty oath required by Union occupiers, hid out. At other times, he pretended to be infirm when unknown soldiers approached, springing up only when he realized they were old friends.[6]

Unionist men in northwest Arkansas fared no better than Confederate sympathizers. John Rutherford and Richard Dye were among the first civilians in the area to swear their loyalty to the Union. Rutherford and Dye's sons had traveled to Missouri to avoid Confederate conscription. In June 1862, the two young men had enlisted in the 1st Arkansas Cavalry (U.S.). The elder Rutherford and Dye were arrested by rebels in 1862 and again in 1863. Guerrilla warfare reduced the two men to military pawns, as historian Rebecca A. Howard notes:

> Dye and Rutherford were at the mercy of Tucker Smith, a man at least a decade their junior, and saved by the threats of their sons, which were passed between the two groups by a woman. In 1861, the men had enough influence in their community to sway a number of others to join the Union cause. A few short

years later they had been reduced to the role of dependents in need of rescue, treated as pawns in contests between guerrilla bands. And for some men, it is important to note, the consequences of this decline in autonomy and power were final. The federal service of R. C. and William Wharton of Madison County, for example, proved inadequate protection for their father, who was murdered for his Union sentiment in late 1863. In summer 1862, William Buttram of Benton County, a known unionist, saw his son murdered by bushwhackers in his own front yard. His house was robbed, and his daughter-in-law and grandchildren were threatened.[7]

For Black men like Mecklin's slave Wesley, guerrilla warfare brought more control over his own life and that of his family. Wesley did much of the work on his master's farm and his wife's master's farm as both slaveholders sought to avoid both Confederate and Union forces. Wesley took advantage of his master's inability to supervise him by serving as a Union spy and helping Union soldiers defend Fayetteville. As Howard argues, "Wesley Mecklin moved freely, made his own money, and even used firearms. Robert Mecklin hid in the house, watched the women take control, and pretended to be more infirm than he actually was. Wesley Mecklin's power and autonomy grew through the war as Robert Mecklin's diminished." African American men made substantial gains as northwest Arkansas households were turned upside down as the result of the guerrilla war.[8]

Writing from Arkansas in 1864, Confederate General Joseph O. Shelby found "the entire country overrun with able-bodied men; recruiting officers quarrelling or sunk in total apathy; predatory bands of thieves roaming over the country at will, killing some, burning the feet of others, and all hungering with the lust of robbery; one officer refusing to report to another, no organizations, no discipline, no arms, no leader, no desire to fight, no anything."[9] For women and African American men, the battle for control of Arkansas created a liminal space that offered greater autonomy.

On Her Own

The Texas Home Front during the Civil War

Letter written by John B. Latimer to his daughter Willia C. Neel, dated November 23, 1863.

Georgia planter Thomas C. Neel emigrated to Texas in 1854 with his wife Willia, daughter Mattie, and a large group of slaves. In 1855, he settled in Ellis County, establishing a large plantation near Ennis, where he grew cotton and wheat. One of the wealthiest men in the county, Neel served as a delegate to the Texas Secession Convention in January 1861 and signed the Articles of Secession. The following August he was elected to the Texas House of Representatives. After completing his two-year term, Neel was elected state senator; however, he became ill before he could take office. He died on September 12, 1863.[1]

This condolence letter, written by Willia's father John B. Latimer, reveals how the Civil War disrupted communication and travel between Texas and Georgia, isolating residents on the frontier. The Union blockade of Southern ports, the invading Northern army, and the scarcity of postal stamps all hampered Confederate mail service. In late September 1863, Willia Neel wrote to her father, a wealthy planter in Sparta, Georgia, informing him of Thomas's death and asking his advice in administering the estate. Latimer never received the letter. In October, Willia wrote another letter, which her father received in mid-November. Without male relatives to assist her, Willia assumed responsibility for probating her husband's estate.[2]

Texas women like Willia Neel shared many of the same circumstances as women in other Confederate states: overseeing legal, financial, and business matters traditionally handled by their male relatives; dealing with inflation and shortages of necessary goods; and waiting anxiously for news from absent loved ones. For Texas women, these experiences were shaped by the state's frontier location and its history.

Texas was annexed by the United States in 1845, which led to war with Mexico. In 1848, the Treaty of Guadalupe Hidalgo ended the war with Mexico and confirmed the Rio Grande as the border between the United States and Mexico. The Compromise of 1850 settled a boundary dispute between Texas and New Mexico. With the boundaries settled, immigrants moved into Texas in increasing numbers. By 1860, the state's population had tripled. Most of these new arrivals settled in the eastern two-fifths of the state. Westward development in Texas did not advance beyond the forts constructed in the 1850s to create a line of defense from Fort Belknap in the north to Fort Clark in the south (a north-south line located about one hundred miles west of present day I-35). These westernmost settlements formed a boundary between Texans and Native Americans, with the former often pushing against the latter, resulting in ongoing conflicts between the two throughout the 1850s and

Letter written by Emily Latimer to her sister Willia C. Neel, dated October 1862, about the scarcity and high price of consumer goods in Georgia: "Looms are in motion every where in this neighborhood, & striped or plaid homespun is already selling from 50 cts to $1.00 where the weavers find the thread. I would like to have a homespun if I can get one before it gets too high."

1860s. Mexican-Texans predominated in south Texas along the Rio Grande, while in the central and eastern parts of the state Germans, Poles, Czechs, and Mexican-Texans were joined by settlers from other areas of the South and the Old Northwest, with natives of the Lower South forming the single largest group. By 1860, Southerners headed three of every four households in Texas.[3]

The diversity of the state's population influenced politics in the secession winter of 1860–1861 and shaped life on the home front during the Civil War. Secessionists in Texas began to consider the issue as early as October 1860, when it became clear that Abraham Lincoln would be elected. Beginning in early December, Texas newspapers printed calls for the election of delegates to a convention, to be held on January 8, 1861, to consider secession. Prominent Unionists, including Governor Sam Houston, attempted to stop the secession movement. Houston convened the state legislature with the hope it would declare the secession convention illegal. Instead the legislature validated the call for the convention, turned the House chambers over to the convention, and adjourned. On February 1, convention delegates voted 166 to 8 for secession. Three weeks later, Texas voters supported the secession referendum. Although secession passed by an overwhelming majority, 18 of the 122 counties casting votes cast majorities against secession, an indication of the strength and organization of the Unionist minority in some areas of the state.[4]

The political divisions that shaped the secession movement influenced life on the Texas home front during the Civil War. Although Texas did not experience large-scale Union occupation, Texas women on the home front "shared many of the same circumstances as women in other Southern states during the war," historian Angela Boswell notes. "As in other Southern states, women's experience also varied due to race, class, and community."[5]

Wealthy, slaveholding women like Willia Neel faced new challenges during the war. Willia had assumed oversight of her husband's business interests during his lengthy absences while he served in the Texas legislature. After Thomas's death in 1863, Willia found herself solely responsible for his estate. None of Willia's letters have survived; however, it is possible to understand her experience by examining the life of another slaveholding woman, Caroline Sedberry. The Sedberrys moved with their slaves from Tennessee to Texas in the early 1850s, settling on five hundred acres of land on the Bosque River, near Meridian in central Texas. From 1861 to 1862, William Sedberry served in the Texas House of Representatives with Thomas C. Neel. In early 1862, William resigned his political office and joined the Confederate army. On the Texas home front, Caroline mothered her children, planted vegetables, carded wool, and sewed, all while managing the business of the farm, including the slaves. When William died in December 1862, Caroline administered his estate. In frontier areas, women like Willia and Caroline often found themselves cut off from their extended family, leaving women to rely on their own resources. Traditional male activities such as raising food and cash crops and administering estates could not wait for male relatives to return home, and as a result more women assumed these responsibilities.[6]

The progress of the Civil War did not affect slavery in Texas to the same degree that it did in other Confederate states. Texas slaves continued to work and live much as they had before the war began. Still, as historian Caleb McDaniel argues, "the lack of serious disruptions to slavery in Confederate Texas does not prove an absence of dissent among enslaved people who were brought there."[7]

In the months before Texas seceded, a slave insurrection panic gripped the state. In February, an enslaved woman in Collin County came under suspicion for setting fire to her master's house. She claimed a white resident had encouraged her, promising to take her to a free state. In May, three slaves known only as Emma, Jess, and Ruben were hanged for allegedly killing their master and his family. Two months later, a series of fires broke out in several Texas communities, including Dallas, Denton, Milford, Waxahachie, and Austin, confirming for slaveholders that abolitionists and slaves were plotting a major revolt. On July 17, William H. Crawford, a white man suspected of being an abolitionist, was lynched in Fort Worth. That same day, Northern Methodist missionary Anthony Bewley, his wife Jane, and their family, traveling by cover of darkness, fled Fort Worth. A posse tracked the Bewleys to Missouri. Capturing Anthony, they took the missionary back to Fort Worth where he was hanged from the same tree where Crawford died. In August, a druggist in Waxahachie was hanged for allegedly giving strychnine to slaves to put in wells. Although the insurrection panic had run its course by mid-September 1860, the "Texas Troubles"—as the press referred to the events—heightened slaveholders' anxiety.[8]

Slaveholders in Texas also worried about the presence of Mexican-Texans or Tejanos. In the 1850s, hundreds or perhaps thousands of Texas slaves escaped to freedom south of the border. Mexico abolished slavery in 1829, and its political leaders made no attempt to discourage runaway slaves who fled to Mexico. Many Mexican-Texans had no use for slavery and some even assisted runaway slaves. Not surprisingly, Anglo Texans believed all Mexicans were "abolitionists at heart." During the Civil War, more than two thousand Mexican-Texans joined the Confederate army, while almost a thousand joined the Union army. Other Tejanos took their families and fled to Mexico during the war. Although some Tejanos along the border in south Texas benefited from the economic boom that resulted from Union naval blockades of the Texas coast, many other Mexican-Texans experienced extreme poverty.[9]

Unionist families in Texas also experienced disruption. After Texas seceded, some Unionist families simply left the state, starting over where their politics would not endanger them. In other families, only the men of the family left, seeking shelter with relatives elsewhere or joining the Union army. William Spangler Condit, a Northern Methodist who emigrated to Texas in 1851 with his wife Jane and their children, fled to Kentucky when the war began. Jane and their children remained in Texas. William's death in Kentucky left Jane alone to manage the family's business in Texas. In other families,

Unionist men went into hiding, relying on family members to supply them with food and clothing. For Unionist families in Texas, vigilantism remained a persistent threat. Dozens of Unionist women were widowed by Confederate sympathizers who had their men rounded up, sometimes tried and sometimes not, and hanged. The most infamous incident happened in Gainesville, north of Dallas, in October 1862, when forty suspected Unionists were hanged. Afterward, many of the widows returned to the places they had come from before moving to Texas. Those who remained in Texas were vulnerable to ongoing harassment.

When the Neels moved to Texas in 1854, they brought with them an unknown number of slaves, including a woman known only as "Mammy Tilda." Tilda was one of two hundred thousand enslaved persons living in Texas at the beginning of the Civil War. During the war, Confederate slaveholders from other Southern states brought with them as many as 150,000 enslaved people. "Refugeed slaves" in Texas were an important source of income for their owners, who often "hired out" their slaves to contractors who paid the slave owner for the slave's labor on cotton plantations, railroads, and iron and salt industries. As a result, the slaves of refugee Confederates endured multiple relocations as their owners sought out economic opportunities. The forced relocation of slaves to Texas "likely swelled the state's population of Unionists and dissenters," according to McDaniel. Although faced with "dangers and obstacles far greater than those that white Unionists faced," refugeed slaves "helped to undermine the Confederacy from within."[10]

Although Texans did not experience Union occupation to the same degree as other Confederate states, the push and pull of different forces on the home front created disruptions and dislocations, leaving everyone changed by the war. How much change depended on an individual's sex, class, race, political affiliation, and geographic location within the state.

Part VII

SYMBOLS

Symbols are powerful political tools. They can take many forms, including visual images, literary characters, and patriotic music. Beginning in the late eighteenth century, British and American abolitionists used visual images to convey the horrors of the slave trade and slavery and to communicate potent moral messages. The image of a kneeling slave crying out "Am I not a man and a brother?" urged viewers to empathize with the enslaved. For readers of Harriet Beecher Stowe's antislavery novel *Uncle Tom's Cabin*, Uncle Tom and the novel's other characters assumed a lifelike presence. In the antebellum period, these antislavery symbols shifted the way people understood slavery and deepened the divide between opponents and supporters of slavery. With the outbreak of war over the issue of slavery, symbols communicated allegiance to the Union or loyalty to the South and slavery. For the newly formed Confederate States of America, new symbols such as flags and music signified Southern states' separation from the United States and their rejection of Northern abolitionism. When Southern Unionists and Northern soldiers and civilians encountered these symbols of Southern unity, they responded with symbols that represented the United States. By arousing patriotic feelings, flags and flag songs encouraged men and women to unite in a common cause, whether preserving the existing Union or establishing a new government.

"The Speechless Agony of the Fettered Slave"

The Symbolism of the Antislavery Movement

Gibbs, Gardner, and Company, American Anti-Slavery Society (publisher), "Am I Not a Woman & a Sister" antislavery hard times token, 1838.

SOURCE: PURCHASED WITH THE ABBIE BOSWORTH WILLIAMS (CLASS OF 1927) FUND MOUNT HOLYOKE COLLEGE ART MUSEUM, SOUTH HADLEY, MASSACHUSETTS, PHOTOGRAPH LAURA SHEA 2015.9.

In late 1837, the American Anti-Slavery Society (AASS) commissioned Gibbs, Gardner, and Company of Belleville, New Jersey, to strike these antislavery tokens, which featured an image of a kneeling female slave with the words "Am I Not a Woman, a Sister?" Advertised in the AASS's newspaper *The Emancipator*, the coins sold for $1 for one hundred coins. In the same advertisement, the AASS also announced plans to issue a second coin with the image of a kneeling male slave. The antislavery tokens were among hundreds of "hard times tokens" produced between 1832 and 1844 to meet the public need for small change. Often these coins carried political messages. The AASS used the financial crisis of the 1830s and 1840s to promote the abolitionist cause by issuing tokens with the most iconic image of the antislavery movement.[1]

Beginning in the eighteenth century, British and American abolitionists used visual images to generate public support for the abolition of slavery and the slave trade. Antislavery iconography evoked a range of emotional responses. Using horror and sympathy together, abolitionists "worked both sides of the [abolitionist] argument simultaneously: through the gothic, [they] exposed the trade in slaves as revolting, and through the sentimental, [they] portrayed the slave as human and antislavery as benevolent." In 1837, at the Anti-Slavery Convention of American Women in New York, the delegates recognized "pictorial representations" as "powerful auxiliaries in the cause of emancipation" and called for an increase in the production of these images "so that the speechless agony of the fettered slave may unceasingly appeal to the heart of the patriot, the philanthropist, and the christian."[2]

Two of the most iconic images of the abolitionist movement—the kneeling slave and the slave ship *Brooks*—were first produced in England. The image of the kneeling slave was created in the factory of ceramicist Josiah Wedgwood in 1787, the same year British activists organized the Society for Effecting the Abolition of the Slave Trade (SEAST). The final design resulted from a collaboration between Wedgwood and a committee of the SEAST. Depicting the kneeling slave in black jasper against a white ceramic background, the cameos were made into pendants, hatpins, and brooches, becoming the most highly sought after fashion accessory of the period. "The ladies now wear the Figure of a Negro in Wedgwood's Ware round their Necks," British author Hester Thrale noted in 1788. The image was also reproduced on tea ware, snuff boxes, and other domestic goods.[3]

The image of the slave ship *Brooks* was also produced by a committee of the SEAST. Built in 1781, the *Brooks* was named for its owner and builder, James Brooks. The ship carried hundreds of enslaved Africans from West Africa to the Caribbean. British abolitionist leader and historian Thomas Clarkson commissioned artist James Phillips to make an engraving of the *Brooks* to highlight the inhumanity of the slave trade. The engraving with its closely packed rows of tiny black figures takes on the appearance of a coffin. By graphically exposing the violence of slavery, the *Brooks* image was meant to shock its audience into action. More than eight thousand copies of the *Brooks* engraving were printed in England. Two wooden models were also created from the *Brooks* engraving, one model commissioned by French abolitionist Comte de Mirabeau and the other by English abolitionist William Wilberforce.

Both images—the kneeling slave and the slave ship—were exported to the United States, where they were widely circulated. In February 1788, Wedgwood sent several cameos to Benjamin Franklin, who was president of the Pennsylvania Abolition Society (PAS). Franklin responded saying he had distributed the cameos among his friends "in whose countenances I have seen such marks of being affected by contemplating the figure of the supplicant (which is admirably executed) that I am persuaded it may have an effect equal to that of the best written pamphlet in procuring favor to those afflicted people." The PAS was also responsible for the dissemination of the *Brooks* image. Philadelphia printer and engraver Matthew Carey published a copy of the engraving in the May 1789 issue of *American Museum*, a prominent monthly magazine that was distributed widely in the United States, Great Britain, and France.[4]

In the 1830s, as the fight for the abolition of slavery in the United States intensified, abolitionists increased their use of graphics to illustrate the cruelty of slavery. American abolitionists used both male and female images of the kneeling slave in their antislavery campaigns. Quaker Benjamin Lundy, editor of the *Genius of Universal Emancipation*, and Boston printer William Lloyd Garrison, who edited *The Liberator*, both used the kneeling slave image. The female version introduced special women's sections of each publication. It was also reproduced on a variety of domestic items such as fire screens, needle bags, chinaware, linen, silk goods, stationery, and other printed ephemera, while the kneeling male slave appeared on a variety of items, including the masthead of *The Liberator* and on the weekly contribution boxes distributed by the Rhode Island Anti-Slavery Society. Supplicant slave images were also printed in the pages of *The Slave's Friend*, a children's antislavery magazine produced by the American Anti-Slavery Society in the 1830s, and in countless abolitionist books, including *The Fountain* and *Authentic Anecdotes of American Slavery*, both written by Lydia Maria Child.[5]

Abolitionists recognized the power of symbols and images "to create an ennobling image of the African, arouse the compassion of white Americans for the plight of the slave, [and] generate outrage among Northerners toward the South." Women in Boston and Philadelphia hosted antislavery fairs where they sold a variety of domestic goods, including pens, bookmarks, quilts, ceramics, and even shoes with "Trample not the Oppressed" printed on the soles. Children's books such as Hannah Townsend's *The Anti-Slavery Alphabet*, which was sold at the Philadelphia Anti-Slavery Fair in 1846 and 1847, used color, graphics, and text to convert the next generation of abolitionists. Antislavery goods appealed to consumers' emotions, unifying them in the cause. In 1852, with the publication of Harriet Beecher Stowe's *Uncle Tom's Cabin*, the production and sale of antislavery-themed goods reached new highs, bringing even more people into the antislavery cause.[6]

This Rhode Island Anti-Slavery Society collection box belonged to the family of Boston printer and abolitionist William Lloyd Garrison.

SOURCE: COLLECTION OF THE SMITHSONIAN NATIONAL MUSEUM OF AFRICAN AMERICAN HISTORY AND CULTURE, GIFT OF THE GARRISON FAMILY IN MEMORY OF GEORGE THOMPSON GARRISON.

"The Little Woman Who Made the Great War"

Harriet Beecher Stowe and Uncle Tom's Cabin

Robert S. Duncanson, *Uncle Tom and Little Eva*, 1853, oil on canvas.

*U*ncle Tom and Little Eva (1853), painted by African American landscape
artist Robert S. Duncanson, features two characters from Harriet Beecher
Stowe's bestselling antislavery novel *Uncle Tom's Cabin* (1852). The oil on
canvas painting, measuring twenty-seven by thirty-eight inches, is patterned
on an illustration drawn by Hammatt Billings for the novel. In the scene
Tom and Eva are sitting in the garden of Augustine St. Clare's villa on Lake
Pontchartrain (Louisiana), the sunset "kindl[ing] the whole horizon into one
blaze of glory, and mak[ing] the water another sky." Eva is reading to Tom
from the book of Revelation when she encounters a passage that suggests the
sunset. She tells Tom she sees in the evening clouds the New Jerusalem with
its "great gates of pearl . . . and . . . beyond them gold." Resting her hand on
Tom, Eva tells him she will be going there, a foreshadowing of her death four
chapters later. As one of the most widely reproduced scenes from *Uncle Tom's
Cabin*, the Lake Pontchartrain scene would have been readily recognizable to
contemporary viewers of Duncanson's painting.[1]

Scenes from *Uncle Tom's Cabin* appeared on framing prints, sheet music
covers, and other ephemera. These representations of characters and scenes
from Stowe's novel were part of a powerful cultural phenomenon known
as "Uncle Tomitudes," a phrase coined soon after the book's publication to
describe the outpouring of Tom-themed merchandise. Within a year of its
publication, *Uncle Tom's Cabin* had sold nearly two million copies in America
and Great Britain, and the novel had been translated into fifteen European
languages. The popularity of Stowe's novel created consumer demand for
Tom-themed items, extending the influence of the novel and transforming it
into an American icon, one closely associated with the Civil War.[2]

The passage of the Fugitive Slave Law of 1850 moved Stowe to write
Uncle Tom's Cabin. The novel features two dramatic antislavery plot lines: one
Northern and one Southern. The Northern narrative, which tells the story
of fugitive slaves Eliza and George Harris and their son Harry who flee to
Canada on the Underground Railroad, emphasizes the immorality of the Fugitive Slave Law. Laws that made property of Black men, women, and children
overshadowed slave life Stowe noted in her opening chapter:

> So long as the law considers all these human beings, with beating hearts and
> living affections, only as so many *things* belonging to a master,—so long as the
> failure, or misfortune, or imprudence, or death of the kindest owner may cause
> them any day to exchange a life of kind protection and indulgence for one of

hopeless misery and toil,—so long as it is impossible to make any thing beautiful or desirable in the best regulated administration of slavery.

In the rocky pass scene, the slave chasers remind George, "We have the law on our side, and the power," to which George replies,

"I know very well that you've got the law on your side, and the power. . . . You mean to take my wife to sell in New Orleans, and put my boy like a calf in a trader's pen, and send Jim's old mother to the brute that whipped and abused her before, because he couldn't abuse her son. You wan't to send Jim and me back to be whipped, and tortured, and ground down under the heels of them that you call masters; and your laws *will* bear you out in it,—more shame for you and them! . . . We don't own your laws; we don't own your country; we stand here as free, under God's sky, as you are; and by the great God that made us, we'll fight for our liberty till we die."

The plight of the Harris family, as one reviewer noted, "wakened in millions of minds" the "sense of a 'higher law' . . . and the deep and ineffaceable conviction of the wickedness of slavery."[3]

The Southern narrative of *Uncle Tom's Cabin* relied on images and stories from popular culture, including abolitionist and other reform literature, slave narratives, religious revivals, and news accounts of slave renditions. Published accounts, such as abolitionist Theodore Dwight Weld's *American Slavery as It Is* (1839), in which Weld collected reports and newspaper clippings, many of them from Southern sources, to show the horrors of slavery, helped to provide the factual basis of *Uncle Tom's Cabin*. As Stowe later recalled, "she kept [Weld's] book in her work basket by day, and slept with it under her pillow at night, till its facts crystallized in Uncle Tom." Stowe also relied on slave narratives by Frederick Douglass (1845), Milton Clarke and his brother Lewis Garrard Clarke (1846), William Wells Brown (1847), Henry Bibb (1849), and Josiah Henson (1849). Although Stowe insisted no one individual served as the model for any character, she derived enough aspects of Henson in creating Uncle Tom that Henson was often referred to as the real "Uncle Tom." Later editions of Henson's autobiography included a parenthetical note on the title page: "Mrs. Harriet Beecher Stowe's 'Uncle Tom'" as well as a preface by Stowe.[4]

These materials informed the Southern narrative, which focuses on the horrors of the domestic slave trade. Uncle Tom is sold away from his wife Chloe and their three children by his owner who is facing financial ruin. Forced to leave Kentucky for New Orleans, Tom bonds with his new master Augustine

St. Clare and St. Clare's daughter, Eva. After their deaths, Uncle Tom is sold again, this time to the sadistic Simon Legree, a Louisiana plantation owner who perversely hates Tom. Legree orders his enslaved Black overseers to whip Tom savagely, resulting in Tom's death. Uncle Tom's stoic response to his suffering and his subsequent death at the hands of Legree transforms Uncle Tom into a symbol of Christ-like suffering made more resonant by Stowe's assertion that Uncle Tom will meet Eva and her father in heaven.[5]

Uncle Tom's Cabin outsold all other novels of the period. "For an immense number of people," nineteenth-century American author Henry James noted, *Uncle Tom's Cabin* was "much less a book than a state of vision, of feeling and of consciousness, in which they didn't sit and read and appraise and pass the time, but walked and talked and laughed and cried and, . . . generally conducted themselves."[6] Stowe's publisher John P. Jewett produced several editions of *Uncle Tom's Cabin*, including an edition known in its time as the Splendid Edition. Published in late 1852, in time for the Christmas season, the Splendid Edition featured more than one hundred illustrations by Hammatt Billings, the artist who had illustrated the first edition of *Uncle Tom's Cabin*.

The popularity of *Uncle Tom's Cabin* created an enormous demand for Tom-themed items such as handkerchiefs, needlework patterns, ceramics, candlesticks, games, puzzles, prints, and paintings. Indeed, *Uncle Tom's Cabin* generated more related merchandise than any other pre-twentieth-century book. The merchandise ranged from inexpensive lithograph prints to expensive porcelain Limoges spill vases produced in France.[7]

Northern response to the novel is only one part of the story of how *Uncle Tom's Cabin* came to symbolize the Civil War. The vehement Southern response to *Uncle Tom's Cabin* and its characters reflected the growing chasm between the North and South. In the South, Stowe's novel was subjected to ferociously negative reviews. Writing in *The Southern Literary Messenger*, George F. Holmes lambasted the popularity of *Uncle Tom's Cabin* and its "false assertions" about slavery: "This slanderous work has found its way to every section of our country, and has crossed the water to Great Britain, filling the minds of all who know nothing of slavery with hatred for that institution and those who uphold it. . . . Mrs. Stowe [is] the mouthpiece of a large and dangerous faction which if we do not put down with the pen, we may be compelled one day . . . to repel with the bayonet." In Athens, Georgia, copies of *Uncle Tom's Cabin* were publicly burned. A bookseller in Mobile, Alabama, was run out of town for selling *Uncle Tom's Cabin* and two other antislavery books. A free Black in Maryland was sentenced to ten years in prison for possessing antislavery material, including a copy of *Uncle Tom's Cabin*.[8]

In December 1862, Stowe met with President Lincoln at the White House to urge him to sign the Emancipation Proclamation. Lincoln reportedly greeted Stowe by saying, "Is this the little woman who made the great war?" Lincoln's greeting was not recorded in print until 1896, the year Stowe died, which has led some scholars to describe the quotation as apocryphal, "emerging from within Stowe family tradition without any textual support or verification from the author herself."

Lincoln's comment has become part of the folklore surrounding Harriet Beecher Stowe and her popular novel, underscoring the ways in which *Uncle Tom's Cabin* reflected and reinforced the sectional divide between North and South in the mid-nineteenth century. After the Civil War, the poet Oliver Wendell Holmes wrote "Two Poems to Harriet Beecher Stowe," which included the lines:

> All through the conflict, up and down,
> Went Uncle Tom and old John Brown,
> One ghost, one form ideal
> And which was false, and which was true,
> And which was the mightier of the two,
> The wisest Sybil never knew,
> For both were real.

Uncle Tom took on a larger-than-life existence, taking on a legendary status much like that of the real-life abolitionist John Brown. During the Civil War, the lives of Uncle Tom and John Brown—one fictional, one real—reminded soldiers and civilians on both sides of the conflict what they were fighting for.[9]

"If you want my flag, you'll have to take it over my dead body"

National and Regimental Flags during the Civil War

Flag of the 12th Texas Cavalry.

On December 29, 1861, Chaplain J. Fred Cox presented this regimental flag to the 12th Texas Cavalry "on behalf of the ladies of the regiment." Made by the wives of the regiment's officers, the flag features the familiar blue St. Andrew's cross and includes characteristics commonly found on Texas Civil War battle flags, including the lack of white fimbriation or edging on the cross and a large central star. The 12th Texas served in the Trans-Mississippi west and saw action in Louisiana, Arkansas, and Missouri. After the war, regimental flag bearer Robert W. Bonner carried the flag home to Texas.[1]

Flags were simultaneously vital pieces of military equipment and important political symbols. Union and Confederate regiments generally carried two flags: a national flag and their regimental colors. National flags distinguished between opposing armies, while regimental flags served as moveable landmarks on the battlefield guiding troop movements in the chaos and confusion of combat.

In the spring of 1861, the provision of a national flag was among the first order of business for the Confederate government. On March 4, the Confederacy introduced its new flag: the Confederate First National Flag, or the "Stars and Bars," retained the colors and general shape of the American flag, featuring two red and one white horizontal bars, a blue canton, and white stars corresponding to each Confederate state. The Confederate flag signaled a break with the past and a desire to establish a new national identity. However, on the battlefield the Confederate First National Flag caused confusion. At the First Battle of Bull Run (Manassas) in July 1861, the similarities between the Union "Stars and Stripes" and the Confederate "Stars and Bars" made it nearly impossible for officers and soldiers to distinguish between Union and Confederate troops. Confederate General P. G. T. Beauregard played an instrumental role in creating a more effective battle flag. Adopting a design first suggested by William Porcher Miles, Beauregard's flag featured a red square background with a blue St. Andrew's cross edged in white and displaying a star for each state. In the fall of 1861, the Army of Northern Virginia (ANV) battle flag was presented to Confederate regiments. The ANV battle flag was one of dozens of different patterns that served as the battle flags of Confederate military units. In 1863, the battle flag was used as the canton on the Confederacy's Second National flag.

Regimental flags embodied the esprit de corps of the unit, setting the regiment apart from others. While most of the flags carried by regiments were produced and issued by the military quartermaster clothing depots, a significant number of regimental flags were produced by local women. As a result, regimental flags served as important reminders of home and often reflected the unique character of the unit. For example, the flag of the 11th New York Infantry, recruited from the city's firemen, included the tools of their trade: a fireman's helmet, ladder, hoses, and an axe; the flag of the 69th New York Infantry, recruited from the city's Irish community, carried a flag with an embroidered Celtic harp and a chain of shamrocks.[2]

Once a company had been mustered, or a regiment organized from a group of companies, the local women set to work producing a flag. Silk was the preferred material, though wool bunting was used and proved more durable than silk. Once the flag was completed, a public ceremony was arranged. Flag presentation ceremonies were emotional, public affairs taking the form of a dress parade, an assembly, a banquet, or a mass meeting. The men of the company or the regiment would line up in the town square, the courthouse steps, the local picnic ground, or some other public space. A representative of the women of the community would make a short presentation and an officer from the company would accept the flag on behalf of his command.[3]

Throughout the North and the South, newspapers published accounts of flag presentations. In June 1861, the women of Leavenworth "prepared a fine regimental flag" for the Kansas 2nd Infantry. On the East Coast, as the 1st Maine Infantry marched south toward Washington, DC, they received flags in Boston and in New York City. The women of West Pratt Street in Baltimore presented the 2nd Maryland Infantry with a "handsome regimental flag, 6 feet by 7, composed of silk with 34 stars embroidered upon a blue field," while the students of the Female College at Bordentown presented a flag to the men of the 4th New Jersey. On September 9, 1861, the men of the 1st North Carolina Infantry formed in dress parade to receive "a very handsome Confederate flag" made by the women of Fayetteville. In some cities, such as Detroit, women raised funds to purchase flags for local units.[4]

Often the construction and presentation of regimental flags was described in patriotic and gendered language by the women who made the flags and the men who received them. In May 1861, at the flag presentation ceremony for the Mercer Guard (Company B, 6th Louisiana Infantry), a Miss Collier gave a short speech: "The present condition of our country requires of every true and loyal heart a helping hand. . . . And as we cannot do more than encourage by our words and actions the noble designs and purposes in which you gentlemen are so gallantly engaged, we would offer willingly to do all within our power to aid and help you in the glorious cause." Captain Thomas Walker received the flag on behalf of the men in his company. "In receiving from your generous hands this appropriate and elegant gift the Mercer Guard are indeed honored," Walker told the women. "It has been consecrated by your fervent prayers, and blessed by your sweet lips; we accept it as a tribute of devoted patriotism and affectionate regard."[5]

One of the more unusual regimental flags was carried by the Texas regiment commanded by Colonel Louis T. Wigfall, a Texas politician and secessionist firebrand. Wigfall's wife Fannie and daughter Louise made the regiment's flag using Mrs. Wigfall's wedding dress to make the flag's lone star. Contemporary accounts also credit Confederate president Jefferson Davis's wife Varina and Mary America Waul, wife of Texas politician Thomas Waul, with helping to sew the flag. In the summer of 1861, in Richmond, Virginia, hundreds witnessed as Jefferson Davis presented the flag to Wigfall and the men of the Texas Battalion (later known as Hood's Texas Brigade). The ceremony, which included patriotic speeches and stirring music played by a brass band, moved a correspondent for the *Dallas Daily Herald* to write, "We felt about six inches taller in hearing our Texas boys so praised and applauded." The flag was later captured at the Battle of Antietam in September 1862. It was returned to the state of Texas in 1905 where it hung in the chamber of the Texas House of Representatives until the 1920s.[6]

Given the symbolic importance of flags, it is no wonder that serving as color bearer was an honor and a serious responsibility. Color bearers and their guards suffered high casualty rates. If the flag bearer was wounded or killed in battle, a member of his guard or another soldier would raise and carry the colors onward. At the Battle of Antietam, in September 1862, the 1st Texas Infantry had nine color bearers wounded or killed. The following summer, at the Battle of Gettysburg, the 24th Michigan had seven color bearers wounded or killed, while the 26th North Carolina lost fourteen color bearers.[7]

Flags that were badly damaged were either put into storage or, in some cases, cut into pieces and distributed among the men of the regiment. In Wisconsin, the regimental flag of the 1st Wisconsin draped the coffin of one of the state's first Civil War casualties. Eighteen-year-old Warren Graham had enlisted for a three-month term of service with the 1st Wisconsin. In July 1861, near Martinsburg, Virginia, Graham was shot three times during the Battle of Falling Waters (also known as the Battle of Hokes Run). He died the following month just as his regiment was mustering out from its three-month service. At Graham's funeral, in Wisconsin, "the old regimental flag, under which he fought and received the fatal wounds, was wrapped around the coffin and his uniform laid above his body." Graham's body was escorted to the church and the cemetery by soldiers and officers of his regiment. After the

Flag of the 1st Texas Infantry, also known as the "Wigfall Flag." Fannie Wigfall, wife of Texas politician Louis T. Wigfall, used her wedding dress to make the star.
SOURCE: TEXAS STATE LIBRARY AND ARCHIVES COMMISSION, AUSTIN, TEXAS.

funeral, the regiment's action at Falling Waters was embroidered into the flag and the regimental flag preserved.[8]

Flags also held importance off the battlefield, carrying political, religious, and emotional symbolism. As the secession crisis unfolded in late 1860 and early 1861 in the Upper South, American flags asserted Union patriotism, while resistance or secession banners signaled a break with old political ties and the declaration of a new national identity. Two weeks after Lincoln's election, the *Charleston* (South Carolina) *Courier* told its readers: "We can scarcely pass through a street without finding additions to the banners, flags, and ensigns that are given to the breeze." In the state's capital of Columbia, the president of South Carolina College claimed that "flags in hands, flags across the streets, flags at printing offices, stores, shops, booths, on omnibuses, in every direction" proved the popularity of secession. Secession banners urged immediate and decisive action: "Strike Now or Never," one banner urged, depicting the image of a coiled rattlesnake that dated from the American Revolution.[9]

Southern Unionists who clung to their American flags in defiance of the Confederacy were valorized during the war and for decades afterward. William Driver, a sea captain from Massachusetts, settled in Nashville, Tennessee, in 1837. Driver brought with him a large American flag, measuring ten feet by seventeen feet, which he flew on holidays. When secession fever took hold in 1860, Driver hid his flag. More than once the old sea captain defended his flag against local Confederates, telling intruders, "If you want my flag, you'll have to take it over my dead body." After Nashville fell to the federal army in February 1862, Driver brought his flag out of hiding, presenting it to the troops of the 6th Ohio Infantry. Driver's flag was the first U.S. flag to fly over a former Confederate state capitol. Later that same year, in Frederick, Maryland, ninety-five-year-old Unionist Barbara Fritchie waved a Union flag from her upstairs window as the occupying rebel forces marched out of town. Quaker poet John Greenleaf Whittier immortalized her "folkloric defiance" of Confederate forces in the poem "Barbara Frietchie."[10]

Flags are powerful symbols. During the Civil War, the American flag asserted the endurance of the Union. The newly designed and constructed Confederate flags helped foster the development of a Confederate identity, while regimental flags rallied the men and reminded them of home. In defeat, Confederate flags, especially those with the blue St. Andrew's cross, became a fixture at Memorial Day observations, veterans' reunions and parades, and other Confederate-related meetings. By the mid-twentieth century, the Confederate battle flag, as the Army of Northern Virginia battle flag is commonly known, began to take on new, more complicated meanings. Its powerful symbolism continues to inform political and cultural debates about the meaning and the legacy of the war, particularly as it relates to race and slavery.

Setting the Beat for War

Popular Music in the North and the South

"The Bonnie Blue Flag" by Harry Macarthy was written in 1861 and quickly became a Confederate sensation.

Just as flags were used to signal Southern states' break with the United States, music celebrated secession and set the tempo for events that transpired across the South in late 1860 and 1861. Music was an integral part of flag ceremonies. "The hoisting of the most important flags—those monumental pieces of bunting that were raised in the major squares and parks of the urban South—featured music as well as booming cannon, firing rifles, and rounds of cheers from the assembled audience," notes historian Robert Bonner. "Brass horn ensembles and drums . . . kept the passions of the crowd at a fever pitch."[1]

Confederate bands played recognized tunes such as the French national anthem "La Marseillaise" and the minstrel song "Dixie." "La Marseillaise," written in 1792 during the French Revolution, had been a favorite of Northerners and Southerners for decades. During the secession winter, as Southern states began to secede, "La Marseillaise" became an interim Confederate anthem. A spirited tune and connected as it was to the revolutionary ideals of France, the song inspired loyalty and emotion from its listeners. Confederates fashioned their own lyrics for "La Marseillaise," offering versions such as "The Southern Marseillaise" (1861) and the "Virginian Marseillaise" (1863). Often "La Marseillaise" was played alongside another Southern favorite, "Dixie." Written in 1859 by Northern composer Daniel Emmett for Bryant's Minstrels, "Dixie" was initially more popular in the North than in the South in part because minstrelsy was not as popular in the South. However, with the secession crisis, "Dixie" quickly became the most popular song in the South. The song's connection to Southern nationalism was reinforced when it was played at Jefferson Davis's inauguration on February 18, 1861. "La Marseillaise" and "Dixie" were played in Charleston after Fort Sumter surrendered and again as the first Confederate flag was raised over the capitol of Richmond. "La Marseillaise" and "Dixie" were Confederate favorites throughout the Civil War even as new songs were written to celebrate the South and the Southern cause.[2]

"The Bonnie Blue Flag" was written by English variety entertainer Harry Macarthy after he witnessed the Mississippi secession convention, which voted eighty-three to fifteen to sever ties with the Union. After the vote was announced, Amanda Smythe, wife of convention secretary Homer Smythe, led a group of cheering women to the platform where they presented the chair of the convention with a blue flag with a white five-pointed star. Inspired by the event, Macarthy wrote "The Bonnie Blue Flag," later adding verses as more Southern states seceded.[3] The song became a Confederate sensation by the summer of 1861, in large part because it had been written especially for the Southern cause. Set to the traditional tune "The Irish Jaunting Car," "The

Bonnie Blue Flag" had a catchy tune and patriotic lyrics that captured the spirit of secession and stirred the hearts of soldiers and civilians alike.

The Bonnie Blue Flag

We are a band of brothers, and native to the soil,
Fighting for the property we gain'd by honest toil;
And when our rights were threaten'd the cry rose near and far:
Hurrah for the Bonnie Blue Flag, that bears a Single Star!

Chorus: Hurrah! Hurrah! For Southern Rights hurrah!
Hurrah for the Bonnie Blue Flag, that bears a Single Star!

As long as the Union was faithful to her trust,
Like friends and like brothers, kind were we and just;
But now, when Northern treach'ry attempts our rights to mar,
We hoist on high the Bonnie Blue Flag, that bears a Single Star!

First, gallant South Carolina nobly made the stand,
Then came Alabama, who took her by the hand,
Next quickly, Mississippi, Georgia, and Florida,
All rais'd on high the Bonnie Blue Flag, that bears a Single Star!

Ye men of valor, gather round the Banner of the Right!
Texas and fair Louisiana join us in the fight;
Davis, our loved President, and Stephens, statesman rare,
Now rally round the Bonnie Blue Flag, that bears a Single Star!

And here's to brave Virginia! The old Dominion State,
With the Confed'racy at length has link'd her fate,
Impell'd by her example, now other States prepare
To hoist on high the Bonnie Blue Flag, that bears a Single Star!

Then here's to our Confed'racy, strong we are and brave,
Like Patriots of old, we'll fight our Heritage to save;
And rather than submit to shame, to die we would prefer,
So cheer for the Bonnie Blue Flag, that bears a Single Star!

Then, cheer, boys, cheer, raise the joyous shout,
For Arkansas and North Carolina have both gone out;
And let another rousing cheer for Tennessee be given
The Single Star of the Bonnie Blue Flag has grown to be Eleven!

Chorus: Hurrah! Hurrah! For Southern Rights, hurrah!
Hurrah for the Bonnie Blue Flag has gain'd th' Eleventh Star![1]

A young Alabama soldier, who saw his first performance of "The Bonnie Blue Flag" in Florida in 1861, recalled the event forty-two years later "as vividly as on the night of its occurrence":

> A gentleman soloist, and a fine singer he was, advanced to the front of the stage bearing a large, blue, silk flag with a golden star in the center. Slowly unfurling the banner he began the song of the "Bonnie Blue Flag." As he named each State in the order of its secession the soldiers from these respective States cheered with the greatest enthusiasm. But as he concluded the last stanza,
>
> "For the lone star of the Bonnie Blue Flag
>
> Has grown to eleven,"
>
> He at the same time reversed the banner, displaying on the opposite side a galaxy of eleven stars, representing the eleven States of our new-born Confederacy. The sentiment, the occasion, the highly dramatic rendition of the whole recitation electrified the great assembly. Every man at once seemed to lose his reason. They sprang to their feet, rushed forward frantically waving their caps and wildling gesticulating, some out of joy beating comrades with fists, others embracing and kissing, still others shouting and yelling like mad men. This reign of Bedlam lasted ten minutes.

In New Orleans, Louisiana, a performance of the song inspired a similar response as the audience "rose to their feet, and yelled and yelled," one soldier later recalled. "The audience . . . caught on to the chorus and it was wafted into the streets, and the whole crowd turned into a Hallelujah meeting." When a police officer tried to quiet one particularly noisy Texas soldier, a small riot broke out.[4]

"The Bonnie Blue Flag" was popular with Confederate women who used the song and its versions to demonstrate their loyalty. "The Homespun Dress," a popular version of "The Bonnie Blue Flag," celebrated the sacrifice of southern women:

> Oh! yes, I am a Southern girl, and glory in the name,
> And boast it with far greater pride than glittering wealth or fame,
> We envy not the Northern girl, her robes of beauties rare,
> Though diamonds grace her snowy neck, and pearls bedeck her hair.
>
> Hurrah! hurrah! for the sunny south so dear,
> Three cheers for the homespun dress the Southern ladies wear.[5]

"The Bonnie Blue Flag" and "The Homespun Dress" became weapons in a war of words between Southern women and occupying Union troops. In Washington, DC, after the fall of Fort Sumter, Lincoln's secretary William O. Stoddard observed how "the tone of the piano-playing part of Washington society . . . is in romantic sympathy with the 'the sunny South,' and there is the perpetual tinkle of the favorite secession airs pouring through the windows, which [women] leave open for the benefit of any Northern vandals who may happen to pass within hearing." The most popular tunes were "Dixie," "The Bonnie Blue Flag," and "Maryland, My Maryland." However, the situation changed when Northern regimental bands arrived in Washington and laid claim to "Dixie." Stoddard recalled that soldiers played it "as if for a wager, and the cheering along the thronged sidewalks answered uproariously. Suddenly, as if a counter spell had been uttered, the weird and mocking power has passed away from the boding melody." The young women "cease[d] playing Dixie," shut "their windows and mournfully declar[d] that the Yankees have stolen even the national music of the South."[6]

The popularity of "The Bonnie Blue Flag" led Northerners to write new versions of the song. The most successful version was written by Colonel James L. Geddes of the Eighth Iowa Infantry while a prisoner of war in Selma, Alabama. Written in protest against the "The Bonnie Blue Flag," Geddes's song "The Bonnie Flag with the Stripes and Stars" accused the South of breaking the bond of friendship between North and South:

> We treated you as brothers until you drew the sword,
> With impious hands at Sumter you cut the silver cord,
> So now you hear our bugles; we come the sons of Mars,
> We rally round that brave old flag which bears the Stripes and Stars.

> We do not want your cotton, we care not for your slaves,
> But rather than divide this land, we'll fill your southern graves.
> With Lincoln for our Chieftain, we'll wear our country's scars.
> We rally round that brave old flag that bears the Stripes and Stars!

> We deem our cause most holy, we know we're in the right,
> And twenty Millions of freemen stand ready for the fight.
> Our bride is fair Columbia, no stain her beauty mars.
> O'er her we'll raise that brave old flag which bears the Stripes and Stars.[7]

Colonel James L. Geddes of the 8th Iowa Infantry wrote "The Bonnie Flag with the Stripes and Stars" as a Northern response to "The Bonnie Blue Flag."

Federal officials recognized the power of music to sustain Confederate morale. In Union-occupied New Orleans, federal authorities targeted A. E. Blackmar, publisher of "The Bonnie Blue Flag." Blackmar was fined three hundred dollars and imprisoned. While Blackmar was in prison, his store and its inventory were destroyed. Union General Benjamin Butler also issued General Order No. 40 banning "The Bonnie Blue Flag." Anyone who whistled, sang, or played "The Bonnie Blue Flag," or anyone in possession of the music, faced a range of penalties from a fine to time in a workhouse.[8]

"The Bonnie Blue Flag" never usurped "Dixie" as the Confederacy's primary anthem. Although the song served a basic need for a Confederate flag song, the Bonnie Blue flag that inspired the song did not resemble any of the several national flags adopted by the Confederacy. Additionally, Harry Macarthy's loyalty to the Confederacy was called into question when he fled the South for Philadelphia in 1864 to avoid the Confederate draft. Still, "The Bonnie Blue Flag" remained one of the Confederacy's most popular anthems, continuing to invoke strong feelings of Confederate patriotism.[9]

Part VIII

TECHNOLOGY

The Civil War occurred in a period of great technological innovation and invention. Technological advances brought more efficient weapons for killing, including the rifle, the minié ball, and the Gatling gun, while the large number of casualties on the battlefield forced the federal government to find better ways to care for the wounded. Although the Union had an established navy, that branch of the service was not prepared to operate on the inland waterways of the Western Theater. The construction of ships for riverine warfare allowed the Union to develop a two-pronged naval attack against the Confederacy. The need for better communications and transport across a broad geographic swath that stretched from the Trans-Mississippi to the Eastern Theaters led to more effective use of prewar technologies, such as the telegraph, railroads, aerial reconnaissance, and photography.

The Great Locomotive Chase

Railroads and Military Strategy

The steam locomotive the *General* is on exhibit at the Southern Museum of Civil War and Locomotive History, Kennesaw, Georgia.

SOURCE: COURTESY OF SOUTHERN MUSEUM ARCHIVES AND LIBRARY, FROM THE COLLECTION OF DAVID W. SALTER.

Early in the morning of April 12, 1862, a group of Northern raiders, led by civilian James J. Andrews, slipped aboard the Confederate locomotive the *General* during a breakfast stop in Big Shanty, Georgia (present day Kennesaw, Georgia). As the raiders sped away with the locomotive, a tender, and three empty boxcars, the stunned conductor William A. Fuller and two other men gave chase. On foot. Near Moon's Station, two miles north of Big Shanty, the men secured a hand car. Reaching Etowah, the Confederates abandoned the hand car and took over the locomotive *Yonah*. Further ahead, the raiders steamed northward in the *General*, breaking tracks and cutting telegraph lines, until they were forced to stop at Kingston to wait for three southbound trains to pass. After an hour-long delay, the raiders set out again, still ahead of Fuller and his men despite the delay. When the Confederates arrived in Kingston, they switched locomotives. Setting out in the *William R. Smith*, the men covered another six miles before a break in the line forced them to stop. Sprinting past the break, Fuller and his companions hailed the locomotive *Texas* as it rolled toward them headed south. Fuller commandeered the *Texas*. Lacking a roundtable to turn the engine around, Fuller ran the train in reverse tender first in pursuit of the *General*. With the *Texas* closing in, the raiders did not have time to refuel and the *General* ran out of steam at Ringgold, just south of the Georgia-Tennessee border, bringing an end to the seven-hour, eighty-mile chase. The raiders abandoned the train, but several were quickly captured. Andrews and seven other raiders were hanged as spies. Six others were exchanged in early 1863. In the North, the raiders were celebrated as heroes; the six who were exchanged received the Medal of Honor, the first such medals to be awarded. A bronze statue of the *General* stands in the Chattanooga National Cemetery surrounded by the graves of some of the raiders. Still, for all its drama, the incident had no military effect.

The Great Locomotive Chase highlights the role of the railroad during the war. In 1862, Chattanooga was an important rail junction, connecting the Deep South to the Confederate armies fighting in Virginia. Andrews and his raiders planned to steal a train and race it north to Chattanooga, destroying rail lines and bridges behind them, thus preventing Confederate reinforcements from reaching Chattanooga by train. The city could then be captured by Union forces advancing from the west. The failure of the raid led to nearly two more years of fighting—and more than forty-seven thousand deaths—before Chattanooga fell to Union forces.[1]

The Civil War was the first instance of the widespread use of railroads in strategic and logistical operations. Railroads transported private passengers, soldiers and military materiel, and freight. The success of military campaigns relied on adequate rail support. General William T. Sherman credited the success of his Atlanta campaign to having "the men and means to maintain and defend them in addition to what were necessary to overcome the enemy." Sustaining Sherman's "100,000-man army and 35,000 animals for the 196-day campaign over 473-mile supply line would have required 36,600 six-mule teams, each hauling 2 tons of freight 20 miles per day," historian John Clark notes. An impossible task given the state of the roads that existed in the region. Not surprisingly, when Sherman abandoned Atlanta to begin his March to the Sea, Sherman's railroad men destroyed the rails back to Chattanooga.[2]

The demands of the war forced fundamental changes in both Northern and Southern railroad practices. At the beginning of the war, the North had more than twenty thousand miles of track compared to the South's nine thousand miles. The Confederacy also lagged the Union in the number of freight cars and locomotives as well as rail and locomotive production. The South's railroads were primarily short-haul lines used to transport cotton or other goods

A trainload of Ohio troops wait for a supply train to pass. Harpers Ferry, Virginia.
SOURCE: CIVIL WAR PHOTO COLLECTION, UNITED STATES MILITARY ACADEMY.

to a river port or steamboat landing. In the North and the South, railroads were privately owned and operated. Moreover, the lack of a standard track gauge, or width between the parallel rails of the tracks, slowed the movement of passengers and freight, often requiring the train to stop and transfer whatever it was carrying to another train with wheels that could fit the next set of rails.

The Union recognized early on the need to assert federal control over the railroads. On January 31, 1862, Congress passed a law authorizing the president to seize the railroads for military use. The Secretary of War was to supervise and direct the rail transportation of soldiers and military goods. The new law also established the United States Military Rail Road (USMRR) as a separate agency. Secretary of War Edwin Stanton appointed former railroad executive Daniel McCallum as head of the USMRR and Herman Haupt, former chief engineer of the Pennsylvania Railroad, was appointed as chief of construction and transportation.

The USMRR transformed the rail system in the North. Track gauge was standardized, and locomotives and cars were built with wheels to fit that gauge. Stanton also worked out a system of fares for soldiers and military freight. It was Haupt, however, who established a five-point plan for "tactical rail generalship." First, military officers were not to interfere in the running of trains. Second, supplies were sent forward only as needed. Third, trains reaching the front were to be unloaded immediately by anyone available. Fourth, trains would run according to a schedule. Trains departed on schedule, fully loaded or not. Extra trains would be used to pick up the slack. And fifth, where sidings prevented opposing trains from passing each other, convoys of trains would travel as a group, each delivering its cargo and returning to base before the next convoy started out.[3]

Haupt also established two divisions within the USMRR: the Construction Corps and the Transportation Corps. The Construction Corps was charged with making rail lines fit for military use. Consisting of professional civil engineers, skilled workmen, and manual laborers, the Construction Corps was organized into self-sufficient divisions that could respond to a crisis in their assigned area, repairing damaged rails and bridges. In May 1862, under Haupt's direction, crews rebuilt a bridge across Potomac Creek in just nine days. As Lincoln later observed, "That man Haupt has built a bridge four hundred feet long and eighty feet high, across Potomac Creek, on which loaded trains are passing every hour, and upon my word, gentlemen, there is nothing in it but cornstalks and beanpoles." The Transportation Corps was responsible for routine maintenance and operation of the trains. Like the Construction Corps, it was organized into divisions, each assigned responsibility for specific sections of the rail system. After the Battle of Gettysburg, crews delivered tons of critical supplies and evacuated thousands of wounded soldiers.

By 1864, Haupt's organizational structure allowed USMRR construction crews to keep pace with the Union armies as they advanced into the Confederacy. USMRR crews repaired track as fast as combat troops could advance, maintaining a steady flow of supplies despite repeated disruption by Confederate troops. During Sherman's Atlanta Campaign, construction crews built seventy-five miles of new track and built eleven new bridges. Union supply trains were rolling into Atlanta one day after Sherman's troops entered the city. Full-time construction crews, posted at intervals along the tracks, along with strategically placed construction trains, kept the rails open despite frequent Confederate raids. The USMRR also supported Grant's drive toward Richmond, keeping supply lines open and allowing Grant to extend his siege lines south and west around Petersburg, even as the men of Lee's Army of Northern Virginia starved from a lack of supplies. On April 9, 1865, after failing to break through Union lines, Lee surrendered his hungry, exhausted army just a few miles from a railroad terminal where a Confederate supply train held desperately needed rations.

Just days later, after the assassination of President Lincoln, the railroads helped the country grieve. On April 21, a seven-car train left Washington, DC, for Springfield, Illinois, following the same route Lincoln had taken to Washington for his inauguration. Thousands lined the tracks to watch the train pass. By the time Lincoln was laid to rest in Springfield, more than seven million people had seen his casket. In a fitting coda, Lincoln's funeral train was the last one operated by the USMRR.

A Scientific Foundation for Medical Care

The Medical and Surgical History of the War of the Rebellion

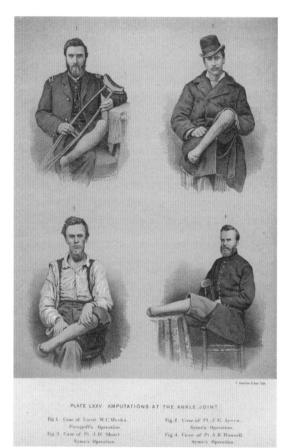

George A. Otis and D. L. Huntington, *The Medical and Surgical History of the War of the Rebellion* (Washington, DC: Government Printing Office, 1883). Private Augustine K. Russell is pictured in the lower-right corner of the image.

SOURCE: CENTRAL LIBRARIES SPECIAL COLLECTIONS, MOODY MEMORIAL LIBRARY, BAYLOR UNIVERSITY, WACO, TEXAS.

Private Augustine K. Russell, Company H, 1st Massachusetts Heavy Artillery, was shot in the left foot during the Battle of Spotsylvania Courthouse in May 1864. The bullet entered Russell's heel and exited through the top of his foot. The regimental surgeon amputated Russell's foot at the ankle joint. Three days later, Russell was transferred to Emory Hospital in Washington, DC, where he received additional medical treatment. By mid-August, Russell's stump "had nearly closed and his general health was good," Acting Assistant Surgeon J. E. Janvrin reported. "The success of this case is attributed in large measure to the method adopted for supporting the flap [that is, the skin covering the stump]."[1] Janvrin had Russell photographed before sending him home on furlough. The photograph and Janvrin's report about Russell's injury and treatment were submitted to the office of the surgeon general. The resulting case study was included in *The Medical and Surgical History of the War of the Rebellion*. Russell is pictured in the lower-right corner of this image.[2]

Described as the country's earliest comprehensive medical monograph, *The Medical and Surgical History of the War of the Rebellion* is a compendium of the experience of Civil War doctors and surgeons. The six-volume history totals more than six thousand pages and is divided equally between disease and surgery (injuries). It includes thousands of case studies documenting the types of disease and injuries military doctors and surgeons could expect to treat, along with examples of treatment. Originally conceived by Surgeon General William Hammond, *The Medical and Surgical History of the War of the Rebellion* was an effort by the Union Medical Department to use the experience of the war for the improvement of medicine.[3]

When the Civil War began, the Union Medical Department was not prepared to meet the demands of war. In 1860, the department had one surgeon general with the rank of colonel, thirty surgeons with the rank of major, and eighty-four assistant surgeons who held the rank of first lieutenant or captain. These officers were part of the general staff of the army and not permanently attached to any regiment or command. Many of these doctors had trained during an era of degraded standards in medicine and medical education: no licensing laws or state recognition of medical societies, few hospitals for training, and an absence of legal regulations for medicine. An insignificant proportion of American doctors were university-educated or had had the opportunity to study abroad where there were more and better educational opportunities. "On the eve of the Civil War, the bulk of American physicians continued to practice bedside medicine, had never used a microscope, and held a physiological conception of disease," notes historian Shauna Devine.

The conditions of war were unlike anything doctors had ever experienced. "The war was overwhelming in its scope," writes Devine, "physicians were forced to deal with diseases and injuries that differed both quantitatively and qualitatively from their usual practice patterns in civilian life." Training camps brought together thousands of men living and fighting in close quarters. Overcrowding, exposure, unsanitary sewage disposal, and a lack of resistance to infectious diseases among the soldier population created conditions that allowed diseases like diarrhea, dysentery, measles, typhoid fever, and pneumonia to thrive. On the battlefield, the fighting resulted in tens of thousands of wounded or dead soldiers.[4]

At the first major engagement of the Civil War, along the banks of Bull Run Creek, medical care of the wounded was hampered by a lack of planning and a shortage of medical supplies. On July 18, 1861, Union Brigadier General Irvin McDowell moved the Army of the Potomac toward Centreville, Virginia. Although it was a hot and humid day, the regiments moved forward on the double-quick through the midday heat. The "hot sun pouring down upon us and the roads so dusty that one can scarcely see his file leader," one soldier recalled. Soldiers who were unable to keep up fell out along the way, many of them suffering from exhaustion and sunstroke. The Union army engaged the enemy at Blackburn's Ford, a minor skirmish resulting in only a few dozen casualties. Still, the battle demonstrated the shortcomings of the Union Medical Department. William S. King, McDowell's medical director, described going out to meet the ambulances returning from the battle:

> [We] soon met the ambulances with the dead, wounded, and disabled men. One soldier had had his face shot away completely. Some in the ambulances were not wounded, but were disabled from sunstroke or exhaustion. . . . A hotel, a church, and large dwelling, were selected by Assistant Surgeon Magruder, and some wounded were placed in them before my arrival. Unfortunately, two of the ambulances had been drawn up on the wrong side of the road, and the division of General Tyler, of twelve thousand troops, marching in close order, filled the passage between our wounded and the church hospital, and we were obliged to wait for two hours . . . before the wounded could be taken out. . . . Water, procured with great difficulty and placed in basins for the purpose of washing the wounded, was snatched up and drank by stragglers, as they passed.

King ordered a volunteer surgeon to treat several seriously injured soldiers. The surgeon refused, claiming the men were not from his regiment and therefore not his responsibility. After seeing to the wounded, a weary King sent an appeal to the surgeon general for additional medical supplies.

On July 21, more than one thousand men were wounded at the First Battle of Bull Run. And once again, King demonstrated his inability to coordinate the care of the sick and wounded. "It was a scene of utter medical chaos," writes medical historian Ira M. Rutkow. "There was no organized evacuation of the injured, and no provisions had been made to have available adequate numbers of field hospitals or even simple first-aid encampments to handle causalities. Everything seemed to have been left to luck or divine intervention."[5]

The congressional appointment of William Hammond as surgeon general in April 1862 marked a turning point in Civil War medical care. Hammond had entered the Army Medical Service in 1849 as an assistant surgeon. After ten years of service in various posts, Hammond resigned from the army to accept a position as chair of anatomy and physiology at the University of Maryland, Baltimore. In April 1861, Hammond treated members of the 6th Massachusetts after they were attacked by a mob of Confederate sympathizers while passing through Baltimore on their way to Washington, DC. Hammond resigned his professorship and rejoined the army. He spent the first few months of the war organizing military hospitals in the Northeast where he gained the respect of the leaders of the United States Sanitary Commission.[6]

Hammond quickly set to work reforming and strengthening the Army Medical Department:

> He added a medical inspecting corps; increased the number of surgeons, assistant surgeons, medical cadets, medical storekeepers and hospital stewards; collaborated with the United States Sanitary Commission and other civilian bodies to support the hiring of female nurses and civilian hospital workers; issued circulars that provided for the formation of the Army Medical Museum and publication of the *Medical and Surgical History of the War of the Rebellion*; built permanent hospitals along scientific standards; created field aid stations and field hospitals; and paved the way for the development of the . . . ambulance and field relief system.

Under Hammond's leadership, the Army Medical Department was reorganized along more scientific and professional standards. Doctors and surgeons who sought army commissions or promotion were required to pass a multipart examination. Hammond increased the number of assistant surgeons assigned to each regiment, developed standardized supply tables listing the officially approved supplies and equipment for the Medical Department, and implemented requirements for all medical data to be recorded and submitted to the Surgeon General's Office.[7]

In May 1862, Hammond issued Circular No. 2 directing medical officers to gather information and submit reports. For example, in the case of amputations, surgeons were to describe the period and nature of the injury; the character of the operation; and the time, place, and result. In cases where postmortem examinations were performed, "accounts of pathological results were to be prepared." Circular No. 2 also provided for the establishment of the Army Medical Museum. Medical officers were "to collect, and to forward to the office of the Surgeon General, all specimens of morbid anatomy, surgical, or medical, which may be regarded as valuable; together with projectiles and foreign bodies removed, and such other matters as may prove of interest in the study of military medicine or surgery."[8]

Hammond's circular created a tremendous body of medical knowledge and made it available to physicians and surgeons. Although some physicians and surgeons submitted reports because they were required to do so (if they wanted to maintain their position in the Union Medical Department), many "got caught up in the general desire for improvement and advancement that characterized the project." Hammond listed clinical instruments, medical texts, and current medical journals on the army medical supply table; he also supported the publication of educational treatises to train and educate physicians and surgeons. As doctors developed new understandings of diseases, such as gangrene, the findings were widely disseminated to doctors in general hospitals, sometimes in the form of orders.

One month after issuing Circular No. 2, Hammond issued Circular No. 5 requiring the cooperation of all medical officers in furnishing data for the publication of *The Medical and Surgical History of the Rebellion*.[9]

The task of preparing the *History* was first assigned to the Army Medical Museum's curators John Hill Brinton and Joseph Woodward. Brinton was responsible for compiling the surgical section, while Woodward was assigned the medical (disease) section. When Brinton left the museum, George Otis took over the surgical section. David Huntington and Charles Smart also helped write and organize the text and illustrations. During the war, Brinton and Woodward redesigned medical department forms and reporting methods to gather the information needed for the project. They gathered research material. The books they collected for the project formed the foundation for the National Library of Medicine.

At the end of the war, the regular staff of the Medical Department had grown to nearly two hundred members, including a surgeon general, an assistant surgeon general, one medical inspector general, and sixteen medical

[Circular No. 5]
Surgeon General's Office
Washington City, D.C., June 9, 1862

It is intended to prepare for publication the Medical and Surgical History of the Rebellion.

The Medical portion of this work has been committed to Assistant Surgeon J. J. Woodward, United States Army, and the Surgical part to Brigade Surgeon John H. Brinton, United States Volunteers.

All medical officers are therefore requested to co-operate in this undertaking forwarding to this office such sanitary, topographical, medical and surgical reports, details of cases, essays, and results of investigations and inquiries as may be of value for this work, for which full credit will be given in the forthcoming volumes.

Authority has been given to both the above named gentlemen to issue, from time to time, such circulars as may be necessary to elicit the desired facts, and the medical officers are desired to comply with the requests why may thus be made of them.

It is scarcely necessary to remind the medical officers of the regular and volunteer services that through the means in question much may be done to advance the science which we all have so much at heart, and to establish land-marks which will serve to guide us in the future.

It is therefore confidently expected that no one will neglect this opportunity of advancing the honor of the service, the cause of humanity, and his own reputation.

William A. Hammond
Surgeon General U.S.A.

inspectors. Another six thousand doctors were mustered into service as either regimental or assistant regimental surgeons between April 1861 and the end of the war. In this same period, there were 85 acting staff surgeons and 5,532 acting assistant surgeons. Under Hammond's leadership, thousands of reports, specimens, and statistics were submitted to the Surgeon General's Office. Over the next twenty-three years, that research would be carefully analyzed and prepared for publication in *The Medical and Surgical History of the War of the Rebellion*.[10]

39

"A curious marine monster"
Ironclads and Riverine Warfare

The *Essex* passed the Vicksburg batteries and reached Baton Rouge, Louisiana, in July 1862.

On January 21, 1863, Union Colonel David Hunter Strother, an artist and journalist prior to the war, visited the USS *Essex*, the first riverine ironclad, while it was anchored in Baton Rouge, Louisiana. Badly damaged during the Battle of Fort Henry, Tennessee, the *Essex* had been rebuilt. The ironclad measured nearly two hundred feet long with a beam of fifty-eight feet and a draft of six feet, nine inches. Displacing one thousand tons, the *Essex* carried a 134-man crew and was capable of 5.5 knots. "She is a curious marine monster and looks very formidable," Strother wrote. "She mounts ten guns ranging in caliber from an old thirty-two pounder to a ten-inch Dahlgren." The hulking *Essex* and her sailors, who "stood around her guns and saluted us with Roman swords," made for a "most grim and piratelike scene," Strother wrote.[1]

Riverine warfare—military operations conducted on rivers and associated waterways—developed early in the Civil War. Union General Winfield Scott proposed a plan to block Southern ports and to invade the Confederacy along its interior waterways, principally the Mississippi. Scott's so-called Anaconda Plan would isolate the South diplomatically and economically, preventing exports and imports from leaving or entering Southern ports and opening vital communication and travel routes into the Confederate interior for Union forces, effectively strangling the South with Union land and naval forces. However, such a plan would require time and resources to implement. In the meantime, impatient Northerners clamored for a more decisive blow against the rebellious South. President Lincoln adopted Scott's plan for a blockade of Southern ports from the Chesapeake Bay to the Gulf of Mexico. It would take three months and a devastating loss at the First Battle of Bull Run before Lincoln incorporated the seizure of western rivers into his military strategy.[2]

Gaining control of the Mississippi and other inland waters was a difficult task. The U.S. Navy had little presence or experience operating on interior waterways other than the Great Lakes. Riverine operations also required a new kind of warship, one capable of mounting large guns with a draft shallow enough and sufficiently narrow to navigate twisting streams. During the Civil War, the army built several types of riverine warships, including timberclads, tinclads, and Cairo- or city-class ironclads, as well as modifying existing ships, such as the river steamer *New Era*, which became the *Essex*.[3]

In the summer of 1861, naval commander John Rodgers negotiated contracts to buy and convert three wooden side-wheel freight-and-passenger Ohio River steamers into timberclad gunboats. The *Tyler*, the *Lexington*, and the *Conestoga* were reinforced to enable them to carry heavy guns, and five-inch-thick oak was installed to provide protection against rifle fire. By mid-August 1861, the three warships were transported to their base at Cairo, Illinois, and commissioned into service. The timberclads saw service along the Cumberland, Tennessee, and Mississippi Rivers, providing an effective stop gap measure until the new ironclads could be brought into service.

Armored with metal plate measuring less than one inch thick capable of protecting only against small-arms fire, tinclads were stern-wheelers and side-wheelers of shallow draft. Draft, or the vertical distance between the waterline and the bottom of the hull, determines the minimum depth of water a boat can safely navigate. With a draft of only two feet, tinclads were developed specifically for service on the shallow rivers that emptied into the Mississippi. Tinclads were highly effective in Union patrol and interdiction operations along these waters. But unlike ironclads they were not sufficiently armored or gunned to take on Confederate naval combatants or major shore batteries. Instead tinclads were used to transport and supply vessels, serve as light replenishment ships, and carry dispatches. During the war, the Union had more than sixty tinclads, thirteen of which were lost.

The Cairo- or city-class ironclads were designed by naval constructor Samuel M. Pook and built by contractor James Buchanan Eads. Named the *Carondelet, St. Louis, Louisville, Pittsburg, Cairo, Mound City,* and *Cincinnati,* the ships were the core of the U.S. Navy's Mississippi Squadron. Pook designed a ship 175 feet in length, with a beam of fifty feet and a draft of six feet. A rectangular casemate, rising above the gun deck at an angle of thirty-five degrees, protected the single paddle wheel in the center of the ship. Eads submitted the lowest bid ($89,600 each). His contract required him to deliver seven vessels to Cairo by October 10, 1861, giving Eads only sixty-five days to construct seven ships. Eads's experience in boat construction proved invaluable. He quickly assembled a four-thousand-man workforce. Installing lights on the docks, construction proceeded around the clock until the ships were delivered in October.

The resulting ironclads were known as "Pook Turtles" for their appearance. The ironclads were

> 175 feet in length, with a beam of 51 feet, 2 inches, draft of 6 feet, and displacement of 512 tons. The flat-bottomed hulls were laid across three keels, with outer keels 10 feet apart from the center to support the wide beam. Their casemates rose above the waterline at a 35-degree angle and were plated with 2.5-inch thick iron plating; the plates themselves were 13 inches wide by 8.5 feet long and locked together with overlapping lips. The wood oak planking of the

casemates on which the iron plates were bolted was 24 inches thick forward and 12.5 inches on the sides and aft.

On the hurricane deck, a conical pilothouse protected the navigator. Below deck were five boilers, three feet in diameter and twenty-five feet long with a brick furnace at each front end. "Each Cairo-class ironclad was armed with 13 guns: three 8-inch smoothbores, four 42-pounder rifled guns, and six 32-pounders, three on the bow, four on each side, and two on the stern."[4]

In addition to the purpose-built ironclad warships, the Union converted river ships, including the *Benton*, a former catamaran snagboat used for pulling debris from the river, and the *Essex*, a converted merchant river ferry. Originally a St. Louis ferry boat—the largest on the Mississippi River—the *Essex* was acquired by the U.S. Army in September 1861 and first converted to a timberclad. When it was commissioned the following month, the *Essex* was armored, and its hull lengthened. In November 1861, the *Essex* was placed under the command of William D. Porter, who used the ironclad for an expedition up the Cumberland River. On January 11, 1862, the *Essex* and the *St. Louis* engaged Confederate gunboats in the Tennessee River near Lucas Bend, Missouri. In February 1862, the *Essex* assisted in the capture of Fort Henry.

The Union attacks on Fort Henry, located on the Tennessee River, and Fort Donelson, located on the Cumberland River, were the first large-scale riverine operations. On February 6, four ironclads—the *Essex*, *Cincinnati*, *Carondelet*, and *St. Louis*—followed by a division of timberclads opened fire on Fort Henry. In the fighting, the *Essex* was struck in the boiler, causing an explosion that killed or wounded thirty-two men, including Porter, who was badly scalded. After several hours of fighting, Confederate forces at Fort Henry surrendered. With Fort Henry secured, attention turned to nearby Fort Donelson. Ulysses S. Grant planned to hold the Confederates within the fort with land forces while the Union flotilla took out the water batteries. Commodore Andrew Foote used the same formation as he had at Fort Henry with four ironclads—the *St. Louis*, *Carondelet*, *Louisville*, and *Pittsburg*—in front and two timberclads in the rear. In the exchange of gunfire, three of the four ironclads were disabled and drifted downstream. The other vessels were forced to withdraw, leaving Union ground forces to continue the attack until the Confederates surrendered on February 16.[5]

On July 22, 1862, the newly rebuilt *Essex* attacked the Confederate ironclad *Arkansas* at Vicksburg, Mississippi, inflicting considerable damage on the Confederate boat. The *Essex* attacked the *Arkansas* a second time, at Baton Rouge, Louisiana, on August 5. In October, the *Essex* was turned over to the navy and thereafter served with the Mississippi Squadron. The gunboat took part in the bombardment of Port Hudson, Louisiana (December 13, 1862), the occupation of Baton Rouge (December 17, 1862), and the bombardment of Whitehall Point, Louisiana (July 10, 1863). The *Essex* played a critical role in both the Siege of Vicksburg (May 18 through July 4, 1863) and the Red River Campaign (March 10–March 22, 1864). From May 1864 through the end of the war, the *Essex* was based in Memphis, Tennessee.

Riverine operations in the Western Theater played a key role in securing the region for the Union. Although riverine operations were not as prominent in the East, the Union navy's control of much of the James River below Richmond aided General Grant's Appomattox Campaign at the end of the war.

The Silk Dress Balloon

Aeronautics in the Civil War

Section of printed silk balloon fabric from a captured Confederate balloon. The craft was constructed of bolts of dress silk by Captain Langdon Cheeves and aeronaut Charles Cevor. Named the *Gazelle*, the balloon saw service during the Peninsula Campaign of 1862. It was captured on July 3, 1862, while being moved aboard an armed tug.

SOURCE: SMITHSONIAN, NATIONAL AIR AND SPACE MUSEUM.

This small piece of fabric, composed of various patterns of dress silk, is all that remains of the *Gazelle*, the first Confederate gas balloon. The balloon was constructed in Savannah, Georgia, in the spring of 1862, by Captain Langdon Cheves Jr., son of the well-known, wealthy South Carolina politician Langdon Cheves Sr. The younger Cheves had been stationed at Port Royal, South Carolina, and had likely seen the Union aeronaut Thaddeus Lowe's balloon in action as it observed Confederate troop movements on the Virginia peninsula. Lacking the supplies available to Lowe in the North, Cheves instead bought up bolts of ladies' dress silk in Savannah and Charleston. The fabric was sewn together and varnished to create the Confederate war balloon, which is often referred to by its nickname, "the Silk Dress Balloon." When the balloon was finished, it was moved to Richmond, Virginia, where the balloon was filled with city gas, attached to a rail car, and transported to the front lines. Confederate officer E. Porter Alexander used the balloon to observe enemy troop movements during the Battle of Gaines' Mill on June 27, 1862. After the battle, the balloon was attached to the Confederate tug *Teaser*. On July 4, the balloon and the boat were seized by Union forces aboard the gunboat *Maritanza*, bringing an end to Confederate aeronautics. The balloon was given to Lowe, who cut it into scraps to give as souvenirs.[1]

The use of balloon technology for military reconnaissance did not originate with the Civil War. Rather, it dates to another military conflict, the French Revolution. Frenchman Jean Francois de Rozier is credited with being the first person to ascend in a balloon. Observing a subsequent balloon ascent in Paris in 1783, Benjamin Franklin noted the possible military value of balloon flight: "[The balloon] might be used for elevating an engineer to take a view of the enemy's army and for conveying intelligence into a besieged town." Over the following decades, experienced aeronauts like John Wise, of Lancaster, Pennsylvania, who by 1847 had logged sixty-two ascensions, brought significant improvements to balloon technology. By the beginning of the war, men like Lowe and Wise as well as John La Mountain had successfully lifted twenty-two-ton payloads, achieved altitudes of two miles, and traveled hundreds of miles nonstop.[2]

On April 20, 1861, just days after the fall of Fort Sumter and the start of the Civil War, Thaddeus Lowe caused quite a stir in Unionville, South Carolina. Lowe, who had been practicing for an Atlantic crossing, had set out from Cincinnati, Ohio, several hours earlier. Viewed with alarm and suspicion by the residents of the new Confederate state, Lowe was threatened with arrest before the president of the local university intervened on Lowe's behalf and provided the aeronaut safe passage back to Cincinnati.

Lowe abandoned his dream of an Atlantic crossing. As Lowe would later recall, "I was fully convinced that the country was facing a severe struggle."[3] He asked one of his financial supporters, Murat Halstead, who was editor of the Cincinnati *Daily Commercial* to write a letter to Treasury Secretary Salmon P. Chase suggesting the army establish a balloon corps under Lowe's command for the express purpose of providing aerial reconnaissance. On receiving Halstead's letter, Chase arranged for Lowe to come to the capitol with the *Enterprise*. With the help of Joseph Henry, secretary of the Smithsonian Institute, Lowe devised a plan to use telegraphic equipment while the balloon was aloft. On June 17, 1861, with Lowe and representatives of the American Telegraph Company aboard, the *Enterprise* ascended on tether lines from the grounds of the Columbia Armory in Washington. From a height of five hundred feet, Lowe transmitted the first telegraphic message from the air:

Balloon Enterprise, Washington, June 17 1861
To the President of the United States:

Sir: This point of observation commands an area nearly fifty miles in diameter. The city, with its girdle of encampments, presents a superb scene. I take great pleasure in sending you this first dispatch ever telegraphed from an aerial station, and in acknowledging my indebtedness to your encouragement for the opportunity of demonstrating the availability of the science of aeronautics in the military service of this country.

Yours respectfully,
T. S. C. Lowe[4]

Soon after Lowe's successful demonstration, Lincoln placed the aeronaut in charge of the new Balloon Corps, a civilian organization established by Lincoln that would serve as part of the Bureau of Topographical Engineers. Lowe was authorized to requisition equipment and labor for the Balloon Corps and to oversee operations. However, the Balloon Corps was essentially a civilian organization and the Bureau of Topographical Engineers was reluctant to provide Lowe with needed supplies, forcing Lowe to use his own equipment and pay his employees out of his own pocket. Still, with Lincoln's assistance, Lowe moved forward with the construction of the Union army's first balloon designed for military use. Costing twelve hundred dollars each to construct, the first two balloons were christened *Union* and *Constitution*. "Each [balloon] displayed its given name," as one historian notes. "The *Constitution* was adorned with a large portrait of George Washington, together with a spread eagle in colors. The *Union* bore the Stars and Stripes. Even the baskets were painted with white stars against a bright blue background." Each balloon was also provided with a wagon train carrying the equipment and supplies needed to operate and maintain each balloon.

In the spring of 1862, the Balloon Corps was transferred from the Topographical Engineers to the Quartermaster Department. Lowe and his balloons were transferred to Fort Monroe to support operations on the Virginia peninsula. During the Peninsula Campaign, Lowe made several ascensions, providing nearly continuous aerial reconnaissance of the region. Lowe carried telegraphic equipment aboard his balloon so he could transmit his observations without descending. Throughout that spring, Lowe's balloons tracked troop movements and army intelligence officers drew maps and made copi-

The Battle of Fair Oaks, 1862. Published by Currier and Ives, circa 1862.
SOURCE: LIBRARY OF CONGRESS.

ous notes all while airborne. At one point, Lowe came under fire from enemy cannons forcing him to descend and move the balloon farther away from the gunfire. On May 4, Lowe telegraphed Union General George McClellan that Yorktown, Virginia, had been evacuated by the Confederates.

The Battle of Fair Oaks, which began on May 31, 1862, was the high point of Lowe's Balloon Corps. On May 31, Lowe telegraphed McClellan that large bodies of enemy troops and wagon trains were moving from Richmond to Fair Oaks. Lowe remained aloft watching the Confederates form a line of battle. Going aloft again the next day, Lowe reported Confederate forces were within five miles of Union forces. During the subsequent battle, Lowe made several ascents with telegraph equipment, "keeping the wires hot with information" of troop positions. "From my own observation and experience," Major General Samuel Heintzelman later told Lowe, "I would consider your balloons indispensable to an army in the field, and should I ever be entrusted with such a command I would consider my preparations incomplete without one or more balloons."[5]

Changes in military command and yet another transfer of the Balloon Corps, this time to the Corps of Engineers, marked the beginning of the end of the Lowe's ambitions for the use of balloons for military reconnaissance. In the spring of 1863, Captain Cyrus Comstock, who oversaw the Corps of Engineers, reduced Lowe's pay by one-third. On May 8, 1863, after the Battle of Chancellorsville, Lowe resigned from the Balloon Corps. The Corps continued for three more months under the supervision of the brothers James and Ezra Allen before it was disbanded.

Part IX

EMANCIPATION

It was not a forgone conclusion that the Civil War would lead to the abolition of slavery. For the first eighteen months of the war, Lincoln resisted efforts to make the Civil War an "abolition war." Writing in 1862 to Horace Greeley, editor of the *New York Tribune*, Lincoln claimed, "My paramount object in this struggle is to save the Union, and it is not either to save or to destroy slavery. If I could save the Union without freeing any slave I would do it, and if I could save it by freeing all the slaves I would do it; and if I could save it by freeing some and leaving others alone I would also do that. That I do about slavery, and the colored race, I do because I believe it helps save the Union; and what I forbear, I forbear because I do not believe it would save the Union." Emancipation was the result of a complex interplay of multiple factors, including, in the words of historian David W. Blight, "the geographical course of the war; the size of the slave population in any given region; the policies enforced at any given time by the Union and Confederate governments through their military forces; and the volition of slaves themselves in seizing their moments to embrace a reasonable chance for freedom." The objects in this part focus on discrete moments in the process of emancipation.[1]

Freedom's Fort

Old Point Comfort, Fort Monroe, and Slavery

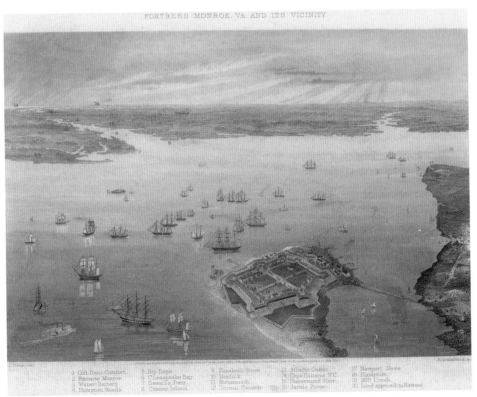

Perspective drawing of Fortress Monroe, Virginia, and its vicinity. Fortress Monroe is located in the bottom of the print to the right of center. The fortress is indicated by the number 2 and the land approach to the fort is indicated by the number 20.

The 565-acre peninsula known as Old Point Comfort, Virginia, is a significant site in African American history. In August 1619, the Dutch privateer the *White Lion* arrived on Point Comfort seeking to trade its cargo of twenty Africans for provisions, the first slave ship to arrive in England's North American colonies. Two hundred years later, enslaved laborers were used to build Fort Monroe on the southern tip of Point Comfort. Construction on the fort began in 1819 and concluded in 1834 under the supervision of Robert E. Lee, who was stationed at the fort from 1831 to 1834. Named for James Monroe, the nation's fifth president and the fourth Virginia slaveholder to hold that office, Fort Monroe covered sixty-three acres. In May 1861, as Virginians voted to secede from the Union, Fort Monroe remained a Union stronghold. As Virginians celebrated their independence from the North, three enslaved men—Shepard Mallory, Frank Baker, and James Townsend—fled to the fort. As they made their own claim for independence, Mallory, Baker, and Townsend set in motion a movement that would transform Fort Monroe into "Freedom's Fort" and, in time, would force a change in Union war aims.[1]

Although not drawn to scale, the map "Fortress Monroe, Va. and Its Vicinity," drawn by Jacob Wells in 1862, helps us to imagine the landscape of Old Point Comfort and the journey Mallory, Baker, and Townsend took on the evening of May 23. The three men had been working to build a Confederate battery at Sewall's Point, near Norfolk. Sewall's Point is visible in the upper left corner of the map, located at the tip of the land mass that juts out from the left border of the map, indicated by the number 7. Sewall's Point and Craney Island, which is located to the right of Sewall's Point (8), form the mouth of the Elizabeth River (9). Old Point Comfort (1) and Fort Monroe (2) are in the bottom center of the map with the land approach to the fort (20) disappearing into the bottom border of the map. Between Sewall's Point and Fort Monroe flows Hampton Roads (4), the five-mile wide natural roadstead formed by the deep-water estuary of the James River (16). The map depicts ships and boats of various sizes traveling Hampton Roads between Sewall's Point and Fort Monroe. The rowboat used by Mallory, Baker, and Townsend would have been one of the smaller boats in the channel.

The three men had learned their owner Charles Mallory planned to take them to the Carolinas "for the purposes of aiding secession forces there." Confronted with separation from their families, the three men chose to embark on a dangerous journey to freedom. As Mallory, Baker, and Townsend rowed their boat across Hampton Roads toward Fort Monroe in the dark, they had no idea what might happen. Even if they survived the crossing, they did not know how they would be received at the fort. The men faced the possibility of being turned away or returned to their master, with the likelihood of severe physical punishment and sale deeper into the South. Still, the men continued to row, drawn forward by their courage and the presence of the Union army in Confederate Virginia.[2]

Slaves understood the significance of Lincoln's election. "There was great excitement in Richmond over the election of Mr. Abraham Lincoln as President of the United States," Virginia slave Thomas Johnson recalled. "We knew he was in great sympathy with the abolition of slavery." A Mississippi mistress noted how much the slaves had "been talking . . . about Lincoln freeing the servants." In March 1861, just one week after Lincoln's inauguration, eight slaves arrived at Fort Pickens, an island installation off the coast of Pensacola, Florida, under Union control. The officer in charge had his men deliver the fugitives to the Pensacola city marshal to be sent back to their owners. Elsewhere in Florida, as well as Virginia and Maryland, enslaved people appealed to Union forces to open their lines. Initially, Union officials responded by enforcing federal law—the Constitution and the Fugitive Slave Act—and returned fugitive slaves to their owners.[3]

Mallory, Baker, and Townsend were not turned away when they reached Fort Monroe. Instead the three met with the commander of the fort, General Benjamin Butler. Having learned the Confederates had been using slaves to construct fortifications in the area, Butler decided it was "a measure of necessity" to keep the men within Union lines. On May 24, when an agent for the slaves' owner arrived at the fort requesting the return of the three fugitives under the provisions of the Fugitive Slave Act, Butler refused to comply. The Fugitive Slave Act, Butler said, "did not affect a foreign country, which Virginia claimed to be." If Charles Mallory would take an oath of allegiance to the United States, Butler would return the three slaves. As Butler expected, Mallory declined.

Under the laws of war, enemy property could be seized. "Property of whatever nature, used or capable of being used for warlike purposes, and especially when being so used, may be captured and held either on sea or on shore as property contraband of war," Butler later explained. Although Butler doubted "there may be property in human beings," he did believe it was legitimate to deprive the enemy of slaves' labor.[4]

On May 30, after a meeting of Lincoln's cabinet, the Secretary of War telegraphed Butler telling him his "contraband policy" had been approved. The secretary's instructions introduced an important distinction that would guide federal emancipation policy until Lincoln issued the Emancipation Proclamation: slaves who entered Union lines voluntarily—like Mallory, Baker, and Townsend—would not be returned to their masters. However, Union troops were warned not to entice slaves away from their masters.

As word of Butler's order spread, enslaved men, women, and children began to stream into Butler's lines. By July 1861, nine hundred freedmen had found their way to Fort Monroe and the adjoining city of Hampton, which was also under Union control. Butler ordered his men to put to work "all able-bodied negroes within your lines," to provide rations for the workers and their families, and to keep accurate records of the slaves, the work they performed, the rations they received, and the names of their owners. Significantly, Butler refused to separate families, retaining children even though he could not plausibly argue for the military necessity of doing so.[5]

For the next few months, the federal government and Union officers and soldiers struggled with the question of what to do about the thousands of slaves who were flooding into Union lines. After Butler's contraband decision, Congress passed the First Confiscation Act, empowering the government to confiscate property, including slaves, used to aid the rebellion, and terminated masters' claims over those slaves who had been used to assist the Confederate military. The act did not address the status of those slaves, however. In July 1862, Congress passed the Second Confiscation Act and the Militia Act. The Second Confiscation Act explicitly freed slaves of all persons "in rebellion." In the spring of 1862, Congress abolished slavery in Washington, DC, and in the western territories. Lincoln also met with representatives from the border states, but he was unable to convince them to adopt a plan for gradual, compensated emancipation.

In the field, military leaders crafted their own solutions to the slave problem, often in direct conflict with the political solutions approved by Congress. In August 1861, John C. Fremont, commander of the Western department at St. Louis, issued his own edict of freedom placing the state of Missouri under martial law and declaring the property of all Missourians fighting against the United States confiscated and liable to use by Union forces. Fremont also pronounced the slaves of Confederate Missourians free. In April 1862, Major David Hunter declared all slaves in Georgia, Florida, and South Carolina free. In both cases, Lincoln modified the orders.

Enslaved people had been running away for decades before the Civil War, seeking freedom in Northern states or in Canada. In times of war, such as the American Revolution or the War of 1812, the dash to freedom by enslaved

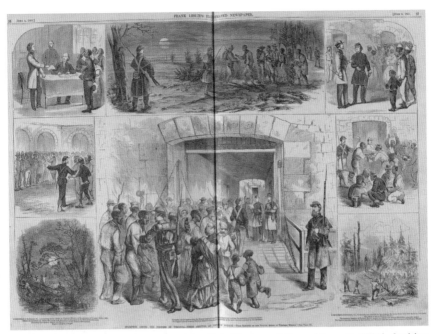

In this two-page spread from *Frank Leslie's Illustrated News* (June 8, 1861), fugitive slaves are shown entering Fortress Monroe seeking freedom and protection after General Benjamin Butler declared fugitive slaves "contraband of war."
SOURCE: LIBRARY OF CONGRESS PRINTS AND PHOTOGRAPHS DIVISION.

men, women, and children accelerated, freeing "tens of thousands." However, when peace returned, slavery continued to expand across the American South. The Civil War was different. As historian Amy Murrell Taylor writes, the war "set in motion hundreds of thousands of men, women, and children—entire families, neighborhoods, and communities—in a mass exodus from slavery that would strain and then destroy the institution once and for all."[6] That this exodus began at Old Point Comfort, a site that witnessed the beginnings of African slavery, has a certain poetic justice.

An Abolition War

The Emancipation Proclamation

Reading the Emancipation Proclamation.
SOURCE: LIBRARY OF CONGRESS PRINTS AND PHOTOGRAPHS DIVISION.

Lucius Stebbins, a book publisher from Hartford, Connecticut, produced and sold the print *Reading the Emancipation Proclamation*, along with a small promotional pamphlet, *Emancipation Proclamation of January 1st, 1864* [*sic*]. The print, which sold for $2.50, portrayed a Union soldier reading aloud the words of the Emancipation Proclamation to a slave family gathered in a small cabin somewhere in the Confederacy. The print was based on a painting by Henry W. Herrick, a New Hampshire–based artist. *Reading the Emancipation Proclamation* is the only print of the period to show a first reading of the Emancipation Proclamation from the point of view of those whom the order was designed to free. It is an accurate portrayal of Lincoln's order. The proclamation itself freed no slave until federal troops had advanced into slave-holding states and liberated the slave population in their wake, or until slaves themselves broke out from the plantations to achieve freedom. As historians Mark Neely and Harold Holzer note, "Slaves were freed by the sword as well as the pen, but Stebbins's was the first print to suggest it."[1]

By the summer of 1862, Lincoln had come to realize the importance of abolition to the Union war effort. He believed emancipation by state action would demoralize the Confederacy as would a great military victory over Confederate forces. Yet neither had happened by mid-summer. Up to this point, the border states refused to accept Lincoln's offers for compensated emancipation. After a failed meeting with border state congressmen in July 1862, Lincoln warned them that if they did not adopt emancipation, slavery might soon "be extinguished by mere friction and abrasion—by the mere incidents of war." After the border state congressmen left Washington, DC, Lincoln shared an early draft of the Emancipation Proclamation with his cabinet. The cabinet was concerned the order might look like an act of desperation by a nearly defeated Union. The cabinet and Lincoln agreed to Lincoln's desire to issue the order, but Lincoln agreed to wait for a military victory. That victory came in September 1862 at the Battle of Antietam. On September 22, Lincoln issued the preliminary Emancipation Proclamation.[2]

Seward and the other members of the cabinet recognized how the Emancipation Proclamation would change the nature of the war and set slavery on the path to destruction. Throughout the second half of 1862, Lincoln pushed hard for the gradualist measures he wanted attached to emancipation: compensation and colonization. To that end, he met with free Black leaders in hopes of convincing them to endorse his colonization plans. Most refused to endorse colonization. "Mr. Lincoln is quite a genuine representative of American prejudices and negro hatred," Frederick Douglass later wrote. Lincoln was "far more concerned for the preservation of slavery, and the favor of the Border Slave states, than for any sentiment of magnanimity or principle of justice and humanity."

The final proclamation, issued on January 1, 1863, made no mention of colonization. It also included provisions for accepting Blacks into military service.

On the fiftieth anniversary of the Emancipation Proclamation, the African Methodist Episcopal church (AME) asked Bishop Henry McNeal Turner to write a reflection on the meaning of the order. Born a free Black on February 1, 1834, in South Carolina, Turner joined the AME church in 1858, becoming an ordained minister and serving as pastor of Israel AME church in Washington, DC. During the Civil War, Lincoln commissioned Turner to the office of chaplain in the Union army, the first Black chaplain in any branch of the military. After the Civil War, Turner served as army chaplain with the Freedmen's Bureau in Georgia. In his essay, Turner recalled the events of that fateful January day:

> I hurriedly went up to the office of the first paper in which the proclamation of freedom could be printed, known as the "Evening Star," and squeezed myself through the dense crowd that was waiting for the paper. The first sheet run off with the proclamation in it was grabbed for by three of us, but some active young man got possession of it and fled. The next sheet was grabbed for by several, and was torn into tatters. The third sheet from the press was grabbed for by several, but I succeeded in procuring so much of it as contained the proclamation, and off I went for life and death. Down Pennsylvania Ave. I ran as for my life, and when the people saw me coming with the paper in my hand they raised a shouting cheer that was almost deafening. As many as could get around me lifted me to a great platform, and I started to read the proclamation.

Overcome with emotion and out of breath after running nearly a mile, Turner handed the paper over to someone else to read.

> Mr. Hinton . . . read it with great force and clearness. While he was reading every kind of demonstration and gesticulation was going on. Men squealed, women fainted, dogs barked, white and colored people shook hands, songs were sung, and by this time cannons began to fire at the navy-yard, and follow in the wake of the roar that had for some time been going on behind the White House. Every face had a smile, and even the dumb animals seemed to realize

that some extraordinary event had taken place. Great processions of colored and white men marched to and fro and passed in front of the White House and congratulated President Lincoln on his proclamation. The President came to the window and made responsive bows, and thousands told him, if he would come out of that palace, they would hug him to death. Mr. Lincoln, however, kept a safe distance from the multitude, who were frenzied to distraction over his proclamation.[3]

When Lincoln signed the Emancipation Proclamation declaring slaves in the states still in rebellion "forever free," he transformed the Civil War from "a war only for Union to a war for Union *and* emancipation. It dashed Confederates' hopes that European nations, particularly England and France, would join them as allies. How could these nations, which had already abolished slavery, wage war against the cause of emancipation? Finally, in invoking God's will for emancipation, the Proclamation gave the war a noble, even a holy, purpose."[4] The Emancipation Proclamation made emancipation a Union war aim and signaled a shift in the conflict and in the direction of the United States.

Troubled Refuge

Contraband Camps

Contraband camp near Baton Rouge, Louisiana, circa 1863.

Between 1861 and 1865, hundreds of thousands of enslaved men, women, and children sought refuge inside Union lines. Throughout the South, wherever the Union army established a presence, contrabands—a phrase first used by General Benjamin Butler at Fort Monroe—fled to Union lines. Traveling for days or even weeks, individually or in groups, refugees carried what few possessions they had to start a new life in freedom. Once behind Union lines, refugees found housing in tents, abandoned buildings, or makeshift shelters. In some cases, such as the contraband camp pictured here in Baton Rouge, Louisiana, camps were established on seized Confederate property, in this case a girls' school. Conditions and treatment once inside the camps varied widely. The population varied from a few dozen to thousands.

Beginning with Fort Monroe in 1861, contraband camps were places where Black men, women, and children staked a claim for freedom. The Emancipation Proclamation and the Thirteenth Amendment provided the military and legal foundation for the abolition of slavery. But what did freedom mean? Harriet Jacobs, a formerly enslaved woman turned reformer, asked that question when she encountered former slaves in Washington, DC, in 1862. "Many were sick with measles, diphtheria, scarlet and typhoid fever," she wrote. "Some had a few filthy rages to lie on; others had nothing but the bare floor for a couch." Jacobs wondered, "Is this freedom?"[1]

In her book *Troubled Refuge: Struggling for Freedom in the Civil War*, historian Chandra Manning spends considerable time reflecting on this image of the camp in Baton Rouge:

> Women and children and a handful of men gather in a large yard. One woman holds a baby on her lap, the fingers of her left hand splayed around the child's back in a grip both indestructibly solid and infinitely tender. Another woman gazes down at a toddler at her feet as he plays with a stick, in the way very small children do. A group of older children kneels in a circle, entranced by a game, possibly marbles, more deserving of their attention than the photographer. A cluster of women sits together in a semicircle, ages and expressions limning a wide arc of human life span and experience. One of the older women bores right into the camera with eyes that say they have seen it all, while one of the younger women looks just as directly with eyes that announce a readiness to face whatever sights might present themselves. Other women look away or down, the shoulders of one in particular expressing sorrow that goes beyond mere sight. To their left stand more women, one holding her chin contemplatively in her hand. Around the edges of the photograph stand dozens more people, often

with arms crossed, too far from the camera for nineteenth-century photography to capture much detail about their faces, but of all ages. The group's size and variety and range of activities insist that life persists, in all its richness and tedium and suffering, in its minutiae and in its vastness.

For freed men, women, and children life in the camps, and with it the experience of emancipation, varied widely, shifting with the progress of the war. Place mattered, as Manning writes, "With few notable exceptions, Union grasp on territory in the West was more tenuous and forces changed base, often repeatedly and sometimes rapidly." In the Eastern Theater, at places like Fort Monroe or the Sea Islands, refugees from slavery tended to stay put once they arrived in a contraband camp. In the West, however, refugees often "floated in and out of multiple camps, but never out of danger. Almost nobody, and nothing, not even freedom itself, stayed in one place for long."[2]

In November 1861, when the Union navy and army captured Port Royal Sound, off the coast of South Carolina, Confederate residents fled, leaving behind nearly ten thousand slaves. The enslaved men, women, and children of the Sea Islands became free by simply staying put. With the Union army in place, other slaves who lived nearby came "singly or in small groups but more often in 'parties of 10, 20, 50 and 100.'" For the freed people on the Sea Islands, life continued much as it had before. Food and housing did not run short because former slaves remained in their dwellings, where they continued to grow vegetables and to keep chickens. Former slaves' most pressing need was for clothing because they had not received their annual allotment of clothing before white Confederates left. Northern benevolent societies sent missionaries and workers south to provide help to freedpeople, providing goods such as cloth and books, establishing schools, and tending to the souls of the newly freed. Still, the proximity of Confederate troops meant kidnapping was a persistent threat. On St. Simons Island, Georgia, freedpeople could not "go very far from our own quarters in the daytime" and after dark did not dare "even to go out of the house" because nearby Confederate troops "would capture any persons venturing out alone and carry them" off. Former slaves who ended up in the hands of slave owners often found themselves forcibly moved away from Union lines, preventing further flights to freedom.[3]

In the Western Theater, the contraband camp at Helena, Arkansas, was established in 1862. As Union general Samuel R. Curtis moved his army from Missouri into Arkansas, thousands of slaves came into his lines. General Curtis did not discourage the flight. Instead he issued certificates of freedom, though he was careful to assure his superiors and the slaveholding Unionists

657. A Negro Family coming into the Union Lines.
[FOR DESCRIPTION OF THIS VIEW SEE THE OTHER SIDE OF THIS CARD.]

"A Negro Family Coming into Union Lines."
SOURCE: LIBRARY OF CONGRESS PRINTS AND PHOTOGRAPHS DIVISION.

in Missouri that escaped slaves got to his lines on their own and without any enticement from him. In Helena, the assistant quartermaster noted that within days of the army's arrival, "a perfect cloud of negroes [were] thrown upon him for subsistence and support." Former slaves found shelter in churches, houses, a barn, and tents. Makeshift structures were clustered together in a part of town named Camp Ethiopia.[4]

Freedom in the camp was fragile. Helena was prone to flooding. The flood waters created conditions that when combined with poor rations, weakened immune systems, and overcrowding caused high mortality rates among the camp's residents. Like other contraband camps, kidnapping and physical violence were persistent threats. In July 1863, after the Battle of Helena, defeated Confederates burned the cabins of Camp Ethiopia and beat and killed many of the inhabitants. That same summer—which was an "an especially horrible time for black people in the western theater," according to historian Thavolia Glymph—nine refugees who had made their way to the camp at Helena found their freedom threatened when the provost marshal at Helena allowed the daughter of the woman who claimed ownership of the men to enter the camp to reclaim them. The superintendent of contrabands protested their reenslavement. The refugees had been "freed by the President's Proclamation," he asserted. "The General Commanding," the provost marshal responded, "would prefer that they should go, for their own good and that of the Government." And because the Emancipation Proclamation had freed them, he wrote, "it would hardly be returning them to slavery."[5]

Northern benevolent organizations such as the American Missionary Association, the Western Sanitary Commission, the North Western Freedmen's Aid Commission, and various groups of Quakers organized to provide food, medicine, doctors, nurses, and teachers. In Washington, DC, a group of Black women organized the Contraband Relief Association in 1862. Initially, the group's efforts focused on aiding freed Blacks in the camps. After the Union army began to accept freedmen for military service, the group expanded its work to include support for Black soldiers. In 1864, the women changed the name of the organization to the Freedmen and Soldiers' Relief Association.

The Emancipation Proclamation accelerated the movement of enslaved people into Union lines and contraband camps. However, for the enslaved in the border states the Emancipation Proclamation had no effect. These states were not in rebellion and, as a result, slaves who were owned by masters who were loyal to the Union were not freed. In Kentucky, slaves who made their way to Camp Nelson were expected to leave the camp and return to enslavement unless they enlisted in the Union army. Of course, this path to freedom was not feasible for the women and children who made their way to camp. Official orders were issued to remove the women and children from the camp. In November 1864, Union soldiers forcibly escorted women and children from the camp and then destroyed their cabins. Freezing temperatures and harsh conditions resulted in more than one hundred deaths.

The public outcry over the expulsion at Camp Nelson caused the Union army to reverse its policy toward refugees. The army began construction on a "Home for Colored Refugees" at Camp Nelson. Those who had been turned away were allowed to resettle at the camp. Still, the women and children were not legally free. Finally, in March 1865, Congress passed an act emancipating the wives, mothers, and children of USCT, thus providing legal protection for the refugees at Camp Nelson and giving additional motivation for Black men to enlist in the military.

Historians of U.S. slavery and emancipation encourage us to see emancipation as "a process rather than a shotgun moment of liberation." For the formerly enslaved men, women, and children who arrived in Union lines, contraband camps were simultaneously places of refuge, "incubators of revolutionary revival," labor camps, slums, battlefields, and sites of "unspeakable violence." Refugee camps were places where Black freedom was claimed and contested many times under "warlike conditions."[6]

A New Birth of Freedom

The Thirteenth Amendment

"Abolishing Slavery." Joint Resolution of the Thirty-Eighth Congress of the United States of America, proposing an amendment to the Constitution of the United States, abolishing slavery.

SOURCE: LIBRARY OF CONGRESS PRINTS AND PHOTOGRAPHS DIVISION.

In 1868, as African American men in the South voted for the first time in national elections, artist and engraver Walter Shirlaw commemorated the passage of the Thirteenth Amendment by creating this decorative print. In a style that mirrored the Declaration of Independence, Shirlaw included the text of the amendment and carefully reproduced the signatures of those in Congress who backed the amendment, including them at the bottom of his print. "For Shirlaw, the Thirteenth Amendment was a new birth of freedom— a newfound declaration of independence—that promised a better America."[1]

The Emancipation Proclamation was a wartime measure and had freed only those slaves in states that were still in rebellion against the United States. Many feared, and rightfully so, the Emancipation Proclamation would be judged unconstitutional when the war ended. To abolish slavery permanently would require a constitutional amendment. Illinois congressman and abolitionist Owen Lovejoy, a radical abolitionist and brother of martyred abolitionist Elijah Lovejoy, drafted the original language of the amendment. On December 14, 1863, Republican James Ashley of Ohio introduced the amendment to the House of Representatives. In the Senate, John Henderson of Missouri introduced similar legislation. The two measures were combined to form a joint resolution. In April 1864, the amendment passed the Senate by a vote of thirty-eight to six, but fell short in the House, where Democrats opposed the amendment, claiming it would alienate Confederates and prolong the war.

It was an election year. Lincoln was up for reelection. His opponent was Democrat General George McClellan. Lincoln knew the outcome of the election relied in part on the successful prosecution of the war. Sherman's capture of Atlanta and Sheridan's success in the Shenandoah Valley helped propel Lincoln to victory in November 1864. With reelection secured, Lincoln began an aggressive campaign to win passage of an amendment from Congress.

On January 13, 1865, the House passed the Thirteenth Amendment by a vote of 119 to 56—two votes above the required two-thirds margin. Spectators in the gallery applauded the vote while the representatives on the floor celebrated. "Some embraced one another," Congressman George W. Julian recalled, "others wept like children."[2]

Although the amendment had received the necessary votes in the House of Representatives, it still required endorsement by three-quarters of the state legislatures for ratification. Northern states quickly approved the amendment, leaving the fate of the amendment to the Southern states, who were in constitutional limbo after the collapse of the Confederacy in April 1865. President

---

Thirteenth Amendment

ABOLITION OF SLAVERY

Passed by Congress January 31, 1865. Ratified December 6, 1865. The Thirteenth Amendment changed a portion of Article IV, Section 2.

Section 1

Neither slavery nor involuntary servitude, except as a punishment for crime whereof the party shall have been duly convicted, shall exist within the United States, or any place subject to their jurisdiction.

Section 2

Congress shall have power to enforce this article by appropriate legislation.[1]

Andrew Johnson, who assumed office after Lincoln was assassinated on April 15, told Southern legislatures that ratification was a prerequisite for restoration to the Union. Southern politicians were reluctant to approve the amendment, particularly its second section, which appeared to legitimate federal intervention to secure civil rights. Mississippi refused to ratify the amendment altogether. Most of the Southern states complied with the president's instruction. On December 18, 1865, Secretary of State William H. Seward, who had helped secure the passage of the amendment in the House, announced to the world that the Thirteenth Amendment was now part of the Constitution.

The ratification of the Thirteenth Amendment ended slavery in the United States. The amendment transformed the Constitution from a document concerned primarily with federal-state rights into a means by which Blacks and other minorities would realize a substantial level of freedom and protection.

To further Black civil rights, Congress passed additional legislation during Reconstruction. The Civil Rights Act of 1866 gave Black citizens "the same right in every state": to make and enforce contracts; to sue and be sued; to provide evidence in court; and to inherit, purchase, lease, sell, and hold personal property. Two years later, the Fourteenth Amendment was adopted, granting citizenship to "all persons born or naturalized in the United States," including former slaves. Thaddeus Stevens, an abolitionist and a member of the House of Representatives from Pennsylvania, played an important role in drafting

FROM WASHINGTON.

ABOLITION OF SLAVERY.

Passage of the Constitutional Amendment.

One Hundred and Nineteen Yeas against Fifty-six Nays.

Exciting Scene in the House.

ENTHUSIASM OVER THE RESULT·

February 1, 1865.

SOURCE: *NEW YORK TIMES.*

both the Fourteenth Amendment and the Reconstruction Act of 1867. Stevens also introduced a slavery reparations bill in 1867, but Congress failed to approve it. In 1870, the Fifteenth Amendment granting Black men the right to vote was adopted. That same year Congress enacted the Civil Rights Act of 1870 to enforce the terms of the Fifteenth Amendment. Five years later Congress passed the last of the major Reconstruction statutes, the Civil Rights Act of 1875, which guaranteed African Americans equal treatment in public transportation and accommodations and service on juries.

Although these measures were important steps forward in securing the civil rights of Black Americans, the Fourteenth and Fifteenth Amendments had loopholes that created opportunities to use poll taxes, literacy tests, grandfather clauses, and legislative redistricting to disenfranchise Blacks in the South. Moreover, in 1883, the Supreme Court declared the Civil Rights Act of 1875 unconstitutional, thus paving the way for Jim Crow laws that would codify racial segregation in all aspects of African American life until the passage of the Civil Rights Act of 1964.[3]

Help Me Find My People

Reconstructing Black Families

Marriage certificate of Peter Thompson and Maria Hall, January 28, 1867.

SOURCE: RECORDS OF THE BUREAU OF REFUGEES, FREEDMEN, AND ABANDONED LANDS (RG 105), CERTIFICATES OF MARRIAGE, 1861–1869 (ENTRY 44), U.S. NATIONAL ARCHIVES AND RECORDS ADMINISTRATION.

For Peter Thompson and Maria Hall, both former slaves, in West Feliciana Parish, Louisiana, this marriage certificate dated January 28, 1867, was more than a legal document recognizing their marriage. It was a symbol of freedom; it was a public announcement of their right to claim control of their marital relationship. "To be free meant having a legitimate social identity that permitted legal marriages and, through those marriages, parental and patriarchal rights meant to support, protect, and provide a haven for freed families," historian Brenda E. Stevenson writes. "Freedom, as such, signified taking on the mantle of respectable and respected man- and womanhood and its gendered connotations, symbolized in part, by the ritualization of marriage."[1]

As emancipation spread across the South during the Civil War, hundreds of thousands of formerly enslaved people claimed control of marital and family relationships. To reconstruct families torn apart in slavery, freedpeople participated in marriage rituals, traveled into dangerous areas to reunite with family members, and, in some cases, filed suit all to rebuild the Black family, which had had no legal standing under slavery.

Enslaved men and women had little control over the marital relationship. As former slave Dora Franks recalled, "Us never had no big fun'als or weddin's on de place. Didn' have no marryin' o' any kin'. Folks in dem days jus' sorter hitched up together an' cal deyse'ves man an' wife." Masters dictated the conditions of marriage: the marriage partner, the marriage ritual, and the end of the marriage. Charles Grandy, an enslaved man from Virginia, resented the lack of choice in a marriage partner. If a man desired a wife, Grandy later recalled, the owner would buy one from a passing trader, so long as the "wife" was cheap and appeared to be fertile. Similarly, marriage rituals, if they were even allowed, were controlled by the master and ranged from the banal to the sadistic. In some cases, the master might speak a few words from the Bible. At its most extreme, the marriage ritual might become, as Stevenson notes, "a site of sadistic control and private, as well as public dehumanization." Stevenson cites the example of slave owner "Big Jim" McClain, who forced his slaves to have "orgies" in his presence, the sexual act serving as the only marital ritual. Slave marriages were impermanent, their duration subject to the whim of the master. Enslaved men and women knew that masters could separate them at any time, as Bethany Veney, an enslaved woman from Virginia, recognized when she married a man named Jerry. Although Bethany was married by a minister, Bethany "did not want him to make us promise that we would always be true to each other, forsaking all others, as the white people do in their marriage service, because I knew that at any time our masters could compel us to break such a promise."[2]

As enslaved men and women gained their freedom, some couples sought help from clergy, provost marshal, missionaries, and the Freedmen's Bureau. In the contraband camp at Hampton, Virginia, Edward and Emma Whitehurst were remarried by Lewis Lockwood, a white Presbyterian minister sent by the American Missionary Association. In the fall of 1861, Lockwood married a total of thirty-two couples in the Fort Monroe and Hampton area. The marriages performed by Lockwood were sanctioned by military authorities, "who were willing to assert federal power to supersede the Southern state laws that had long denied enslaved people the legal right to marry," notes historian Amy Murrell Taylor. "And [Lockwood] set a precedent that missionaries and military authorities would follow all across the South, as weddings became commonplace inside Union lines throughout the four years of war." The Whitehursts were among the very first ex-slave couples to be legally married by federal authorities during the war. When the Freedmen's Bureau was established by an act of Congress on March 3, 1865, the bureau continued the practice of solemnizing former slave marriages.[3]

Not all couples sought marriage or remarriage. Nor were all reunions of separated husbands and wives joyful ones. Eliza Bogan met her husband Dennis in the contraband camp in Helena, Arkansas. Dennis was Eliza's fourth husband. In 1869, under pressure from Samuel Brooks, their employer, Eliza and Dennis were legally married by Brooks who, as justice of the peace, officiated at the ceremony. The Bogan marriage was an unhappy one. Eliza described Dennis as a "bad fellow" who had a habit of "running out after women." Their legal marriage did not change that. "There was not any difference in our Relations before and after we had the ceremony," Eliza recalled. To the east, in South Carolina, freedpeople Sarah and her husband Jim worked for the teachers. In slavery, Sarah had had six children and five husbands, "or men with whom she was obliged to live, as she was sold from one master to another." During the war, as Jim and Sarah prepared to abandon the plantation, her former husband Campbell showed up to reclaim Sarah. A fight between Jim and Campbell ended with Jim winning Sarah and her children. "It may be that the conflict truly was resolved through physical confrontation between the two men," historian Heather Andrea Williams writes, "it may also be that Sarah chose to remain with Jim."[4]

Contraband camps could be places of reunion as well as dislocation. Formerly enslaved men, women, and children arrived in the camps looking for kin. "This is the rendezvous. They come here from all about, from Richmond and 200 miles off in North Carolina," a Virginia superintendent wrote. One refugee woman longed for reunion on her island camp: "I always look out when the boat comes, thinking its my children." A missionary wrote, "We sometimes witness the unexpected meeting of scattered members of a family. When the [boat] was at the Craney Island wharf, a little girl who had wondered where she should go . . . strolled upon the deck of the steamer and found in one of the hands her father!"[5]

When seventeen-year-old Mary received her "free papers" in 1863, she set out with a basket of food, a basket of clothes, and a little money in search of her mother, who was rumored to be in Texas. Armstrong knew she was headed into a war zone—slavery was still very firmly entrenched in Texas—but her reasons for doing so were powerful. "Away I goin' to find my mamma," Mary later recalled. Keeping her freedom papers hidden in her dress, Armstrong avoided being sold back into slavery. "Freedom's function was a claim to [Mary's] kin—a material corporeal being together, of knowing her mother existed, knowing her location," notes historian Abigail Cooper. "Mary was a seventeen-year-old black girl with free papers hidden in her bosom traveling alone into spaces where she was considered walking currency, but the risk was of only secondary importance to finding her mother." Mary located her mother in Wharton County, Texas: "Lawd me, talk 'bout cryin' an' singing' an' cryin' some more, we sure done it." Having found her mother, Mary remained with her "'til I gets married in 1871 to John Armstrong an' then we all comes to Houston."[6]

The search for lost family continued long after the collapse of the Confederacy in 1865. In one noteworthy case, a formerly enslaved mother went to court to seek the return of her children, who had been kidnapped and taken to Cuba in early 1863. In mid-December 1862, Rose Herera, an enslaved woman in New Orleans, got into an altercation with Carmelite Roland, the aunt of Herera's owner Mary De Hart. Herera was arrested on the charge of assault and jailed. De Hart visited the jail to pressure Herera to go Cuba. In May 1862, Mary De Hart's husband had fled to New Orleans ahead of the Union occupation of that city. Mary De Hart planned to join her husband in Havana, New Orleans' sister city, where hundreds of Confederates had taken refuge. De Hart wanted to take Herera and her children to Cuba. Herera, however, refused to leave her family, including her mother and her husband. De Hart resorted to threats; she would take Herera's three children in her possession to Cuba with or without Rose. In January 1863, Mary De Hart made good on her threat.

In January 1865, Mary De Hart returned to New Orleans alone to visit friends and family. During the two years she had been gone, much had changed. In September 1864, after two years of Union occupation of New Orleans, a new state constitution was ratified, formally abolishing slavery. That same year, Rose's husband had died of disease and Rose had given birth to another child. Rose learned that De Hart had returned to the city. She begged De Hart to return her children, but De Hart refused. Herera pursued legal action. In May 1865, General Nathaniel Banks adjudicated the case and found for Herera. The following spring, after some arm twisting by the U.S. consul general in Havana, Mary De Hart finally returned the Herera children to New Orleans to be reunited with their mother.[7]

Freedpeople continued to search for lost families into the twentieth century. African Americans placed "Information Wanted" notices in newspapers like the *Christian Recorder*, the *Black Republican*, and the *Free Men's Press*. "The quest to unite with long-lost loved ones was *central* to the meaning of freed," notes historian Adam Rothman. "Wives searched for their husbands, and husbands for their wives. Parents searched for their children, and children for their parents." In addition to newspaper notices, African Americans "wrote letters to government officials and church leaders, and retraced their paths through the landscape of severance and sale." Fifty years after the end of slavery, African Americans continued to search for family members, which suggests that deep family ties endured the worst abuses of slavery.[8]

Part X

LEGACY

History does not refer merely, or even principally, to the past. On the contrary, the great force of history comes from the fact that we carry it within us, unconsciously controlled by it in many ways, and history is literally present in all that we do.

—James Baldwin

More than 150 years after the end of the Civil War, Americans continue to wrestle with the war's legacy. Passage of the Thirteenth, Fourteenth, and Fifteenth Amendments abolished slavery and granted citizenship to former slaves and the right to vote to African American men. However, by the 1870s, with the end of Reconstruction, Southern state governments effectively nullified the Fourteenth and Fifteenth Amendments as segregation and disenfranchisement, known as Jim Crow, took hold across the South. For the next century, Black Americans were targeted in a widespread campaign of intimidation, economic oppression, physical violence, and murder. Only with the rise of the Civil Rights Movement in the mid-twentieth century did Americans begin to confront the racial legacy of the Civil War. Race remains at the center of debates about the display of Confederate iconography and the memorialization of the Confederate past. As the objects in this part make clear, confronting the legacy of the Civil War is an ongoing process, one that will not end unless there is, in the words of author Ta-Nehisi Coates, "a revolution of the American consciousness, a reconciling of our self-image as the great democratizer with the facts of our history."[1]

"I Won't Be Reconstructed"

Southerners and Confederate Defeat

Colonel Joseph O. Shelby, taken at Boonville, in 1864, after he took Boonville.

SOURCE: [OFFICIAL PROCEEDINGS OF 1ST ANNUAL REUNION OF MISSOURI DIVISION, UNITED CONFEDERATE VETERANS. [SHS 005099-1]]. THE STATE HISTORICAL SOCIETY OF MISSOURI, PHOTOGRAPH COLLECTION.

One of the more colorful stories surrounding the collapse of the Confederacy involves this man, General Joseph O. Shelby, a Confederate cavalry officer who served in the Trans-Mississippi Theater. At the time of Lee's surrender, Shelby and his men were in the southwest Arkansas–northeast Texas region. The prevailing sentiment among Shelby and his men was to prolong the fight. Confederate president Jefferson Davis had fled Richmond and was rumored to be making his way west to link up with the fifty thousand Confederate troops still in the field under the command of General Edmund Kirby Smith, who was headquartered in Shreveport, Louisiana.[1] Shelby called his troops to order and asked for volunteers to go to Mexico, where they would establish a Confederate presence. Shelby and several hundred men, with their cannons, arms, and ammunition, traveled across Texas, reaching San Antonio on June 15, 1865. San Antonio was packed with Confederates who were fleeing from federal forces, including the governors of Louisiana, Missouri, and Texas as well as several Confederate officers. Many of these Confederates were also considering exile in Mexico or elsewhere in Latin America.

Rearmed and reprovisioned, Shelby and his men left for Eagle Pass on the Rio Grande. The exact date Shelby crossed the Rio Grande is unknown. What is well known is the story of how Shelby and his men sank their flag—"The last flag to fly over an organized Confederate force"—in the Rio Grande. In Piedras Negras, Shelby and his men encountered the rebel forces of Benito Juárez. After selling all their arms, except their revolvers and carbines, to the rebels, the Confederates continued south toward Mexico City. Arriving in Mexico City, Shelby and his men offered their services to French-imposed emperor Maximilian, who declined their offer and received them only as immigrant settlers.

For many Confederate holdouts, the Trans-Mississippi Department—which encompassed Missouri, Arkansas, western Louisiana, Texas, and the Indian Territory (Oklahoma)—held the last "flickering flame" of hope for the Confederacy. On April 21, Smith issued a proclamation, exhorting his men to "stand by your colors—maintain your discipline. The great resources of this department, . . . and the Providence of God [will] be the means of checking the triumph of our enemy and of seeing the final success of our cause." Shelby urged his men to remain strong: "We will do this: we will hang together, we will keep our organization, our arms, our discipline, our hatred of oppression . . . [preferring] exile to submission, death to dishonor."[2]

In Shreveport, Smith considered his future. On May 2, he wrote to Louisiana businessman Robert Rose, who had frequent business dealings in Mexico, asking him to establish unofficial communications with Maximilian. "There is under my command an army of 60,000 men, [and] of those there are 9,000 Missourians who have been driven from their homes . . . who . . . would no doubt, upon favorable inducements . . . take service with the power so favoring them," Smith wrote. Six days later, Smith met with his federal counterpart, who brought Grant's Appomattox terms. Smith rejected them but asked the man to delay his return until Smith could attend a meeting with the Trans-Mississippi governors in nearby Marshall, Texas.

At that meeting, held in the home of former Senator Louis T. Wigfall, Smith, Shelby, and the governors discussed a strategic retreat to Mexico. Smith was asked to take command of the expedition, but Smith insisted on waiting for orders from Davis. Smith compiled a list of conditions for surrender, which he presented to the federal emissary when Smith returned to Shreveport. The emissary handed over the terms to his superior. In the meantime, Smith announced his plan to move his headquarters from Shreveport to Houston, where he believed there were enough loyal soldiers to form a core of resistance. However, when Smith arrived in Houston, he learned most of the Confederates had surrendered. "Soldiers, I am left a commander without an army—a General without troops," Smith said in his farewell address. "You have made your choice. It was unwise and unpatriotic, but it is final." On June 2, he signed the surrender documents.[3]

In Louisiana, Lieutenant Charles W. Read hoped to sail his ship, the CSS *William H. Webb*, to Mexico. He left the dock at Alexandria and headed down the Red River to the Mississippi. At the mouth of the Red River, the *Webb* came under fire from a Union squadron. Sailing past the New Orleans defenses, with a pair of Union steamers in hot pursuit, Read continued toward the final gauntlet at Forts Jackson and St. Philip. Sixty miles from the forts, Read and the *Webb* encountered the USS *Richmond*. Read ran his ship ashore, where the crew set fire to the craft before escaping into the underbrush. Federal patrols soon captured the Confederate sailors, bringing an end to their escape attempt.

After the war, many Confederates, including Shelby, joined in the establishment of the Carlotta colony in Córdoba, Mexico. Matthew Maury, who had served as an agent of the Confederate navy in England, had been on his return journey to Richmond when he learned of Lee's surrender. Rather than continue to Virginia, Maury decided instead to go to Mexico, where he quickly organized a colonization project to attract Southerners to Mexico. Appointing agents throughout the South as well as New York, Baltimore, Boston, and other Northern cities, Maury set to work promoting the new colony. The colony did not last long. By 1867, most of the colonists, including Shelby, had returned to the United States.

Tens of thousands of Confederate exiles also established colonies in Brazil, Honduras, and Venezuela. Brazil had been a strong Confederate ally during the war, harboring and supplying Confederate ships. Significantly, in 1865, slavery was still legal in Brazil (unlike Mexico). Brazilian emperor Dom Pedro II wanted to expand and upgrade cotton cultivation in his country and offered attractive terms to Confederates willing to relocate. The most successful of the American settlements in Brazil was founded by former Alabama senator William Norris in 1865 near the village of Santa Barbara D'Oeste in the state of Sao Paulo. Although many Americans eventually returned to the United States, many Confederados remained. Their descendants have maintained close ties to their Southern heritage despite generations of assimilation into Brazilian culture. As former president Jimmy Carter observed during a visit to the area in 1972, "The most remarkable thing was, when they spoke they sounded just like people in South Georgia."[4]

A popular, angry postwar Confederate anthem, "Good Old Rebel," captured the defiance of Shelby, Maury, and other Confederates:

> Oh, I'm a good old Rebel soldier, now that's just what I am;
> For this "Fair Land of Freedom" I do not give a damn!
> I'm glad I fought against it, I only wish we'd won.

Another variation of the song, titled "The Unreconstructed Rebel," celebrated Shelby's desire to flee to Mexico:

> I won't be reconstructed, I'm better now than then.
>   And for a Carpetbagger I do not give a damn.
> So it's forward to the frontier, soon as I can go.
>   I'll fix me up a weapon and start for Mexico.

This anthem to Southern defiance remained popular into the twentieth century. Indeed, variations of "Good Old Rebel" may be found on YouTube, where its account of the Confederacy and the Confederate soldier reinforces a particular popular memory of the Civil War, the Confederate cause, and Southern identity.[5]

Memorializing the Dead

Race, Heritage, and the Lost Cause

In the spring of 1865, Black Charlestonians cleaned up and built a fence to protect the Union burial ground at the Washington Race Course.

SOURCE: LIBRARY OF CONGRESS PRINTS AND PHOTOGRAPHS DIVISION.

In April 1865, nearly thirty Black men from Charleston, South Carolina, cleaned up the grounds and raised the graves of the more than 250 Union soldiers who had died in the prisoner of war camp at the Washington Race Course and Jockey Club. The men constructed a fence and an archway over the gate inscribed with the words "Martyrs of the Race Course." On May 1, several thousand people, many of them African Americans, turned out to dedicate the cemetery, the first Decoration Day ceremony. Three thousand Black schoolchildren marched around the race course, singing "John Brown's Body." Three hundred Black women, who represented the Patriotic Association, a group organized to distribute clothing and other goods to freedpeople, carried baskets of flowers, wreaths, and crosses to the cemetery. The men of the Mutual Aid Society, a benevolent association of African American men, marched around the track and into the cemetery. The men, women, and children dropped flowers on the graves, so many flowers that "not a speck of earth could be seen." The parade then made its way out of the cemetery, leaving a small group of former slaves to dedicate the cemetery. The dedication included prayers, Bible readings, and spirituals. After the ceremony, the small group joined the crowds at the judges' stand, where they listened to speeches by Union officers, Black ministers, and abolitionist missionaries.[1]

The first national Memorial Day was celebrated on May 30, 1868, at Arlington National Cemetery, where both Union and Confederate soldiers were buried. Other cities and towns claimed to have observed earlier versions of Memorial Day, or Decoration Day as it was originally called. For example, this photograph from the American Civil War Museum shows a group of women standing beside what appears to be an arch. According to the donor's statement, this is a photograph of the First Memorial Day, held in Petersburg, Virginia, on June 9, 1865, when Nora Fontaine Maury Davidson and her schoolchildren visited Blandford Cemetery in Petersburg, where they decorated the graves of the soldiers who had died a year earlier defending Petersburg.[2]

Although Memorial Day ceremonies in the North and the South were similar, there were differences in the ways in which each region memorialized the dead. In the North, Union men took the lead in organizing Memorial Days. The commemoration at Arlington National Cemetery originated from a request by General John A. Logan, commander of the Grand Army of the Republic (GAR). Logan called on all Union veterans to hold ceremonies and decorate the graves of the Union dead. In 1868 and 1869, Logan called for a national commemoration. In "almost every city, village, and hamlet

The inscription on this photograph reads, "Petersburg, Virginia claims the first observance of this sacred day."

SOURCE: AMERICAN CIVIL WAR MUSEUM, UNDER THE MANAGEMENT OF VIRGINIA MUSEUM OF HISTORY AND CULTURE (098.13.02225).

church-yard in the land," charged Logan's circular, those who died to "suppress the late rebellion" were to be honored annually "while a survivor of the war remains." In 1868, in the North, in addition to the commemoration at Arlington National Cemetery, ceremonies were held in 183 cemeteries in twenty-seven states. By the following year, 336 cities and towns in thirty-one states (including the South) held Decoration Day ceremonies. In 1873, the New York legislature designated May 30 a legal holiday for the purposes of celebrating Decoration Day. By 1890, every other Northern state had adopted the holiday.[3]

The GAR routinely called on loyal women and children to help decorate soldiers' graves. In 1868, in Chambersburg, Pennsylvania, the local women held a festival to raise money for a monument to the Franklin County soldiers "who fell fighting against treason." In 1874, the Canby Post of the GAR invited fifty-two young ladies, all dressed in white, to decorate the cemetery. Northern women organized the Women's Relief Corps (WRC) in 1879. The WRC evolved out of women's memorial work in the 1860s and 1870s and their wartime relief efforts. In 1883, GAR commander Paul Van Der Voort invited the various ladies' organizations to form a national organization that might unite to assist the GAR in its work. The women's association would serve as an auxiliary—a separate and subordinate association—to the GAR. Within months more than twenty women's associations from sixteen states had organized under the WRC banner. The WRC insisted—with the approval of Van Der Voort—on offering membership "to any loyal woman regardless of her kinship to a Union veteran." Numerous women objected, believing membership in such organizations should be limited to the women who could claim kinship to a Union veteran. These women organized their own societies, such as the Ladies' Aid Society (LAS), which served as an auxiliary to the Sons of Union Veterans (SUV). Founded in 1865, the LAS limited its membership to the mothers, wives, sisters, daughters, and granddaughters of Union veterans or members of the SUV. Similar organizations sprang up, including the Ladies of the GAR in Chicago in 1886, which admitted only women of "good moral character" who were the wives or blood kin of an honorably discharged Union veteran.[4]

In the South, women led efforts to honor and eulogize the Confederate war dead. Southern memorialization efforts varied from state to state, often celebrating Memorial Day on different days. The two most common dates were April 26 and May 10, the day of General Joseph E. Johnston's surrender (1865) and the anniversary of Stonewall Jackson's death (1863). In Louisiana, June 3 was selected as Memorial Day in honor of Jefferson Davis's birthday. Other memorial efforts in the South also relied on local organizations and were influenced by local conditions. In May 1865, just one month after Lee's surrender, women in Winchester, Virginia, organized the state's first Ladies' Memorial Association. Mary Dunbar Williams and her sister-in-law Eleanor Williams Boyd had heard the story of a farmer who had plowed up the bodies of two Confederate soldiers while preparing his land for planting. Disturbed by the lack of proper burials for Confederate soldiers, the two women called together local women who had volunteered in the hospitals during the war. The Ladies' Memorial Association had two immediate objectives: to gather the Confederate war dead within a fifteen-mile radius and inter them in one cemetery and to establish an annual tradition of decorating soldiers' graves.

In 1866, Congress approved the financial support necessary for gathering the remains of Union soldiers buried in "the States lately in rebellion." Crews traveled throughout the South scouting for grave sites and organizing cemeteries for Union soldiers. By 1870, three hundred thousand Union soldiers had been reinterred in seventy-three national cemeteries, seventeen of which were located in Virginia.

The presence of the U.S. Burial Corps in the South angered Southerners. Newspapers claimed Union burial crews were violating the graves of Confederate soldiers, "digging up skeletons of [Confederate] soldiers" and "selling them to be ground for manure." Other reports claimed burial crews "cut the bodies in four pieces, burying the same in four pieces, and thus receive $32 instead of $8 [per body]." The well-tended, neatly arranged cemeteries for Union dead stood in sharp contrast to the shallow graves of the Confederate dead. The graves of Confederate soldiers were often uprooted by farmers and scavenging animals. The care rendered only to the Union dead "proved to [ex-Confederates] that northern officials intended to subjugate the Confederate South rather than place the region on an equal footing with the North." Not surprisingly, the reinternment of Union war dead accelerated the organization of additional LMAs in the South. In Petersburg, Virginia, the city's women met to discuss the state of Confederate graves just two weeks after a Union detail began work on a permanent national cemetery in the vicinity.[5]

In the months and years after the Civil War, Northerners and Southerners faced the formidable task of memorializing the more than six hundred thousand war dead. Initially, these memorial ceremonies were occasions of sacred bereavement. However, with the end of Reconstruction, these events became the tool of partisan memory. In the South, memorializing became opportunities to celebrate the Confederate cause and reassert white supremacy. The rituals that developed around the memorialization reinforced the Lost Cause ideology. As historian Caroline Janney points out, the "enduring memories and celebrations of the Confederacy that remain with us today"—such as the display of the Confederate flag, the construction of Confederate monuments, the activities of Confederate heritage organizations such as the Sons and Daughters of the Confederacy, and the arguments "over whether or not slavery was a catalyst for the war"—came from Northern and Southern efforts to memorialize the dead.[6]

Reconciliation and Reunion

Blue and Gray Reunions in the Post–Civil War Era

A Union soldier and a Confederate soldier shake hands at the seventy-fifth anniversary reunion of the Battle of Gettysburg.

SOURCE: MUSSELMAN LIBRARY, GETTYSBURG COLLEGE, GETTYSBURG, PENNSYLVANIA.

In 1938, nearly two thousand Union and Confederate veterans gathered in Gettysburg, Pennsylvania, for the seventy-fifth anniversary of the Battle of Gettysburg. Twenty-six trains transported the veterans to a temporary settlement that included 3,800 tents, 20 miles of electrical wiring, 27 cases of whiskey, and a fleet of wheelchairs. National Guardsmen and Boy Scouts served as traveling companions for the veterans, whose average age was ninety-four. Across the country, from Montana to Wisconsin to Kansas, Indiana, Tennessee, Oklahoma, and beyond, newspapers carried stories of local veterans who traveled to Gettysburg for the reunion. It would be the last Blue and Gray reunion at Gettysburg.[1]

After the Civil War ended, veterans sought out opportunities to gather together, to relive their shared experience of the war, to celebrate their heroic deeds, and to commemorate the sacrifices of their fallen comrades. From the 1860s through the 1870s, these reunions were organized by regiment, corps, or other fraternal associations such as the Grand Army of the Republic (GAR). Only in the 1880s and 1890s, as the nation excised African Americans from its collective memory of the war, did veterans begin to gather in Blue and Gray reunions, which became sites of national reconciliation. "Neither space nor time was allowed at Gettysburg for considering the causes, transformations, and results of the war; no place was reserved for the legacies of emancipation or the conflict and unresolved history of Reconstruction," writes historian David W. Blight of the 1913 Gettysburg reunion. "Because the planners had allowed no space for surviving black veterans, they had also left no space on the programs for a discussion of that second great outcome of the war—the failures of racial reconciliation."[2]

Still, sectional acrimony did come up at these reunions. At the twenty-fifth reunion, in 1887, as Confederate veterans of General George E. Pickett's division prepared to meet with their former adversaries in General Alexander S. Webb's Philadelphia brigade at Gettysburg, the first Blue and Gray meeting reunion on the hallowed battlefield, U.S. Army Adjutant General R. C. Drum suggested returning the more than 550 flags captured from Confederates during the war. The membership of the Grand Army of the Republic, the Union veterans' organization, was indignant. At a meeting of the GAR in New York, Lucius Fairchild said he felt confident that 350,000 GAR men would "rise as one man in solemn protest against any such disposition of the trophies won at such fearful sacrifice of blood." Those present at the meeting "heartily endorsed his blistering attack." Additionally, tensions among the veterans who planned to attend the reunion nearly derailed the gathering before it began.

Confederate veterans questioned the loyalty of their brethren who planned to attend, while Northerners raised a ruckus over rebel plans to place a memorial at the so-called High Water Mark of the Confederacy. By July, however, the veterans had made concessions and nearly five hundred Philadelphia Brigade veterans and their families welcomed some two hundred Confederate veterans to Gettysburg.[3]

In 1913, more than fifty thousand Union and Confederate veterans gathered for the fiftieth anniversary of the Battle of Gettysburg. On July 3, almost exactly fifty years to the moment of Pickett's Charge, five hundred Confederate survivors marched across the field toward their former foes, where Southerners and Northerners clasped hands across the wall. Virginia governor William H. Mann captured the reconciliationist spirit of the reunion, declaring, "There is no North and no South, no rebels and no Yanks. All is one great nation." Speaker of the House Champ Clark, who was a teenager in 1863, asserted, "It was not Southern valor, or Northern valor. It was thank God, American valor." Newspapers across the country declared the "death of sectionalism." However, even among those veterans who attended the reunion in 1913, there were many who did not embrace reconciliation. In one incident, "a raucous fight" broke out between the son of a Confederate major and a Union veteran over the younger man's disparaging comments about Lincoln. Eight men suffered stab wounds from the resulting melee. By 1913, Blue and Gray reunions and the pageantry of reconciliation, built on shared military experience, had reached a high point. Still, so long as the war generation survived, as historian Caroline Janney notes, "so would vestiges of sectional rancor and animosity."[4]

By 1938, as the veterans from both sides gathered for what would be the final reunion of the Blue and Gray, the influence of the war generation on the commemoration of the war had waned significantly. The plan for the seventy-fifth reunion came from local and state commissioners under the leadership of Gettysburg Chamber of Commerce Secretary Paul Roy, who hoped to use the event to "sell" Gettysburg to the nation. Unlike the 1913 reunion, the 1938 gathering brought in a much larger number of tourists. "Automobile travel, improved highways, and increased focus on catering to families ensured both access to Gettysburg and an enjoyable experience upon arrival," one historian notes. The veterans who were present for the reunion "were largely for the benefit of the tourists searching for an authenticated experience of the past." The 1938 reunion marked the end of veterans' direct influence on the commemoration of the battle and the war and a "shift from veterans' commemoration to modern commemoration for the nation."[5]

The reunion at Gettysburg did much to encourage harmony between the North and the South, but sectional reconciliation came at the expense of Black memory of the Civil War. At the fiftieth anniversary, Black veterans were not invited to participate although many Blacks labored to build the camp, cook for the veterans, and perform other menial services. At the seventy-fifth anniversary, little had changed. The small number of Black veterans were not officially acknowledged, nor were they present at any of the major events. Not surprisingly, the nearly two hundred thousand Black men who served in the Union army and navy were not mentioned at either event. Also missing from both gatherings was any mention of slavery or segregation. Instead the reunions remained very much events for white Americans with "the battle-field essentially . . . a giant stage set for an epic fictional performance with a cast of thousands, who were drafted to represent a vision of the Civil War as Americans of the Jim Crow era wished to see it."[6]

The Black Confederate Story

Civil War History and Memory in the Age of the Internet

Andrew Chandler with his slave Silas Chandler.

In 1861, seventeen-year-old Andrew Chandler celebrated his enlistment in the Palo Alto Guards (later Company F, 44th Mississippi Infantry) by sitting for a photograph. Posing with Andrew was Silas Chandler, his body servant or camp slave. Silas, who was seven years older than Andrew, had been with the Chandler family since birth. Born in Virginia, Silas was taken to Mississippi as a toddler when Gilderoy Chandler, Andrew's father, followed the expansion of cotton production to the Deep South. Andrew and Silas are both wearing Confederate uniforms and brandishing a variety of weapons, including a pinfire pistol, a revolver, a pepperbox, a rifle, and two large bowie knives. "There is an almost comic element in Andrew's attempt to cram in as many weapons—very likely studio props—into the photograph," notes historian Kevin Levin. "One can easily imagine an excited Andrew requesting each weapon in an attempt to complete the scene and satisfy his own ideas of martial manhood on the eve of the war." Notwithstanding the military uniforms and the weapons, the relationship between Andrew and Silas was clearly defined by their respective roles as the eldest son of a wealthy slaveholder—the Chandler estate included thirty-five slaves—and his slave.[1]

This tintype is at the center of the debate about the role of African Americans in the Confederate army. In the late 1970s, claims began to emerge that the Confederate government recruited significant numbers of Black men into the army. Levin credits the rise of these claims to a shift in popular memory of the Civil War in the wake of the Civil Rights Movement. "During this period," Levin explains, "historians placed increasing emphasis on slavery as a cause of secession and war; its maintenance as central to the Confederate war effort; and emancipation as one of the war's most significant results, along with the preservation of the Union." The Sons of Confederate Veterans began to promote stories of Black Confederate soldiers to counter this shift. If they could demonstrate that free and enslaved Black men fought for the Confederate cause, they could continue to celebrate their Confederate heritage without appearing "racially insensitive or worse."[2]

In 2009, Andrew Chandler Battaile Jr., a direct descendant of Andrew Chandler, appeared on an episode of *Antiques Roadshow* with this tintype. Wes Cowman conducted the appraisal. He left the interpretation of the image to Battaile, who claimed the two men had "worked the fields together, and continued to live closely throughout the rest of their lives." Andrew and Silas had "fought in four battles together," according to Battaile. Silas had even saved Andrew's leg from amputation. Battaile cited a recent reunion of the two sides of the family, but failed to mention "that at least one of Silas's descendants had already removed the Southern Cross of Honor placed on his grave by the SCV [Sons of Confederate Veterans] back in 1994." Battaile did not clarify Silas's legal status as a slave, nor did he explain his relationship to Andrew and his role in the army.

In 2011, Cowan returned to television, this time on an episode of PBS's *History Detectives*, where he worked with several experts to examine more closely the Chandler narrative. The resulting research dismissed claims that Silas was a soldier. As Levin points out, "The episode did more than just challenge historical claims about the Confederacy and African Americans; it also introduced the Lost Cause myth as a way to understand how the Chandler story was manipulated decades after the war." The Chandler story was part of a larger attempt by Southerners to justify the war. In the late nineteenth and early twentieth century, notes historian Mary Frances Berry in the *History Detectives* episode, "part of that justification was to say that slaves fought for the Confederacy, slaves were loyal to their master." As far as the relationship between Andrew and Silas, Berry noted "that we can never know" owing to the role of "compulsion" and "force" in the master-slave relationship. In 2014, Battaile sold the tintype to the Library of Congress for an undisclosed amount.[3]

The myth of the Black Confederate is a manifestation of the Lost Cause narrative of the loyal camp slave. During the Civil War, impressed slaves performed all kinds of work for the Confederacy. Indeed, as we have seen, it was this work by enslaved men that led General Benjamin Butler to enact his contraband policy at Fort Monroe, Virginia, in 1861. However, these camp slaves or body servants were located outside the military hierarchy and did not serve as soldiers. After the war, the image of the loyal camp slave was central to the Lost Cause narrative. The loyalty of slaves reinforced Southerners' claims that slavery and race were not central to the Confederate cause. In the late nineteenth and early twentieth century, former camp slaves attended Confederate reunions. Their status as former slaves (not soldiers) was clear. A photograph from a Confederate reunion in Tampa, Florida, in 1927 shows one Black attendee who is wearing a white ribbon marked "Ex-Slave."

The myth of the Black Confederate gained traction with the rise of the Internet and the increased availability of inexpensive, easy-to-use digital tools that have provided greater access to primary source materials, such as photographs, pension records, and newspaper articles. The myth of the Black Confederate may be found on hundreds of websites, social media pages, and discussion boards. Unfortunately, on many of these sites, the analysis of primary sources is shallow, uninformed, frequently decontextualized, and inaccurate. For example, in a 2011 dustup between Ann DeWitt, one of the proponents of the Black Confederate myth, and historian Andy Hall, Hall points out DeWitt's misreading of a document and her subsequent erroneous conclusions. "Forget *interpretation*. Forget *analysis*. Forget trying to *understand the document within the context of the time and place it was written*; these people don't even seem capable of *reading* the documents they cite," Hall concluded.[4]

More troubling are instances of intentional manipulation of primary sources to support the Black Confederate narrative, though such examples are rare. One of the more popular examples involves a photograph incorrectly identified as being a photograph of Black soldiers in the Louisiana Native Guard. The image was originally published in 1973 in *Civil War Times Illustrated*, where it was clearly identified as a photograph of Black Union soldiers taken at Camp William Penn in 1864. At some point after its publication, the original photograph was scanned and digitally manipulated. The original photograph showed a white officer on the left side of the image and a door frame on the right side. Both were removed in what was likely an effort to convince the viewer the image was taken in the field. A new label was added to image: "1st Louisiana Native Guard 1861." It was advertised and sold online as "Members of the first all Black Confederate Unit organized in New Orleans in 1861."[5]

The photograph of Andrew and Silas Chandler is perhaps the most popular image associated with the Black Confederate myth. It has been reproduced on consumer goods, book covers, and museum exhibits. For a time, the National Park Service promoted the Black Confederate myth. The Corinth Interpretive Center at Shiloh included the photograph of Andrew and Silas with a caption that obscured the true nature of their relationship: Silas was misidentified as Andrew's "former slave" and the text claimed "both boys fought together at Chickamauga." However, the story of the Black Confederate has not had any support among academic historians, including Levin, who is the foremost authority on the Black Confederate myth.[6]

"The battle over the memory of the black Confederate soldier is one small part of a much larger conversation about the meaning and legacy of our civil war that Americans will continue to debate," Levin concludes. The Black Confederate represents the challenge of coming to terms with the history of slavery and race in America. Although the Black Confederate myth remains popular in some circles, mainstream culture has largely rejected it.[7]

Stone Mountain

Confederate Monuments in the Twenty-First Century

Stone Mountain, Georgia.
SOURCE: MARY H. FARMER.

It took nearly sixty years to create Stone Mountain. Located less than twenty miles east of Atlanta, Georgia, the 825-foot dome of Stone Mountain rises an impressive 1,683 feet above sea level on a path once used by Creek Indians. A carving of Robert E. Lee, Jefferson Davis, and Stonewall Jackson—the Lost Cause trinity—is etched into the rock's side. It is the world's largest piece of sculpture. Lee is as tall as a nine-story building, while Davis's nose is the size of a sofa. Created as a monument to the Confederacy, for many Stone Mountain is the world's largest shrine to white supremacy.

The plans for Stone Mountain began in 1914 when Caroline Helen Jemison Plane, who would lead the Atlanta chapter of the United Daughters of the Confederacy, and the Stone Mountain Memorial Association decided to carve a memorial on the side of Stone Mountain. The following year, William Simmons, a minister and organizer for fraternal organizations, was inspired by D. W. Griffith's silent film *The Birth of a Nation* to restart the Ku Klux Klan (KKK). Credited as the first feature-length film, *The Birth of a Nation* celebrated the heyday of the early KKK. Simmons planned to hold the induction ceremonies at Stone Mountain the week before the movie's opening in Atlanta.

In November, a small group, including fifteen robed and hooded "charter members" of the new organization, met at the summit of Stone Mountain. Among those present were two elderly members of the original Klan and several men who had participated in the recent lynching of Leo Frank, the Jewish superintendent of an Atlanta factory wrongfully convicted of the murder of a thirteen-year-old Christian girl. The men set up a flag-draped altar, opened a Bible, and burned a sixteen-foot cross as part of an initiation ceremony. For the next fifty years, Stone Mountain was the site of an annual Labor Day cross-burning ceremony. Stone Mountain was "*the* sacred site to members of the second and third national klans."[1]

In 1916, the recently incorporated Stone Mountain Confederate Monumental Association (SMCMA) hired Gutzon Borglum, an Idaho sculptor who would later carve Mount Rushmore, to carve Robert E. Lee leading his troops across the mountain's summit. The project was delayed by World War I. It restarted in 1923 only to stall again in 1925—with only the head of Lee carved—when a rift between the sculptor and the SMCMA over artistic control ended with Borglum fired. The sculpture remained unfinished through the Great Depression of the 1930s. In 1941, Governor Eugene Talmadge formed the Stone Mountain Memorial Association to continue work; however, world events intervened once again when the United States entered World War II. In the 1950s, interest and funding in the Confederate memorial was revived.

As the Civil Rights Movement gained momentum, segregationists hoped the Stone Mountain memorial would serve as a reminder of white supremacy. In 1958, the state of Georgia purchased Stone Mountain and made it into a state park. The state and the Stone Mountain Memorial Association, which had organized in 1958, agreed to carve images of Robert E. Lee, Thomas "Stonewall" Jackson, and Jefferson Davis. Plans were also made to construct a plaza at the mountain's base. The memorial was dedicated in 1970.

Stone Mountain reflects the difficult task of what to do with Confederate monuments. Since 2015, when white supremacist Dylann Roof murdered nine members of Emanuel Church in Charleston, South Carolina, Stone Mountain, like other Confederate memorials, has come under increased scrutiny. Stone Mountain, "with its controversial carving and ugly racist history, has come to play a complicated role—not as a central issue, exactly, but as a looming presence, imbued with the volatile power of Confederate remembrance and racial resentment." There have been calls to remove the carving. However, the sheer task of removing the sculpture would require "blowing it off piece by piece with explosives." The carving is protected by Georgia state law and is the centerpiece of Georgia's most visited tourist site. Other suggestions include using the museum spaces around the mountain to tell "a more complete, unvarnished story of Stone Mountain's past." Another proposal calls for adding a bell tower on top of the mountain, evoking Dr. Martin Luther King Jr.'s 1963 "I Have a Dream" speech—"Let freedom ring from Stone Mountain of Georgia!"[2]

The Sons of Confederate Veterans, the League of the South, and others have been vocal in their defense of Stone Mountain. Less than two months after the murders in Charleston, seven hundred people rallied at Stone Mountain, "convinced their way of life and legacy were under attack." The proposed bell tower has drawn similar protests.

Still, as far as Confederate monuments are concerned, Stone Mountain is a unique challenge. The carvings of Lee, Jackson, and Davis are embedded forty-two feet into the heart of the mountain. As other Confederate monuments are pulled down or defaced, Stone Mountain has continued to stand, rendered impervious to destruction by its formidable size. For now, the fate of the carving remains in limbo.

Afterword

George Floyd Mural, Portland, Oregon, June 2020.
SOURCE: LORAINE SCHMITT.

In May 2020, as I was completing the revisions of this manuscript, the world learned of the murder of George Floyd by police officers in Minneapolis, Minnesota. In the days and weeks that followed, the response to Floyd's killing was unprecedented. The deaths of Trayvon Martin, Tamir Rice, Botham Jean, Michael Brown, Eric Garner, and many others had triggered outrage and demonstrations. The Black Lives Matter (BLM) movement, formed in 2013 after the acquittal of the murderer of Martin, has been an important voice for change. However, after Floyd's death, it was "as if a dam had broken," notes historian Annette Gordon-Reed. Thousands of people in each of the fifty states participated in protests, voicing their solidarity with Floyd and BLM. The more violent demonstrations resulted in the destruction of property and the toppling of monuments, many but not all of them Confederate. On June 21, historian Kevin Levin listed twenty-eight Confederate monuments or memorials that had been removed or relocated in the previous three weeks. Seven of those monuments/memorials had been brought down by protesters. It was, as Levin notes, "the most sustained push to remove Confederate monuments from public spaces in recent history." As monuments were coming down, murals started going up as artists from Portland, Oregon, to Greensboro, North Carolina, created tributes to Floyd and other victims of racial violence.[1]

Also significant was the groundswell of response from dozens of institutions, industry groups, and others, each posting statements on the killing of Floyd, BLM, and racist violence in the United States. The list is unprecedented: the American Association of University Professors, the American Hospital Association, the American Historical Association, the National Council on Public History, the American Library Association, and the Jewish Family and Children's Service of Minneapolis, to name just a few. Secretary of the Smithsonian Lonnie G. Bunch III called on the museum field to do more to address racial injustice: "Will we join the struggle to seek justice and equality? Will we heed the call of courageous figures through history who spoke out against slavery, marched on for voting rights, and sat in for basic equality? Will we challenge the nation to live up to its founding ideals? In the memory of those taken from us and for the good of the country, I hope that we do."[2]

It remains to be seen whether the museum field and American society more generally will do just that. "The United States is, apparently, living through one of those punctuation points in history that, seemingly out of the blue, arrive to spur societal change," Gordon-Reed writes. Perhaps this punctuation point will force a reckoning with the history of slavery and race and legacy of the Civil War and create lasting change.[3]

Notes

PREFACE

1. Julie L. Holcomb, "In His Letters to His Wife, Lieutenant Samuel N. Kennerly of the 25th South Carolina Told of the Toll of War," Eyewitness to War, *America's Civil War* 15 (November 2002): 30; "The Edisto Rifles: A History of This Gallant Corps from Its Organization," *Orangeburg Democrat*, July 18, 1879; Julia Henrietta Culler Houser, Find A Grave, https://www.findagrave.com/memorial/57416145/julia-henrietta-houser, accessed September 22, 2019.

2. Samuel N. Kennerly Papers, 1861–1864, finding aid, The Pearce Museum at Navarro College, https://pearcecollections.pastperfectonline.com/archive/7E3109F1-42EF-11D9-AF14-096843515300, accessed September 22, 2019.

3. Founded in 1975, Elderhostel began as a learning program for older adults. By 2010, more than four million adults had taken Elderhostel programs. That year, Elderhostel rebranded itself as Road Scholar. See *Road Scholar*, https://www.roadscholar.org/about/our-story, accessed April 13, 2018.

4. Kenneth W. Rendell, *History Comes to Life: Collecting Historical Letters and Documents* (Norman: University of Oklahoma Press, 1995), 1.

5. Teresa Barnett, *Sacred Relics: Pieces of the Past in Nineteenth-Century America* (Chicago: University of Chicago Press, 2013), 80. See also Julie L. Holcomb, "The Timothy O. Webster Papers and the Pearce Civil War Collection: Using Civil War

Military Collections for Women's History," *Collections: A Journal for Museum and Archives Professionals* 14 (Summer 2018): 365–82.

6. Megan Kate Nelson, *Ruin Nation: Destruction and the American Civil War* (Atlanta: University of Georgia Press, 2012), 229–30. Shaw, as quoted in *Sacred Relics*, 90.

7. Barnett, *Sacred Relics*, 80. Timothy B. Smith credits these visitors with sustaining "efforts to preserve and mark significant sites. . . . As time passed, soldiers began to take the logical step toward marking what tourists saw, beginning an early form of battlefield preservation through interpretation." Timothy B. Smith, *Altogether Fitting and Proper: Civil War Battlefield Preservation in History, Memory, and Policy, 1861–2015* (Knoxville: University of Tennessee Press, 2017), 2.

8. As quoted in Barnett, *Sacred Relics*, 89.

9. Trowbridge, as quoted in Barnett, *Sacred Relics*, 81. Barnett notes that in 1869 an account of the dedication of a Gettysburg monument that appeared in *Harper's Weekly* included illustrations showing people digging bullets from logs and searching the ground for souvenirs. See Barnett, *Sacred Relics*, 85.

10. Barnett, *Sacred Relics*, 141–60. Quotes are from Barnett, *Sacred Relics*, 145. See also James Marten, *Sing Not War: The Lives of Union and Confederate Veterans in Gilded Age America* (Chapel Hill: University of North Carolina Press, 2011), 138–46.

11. Barnett, *Sacred Relics*, 106–40. Confederate Museum, as quoted in Barnett, *Sacred Relics*, 109.

12. Harold Holzer and the New York Historical Society, *The Civil War in 50 Historic Objects* (New York: Viking, 2013); Neil Kagan and Stephen G. Hyslop, *Smithsonian Civil War: Inside the National Collection* (Washington, DC: Smithsonian Books, 2013). For examples of military-focused books, see *Echoes of Glory: Arms and Equipment of the Union* (Alexandria, VA: Time-Life Books, 1991) and *Echoes of Glory: Arms and Equipment of the Confederacy* (Alexandria, VA: Time-Life Books, 1996).

13. See James Oliver Horton and Lois E. Horton, eds., *Slavery and Public History: The Tough Stuff of American History* (Chapel Hill: University of North Carolina Press, 2009).

INTRODUCTION

1. *The Fugitive Slave Law and Its Victims*, revised and enlarged edition (New York: American Anti-Slavery Society, 1861), 4.

CHAPTER 1. FOR SALE—"A DAY I'LL NEVER FORGIT"

1. James and Josiah Huie to Samuel Guy, Bill of sale for four slaves, March 31, 1824, American Slavery Documents Collection, David M. Rubenstein Rare Book and Manuscript Library, Duke University.

2. Thavolia Glymph, *Out of the House of Bondage: The Transformation of the Plantation Household* (New York: Cambridge University Press, 2008), 2.

3. In addition to the bills of sale already cited, see William Guy to Samuel Guy, Bill of sale for one slave girl, March 1, 1811; Montfort Stokes to Samuel Guy, Bill of sale for one slave woman, November 1, 1816; Joseph and Margaret Lawrence to Samuel Guy, Bill of sale for two slaves, May 12, 1817; William Astin to Samuel Guy, Bill of sale for one slave girl, February 11, 1818; Alexander Hogan to Samuel Guy, Bill of sale for one slave girl, February 9, 1828; all in American Slavery Documents Collection, David M. Rubenstein Rare Book and Manuscript Library, Duke University. For more information on Bill, see *Fayetteville Weekly Observer*, July 31, 1823; August 14, 1823; August 21, 1823; *Western Carolinian*, September 16, 1823; September 23, 1823.

4. Astin to Guy, Bill of sale, February 11, 1818.

5. Daina Ramey Berry, *The Price for Their Pound of Flesh: The Value of the Enslaved, from Womb to Grave, in the Building of a Nation* (Boston: Beacon Press, 2017), 18.

6. *The Journal* (Salisbury, North Carolina), June 29, 1830; Jonathan B. Pritchett, "The Interregional Slave Trade and the Selection of Slaves for the New Orleans Market," *The Journal of Interdisciplinary History* 28 (Summer 1997): 75n28.

7. Daina Ramey Berry, "'We'm Fus' Rate Bargain': Value, Labor, and Price in a George Slave Community," in *The Chattel Principle: Internal Slave Trades in the Americas*, ed. Walter Johnson (New Haven, CT: Yale University Press, 2017), 64.

8. Josiah Henson, *The Life of Josiah Henson, Formerly a Slave, Now an Inhabitant of Canada, as Narrated by Himself* (Boston: A. D. Phelps, 1849), 3–4; Jared Brock, *The Road to Dawn: Josiah Henson and the Story That Sparked the Civil War* (New York: Public Affairs, Hachette Book Group, 2018), 19–22.

9. Berry, "'We'm Fus' Rate Bargain,'" 65.

10. "Copy of inventory and sale list of the estate of Samuel Guy decd.," January 15, 1829, North Carolina County, District, and Probate Courts.

CHAPTER 2. GOOD CREDIT, GOOD PRICES, AND GOOD PROFITS

1. U.S. Department of the Interior, National Park Service, National Register of Historic Places Inventory, Nomination form for Franklin and Armfield Office, 1976.

2. Calvin Schermerhorn, *The Business of Slavery and the Rise of American Capitalism, 1815–1860* (New Haven, CT: Yale University Press, 2015), 124–68; Walter Johnson, *Soul by Soul: Life Inside the Antebellum Slave Market* (Cambridge, MA: Harvard University Press, 1999), 47–48.

3. Baptist, *The Half Has Never Been Told*, xxii, 321–22.

4. Schermerhorn, *The Business of Slavery*, 158–59; Edward E. Baptist, *The Half Has Never Been Told: Slavery and the Making of American Capitalism* (New York: Basic Books, 2014), 238–40.

5. *Liberator*, March 18, 1837; Robert H. Gudmestad, "Slave Resistance, Coffles, and the Debates over Slavery in the Nation's Capital," *The Chattel Principle: Internal Slave Trades in the Americas*, ed. Walter Johnson (New Haven, CT: Yale University Press, 2004), 72–90.

6. Nomination form for Franklin and Armfield Office.

7. U.S. Department of the Interior, National Park Service, National Register of Historic Places Inventory, Nomination form for Franklin and Armfield Office, 1976. See also "Alexandria to Buy Freedom House Museum," *WTOP News*, January 7, 2020, https://wtop.com/alexandria/2020/01/alexandria-to-buy-freedom-house -museum/, accessed March 10, 2020.

CHAPTER 3. BUY FOR THE SAKE OF THE SLAVE!

1. See chapter 33 for a discussion of the symbolism of the antislavery movement.

2. For an introduction to Quakerism and the Society of Friends, see Pink Dandelion, *The Quakers: A Very Short Introduction* (New York: Oxford University Press, 2008).

3. Marcus Rediker, *The Fearless Benjamin Lay: The Quaker Dwarf Who Became the First Revolutionary Abolitionist* (Boston: Beacon Press, 2017).

4. Julie L. Holcomb, *Moral Commerce: Quakers and the Transatlantic Boycott of the Slave Labor Economy* (Ithaca, NY: Cornell University Press, 2016), 13–35. See also Geoffrey Plank, *John Woolman's Path to Peaceable Kingdom: A Quaker in the British Empire* (Philadelphia: University of Pennsylvania Press, 2012).

5. Holcomb, *Moral Commerce*, 36–62, 89–122, 141–46, 161–68, 170. For the destruction of Pennsylvania Hall, see chapter 5.

6. Holcomb, *Moral Commerce*, 170–79; Ruth Nuermberger, *The Free Produce Movement: A Quaker Protest against Slavery* (Durham, NC: Duke University Press, 1942), 83–99.

7. Susan Drinan, "Artifact: Free Labor Pinafore," *The Encyclopedia of Greater Philadelphia*, https://philadelphiaencyclopedia.org/archive/artifact-free-labor -pinafore/, accessed October 1, 2018.

8. Holcomb, *Moral Commerce*, 188–93.

CHAPTER 4. STRIKING A BLOW FOR FREEDOM

1. David Walker, *Appeal to the Coloured Citizens of the World*, reprinted in *Documents Decoded: Abolitionist Movement*, ed. Christopher Cameron (Santa Barbara, CA: ABC-CLIO, 2014), 57–105; Manisha Sinha, *The Slave's Cause: A History of Abolition* (New Haven, CT: Yale University Press, 2016), 205–7.

2. Sinha, *The Slave's Cause*, 9, 17, 28, 47, 201, 204; Richard S. Newman, "Prince Hall, Richard Allen, and Daniel Coker: Revolutionary Black Founders, Revolutionary Black Communities," in *Revolutionary Founders: Rebels, Radical, and Reformers in the Making of a Nation*, ed. Alfred E. Young, Gary B. Nash, and Ray Raphael (New York: Alfred A. Knopf, 2011), 306.

3. Peter P. Hinks, *Awaken My Afflicted Brethren: David Walker and the Problem of Antebellum Slave Resistance* (University Park: Pennsylvania State University Press, 1997), 29–40.

4. Walker, *Appeal to the Coloured Citizens*; Sinha, *The Slave's Cause*, 205, 207.

5. Benjamin Quarles, *Black Abolitionists* (New York: Oxford University Press, 1969), 16–17; "David Walker," *Africans in America*, Part 4: 1831–1865, WGBH Educational Foundation, 1998, https://www.pbs.org/wgbh/aia/part4/4p2930.html/, accessed October 2, 2018. See also Community Change, Inc., *The David Walker Memorial Project*, http://www.davidwalkermemorial.org/home/, accessed October 2, 2018.

CHAPTER 5. "I *WILL BE* HARSH AS TRUTH, AND AS UNCOMPROMISING AS JUSTICE"

1. Beverly C. Tomek, *Pennsylvania Hall: A "Legal Lynching" in the Shadow of the Liberty Bell* (New York: Oxford University Press, 2014), 70–71; *History of*

Pennsylvania Hall, which was Destroyed by a Mob, on the 17th of May 1838 (Philadelphia: Merrihew and Gunn, 1838), 11.

2. *History of Pennsylvania Hall*, 137; Tomek, *Pennsylvania Hall*, 119–35.

3. Tomek, *Pennsylvania Hall*, 170.

4. Tomek, *Pennsylvania Hall*, 6; Thomas Skiles to Nathaniel Ellmaker, Bill of sale for York, December 9, 1782, Heritage Center Collection, Lancasterhistory.org, Heritage Center Collection.

5. "Garrison's First Anti-Slavery Address in Boston. Address at Park Street Church, Boston, July 4, 1829," *Old South Leaflets* (Boston, 1907); *The Liberator*, January 1, 1831.

6. Jean R. Soderlund, "Priorities and Power: The Philadelphia Female Anti-Slavery Society," in *The Abolitionist Sisterhood: Women's Political Culture in Antebellum America*, ed. Jean Fagan-Yellin and John C. Van Horne (Ithaca, NY: Cornell University Press, 1994), 67–88.

7. Tomek, *Pennsylvania Hall*, 174, 177.

CHAPTER 6. BLEEDING KANSAS, BLEEDING SUMNER

1. David Tatham, "Pictorial Responses to the Caning of Senator Sumner," *American Printmaking Before 1876: Fact, Fiction, and Fantasy* (Washington, DC: Library of Congress, 1975), 11–19: Joanne B. Freeman, *The Field of Blood: Violence in Congress and the Road to Civil War* (New York: Farrar, Straus and Giroux, 2018), 214–34.

2. Tatham, "Pictorial Response to the Caning of Senator Sumner," 14–15.

3. Freeman, *The Field of Blood*, 214; R. J. M. Blackett, *The Captive's Quest for Freedom: Fugitive Slaves, the 1850 Fugitive Slave Law, and the Politics of Slavery* (New York: Cambridge University Press, 2018), 7–14; Tatham, "Pictorial Response to the Caning of Senator Sumner," 13. See also Stephen E. Maizlish, *A Strife of Tongues: The Compromise of 1850 and the Ideological Foundations of the American Civil War* (Charlottesville: University of Virginia Press, 2018).

4. Freeman, *The Field of Blood*, 218–21; Tatham, "Pictorial Response to the Caning of Senator Sumner," 15.

5. Freeman, *The Field of Blood*, 223, 224; Tatham, "Pictorial Response to the Caning of Senator Sumner," 13.

6. Freeman, *The Field of Blood*, 230–31; Tatham, "Pictorial Response to the Caning of Senator Sumner," 18.

CHAPTER 7. "A MAN KIDNAPPED!"

1. *The Liberator*, June 2, 1854; Library of Congress, "The Popularity of Broadsides," *Printed Ephemera: Three Centuries of Broadsides and Other Printed Ephemera: Introduction to Printed Ephemera Collection*, https://www.loc.gov/collections /broadsides-and-other-printed-ephemera/articles-and-essays/introduction-to -printed-ephemera-collection/the-popularity-of-broadsides/, accessed November 25, 2018. See also Albert J. Von Frank, *The Trials of Anthony Burns: Freedom and Slavery in Emerson's Boston* (Cambridge, MA: Harvard University Press, 1998).

2. James Oliver Horton and Lois E. Horton, *Black Bostonians: Family Life and Community Struggle in the Antebellum North*, revised edition (New York: Homes and Meier, 1999), 106, 108, 112–13; R. J. M. Blackett, *The Captive's Quest for Freedom: Fugitive Slaves, the 1850 Fugitive Slave Law, and the Politics of Slavery* (New York: Cambridge University Press, 2018), 409.

3. *Liberator*, October 18, 1850.

4. Unlike broadsides, handbills are smaller and printed on both sides.

5. *Boston Daily Atlas*, July 6, 1854.

CHAPTER 8. "HONEST OLD ABE IS BOUND TO WIN"

1. Richard Carwardine, *Lincoln: A Life of Purpose and Power* (New York: Alfred A. Knopf, 2006), 97–99; Gretchen Guidess and Christine Puza, "Old Abe Rides Again: A Long-Unseen Campaign Banner Is Restored for Exhibition," *Art Conservator* 10 (Winter 2015): 4; L. Ashton Thorp, *Manchester of Yesterday: A Human Interest Story of Its Past* (Manchester, NH: Granite State Press, 1939), 291.

2. Michael F. Holt, *The Election of 1860: A Campaign Fraught with Consequences* (University Press of Kansas, 2017), 36–37, 44, 80–81, 88–133; Douglas R. Edgerton, *Year of Meteors: Stephen Douglas, Abraham Lincoln, and the Election That Brought on the Civil War* (New York: Bloomsbury Press, 2010), 110–75.

3. "J.B." is a reference to incumbent president James Buchanan.

4. "Old Fogies" is a reference to the maturity of the men the Constitutional Union Party considered for its nomination. Of the ten men who received votes on the first

ballot, none was younger than fifty and only four were younger than sixty. See Holt, *The Election of 1860*, 81.

5. "Up Salt River" is a nineteenth-century reference to political downfall.

6. The "Wide-Awakes" were a political club organized in support of Abraham Lincoln.

7. "Giant killer" is a reference to Lincoln and his opponent, Stephen Douglas, who was nicknamed the "Little Giant" because he was short in physical stature but a forceful figure in politics.

8. "Lincoln & Hamlin" (n.p., 1860).

9. Guidess and Puza, "Old Abe Rides Again," 4–6; Carwardine, *Lincoln*, 98.

10. Carwardine, *Lincoln*, 129–31.

CHAPTER 9. THE UNION IS DISSOLVED!

1. Smithsonian National Museum of American History, Division of Military History and Diplomacy, "The Union Is Dissolved!" broadside, The Price of Freedom: Americans at War, https://amhistory.si.edu/militaryhistory/collection/object.asp?ID=87/, accessed December 29, 2018.

2. Eric Fettmann, "Charleston Mercury," in *Encyclopedia of the American Civil War: A Political, Social, and Military History*, ed. David S. Heidler and Jeanne T. Heidler (Santa Barbara, CA: ABC-CLIO, 2000).

3. "A Declaration of the Immediate Causes Which Induce and Justify the Secession of the State of Mississippi from the Federal Union," in *The U.S. Constitution and Secession: A Documentary Anthology of Slavery and White Supremacy*, ed. Dwight T. Pitcaithley (Lawrence: University of Kansas Press, 2018), 100–101.

CHAPTER 10. "STRIKE FOR YOUR ALTARS AND YOUR FIRES!"

1. Edison H. Thomas, *John Hunt Morgan and His Raiders* (Lexington: University Press of Kentucky, 1985), 34–45.

2. As quoted in James M. McPherson, *Battle Cry of Freedom: The Civil War Era* (New York: Oxford University Press, 1988), 276–307. The transmountain counties of western Virginia separated from Confederate Virginia and later formed the new state of West Virginia. See McPherson, *Battle Cry of Freedom*, 297–306.

3. Thomas, *John Hunt Morgan and His Raiders*.

4. *Harper's Weekly*, August 16, 1862.

5. In the early nineteenth century, Fitz-Greene Halleck was America's premier poet. "Marco Bozzaris," his poem about an episode from the Greek revolution, was widely reprinted in the nineteenth century. The poem was reportedly a favorite of the poet Emily Dickinson. See Jeffrey Gray, Mary McAleer Balkun, and James McCorkle, eds., *American Poets and Poetry: From the Colonial Era to the Present* (Santa Barbara, CA: ABC-CLIO, 2015), 241–43.

6. Thomas, *John Hunt Morgan and His Raiders*, 72–112.

CHAPTER 11. SECURING ALLIANCES

1. Commonly referred to as the "OR," the 128-volume *Official Records* "provide the most comprehensive, authoritative, and voluminous referent on Civil War operations." See "The War of the Rebellion: Official Records of the Civil War," Department of History, The Ohio State University, https://ehistory.osu.edu/books /official-records, accessed January 28, 2019.

2. Thomas W. Cutrer, "Harrison, James Edward," *Handbook of Texas Online*, https:// tshaonline.org/handbook/online/articles/fhaac/, accessed January 28, 2019.

3. Richard B. McCaslin, "Bourland, James G.," *Handbook of Texas Online*, https:// tshaonline.org/handbook/online/articles/fbo38/, accessed January 28, 2019. In October 1862, in Gainesville, Texas, forty suspected Unionists were hanged, and two others were shot while attempting to escape. Most were innocent of the abolitionist sentiments for which they were tried. See Richard B. McCaslin, "Great Hanging at Gainesville," *Handbook of Texas Online*, https://tshaonline.org/handbook/online /articles/jig01/, accessed January 28, 2019. See also Richard B. McCaslin, *Tainted Breeze: The Great Hanging at Gainesville, Texas, 1862* (Baton Rouge: Louisiana State University Press, 1994).

4. Charles A. Hamilton to Edward C. Clark, July 7, 1861, Governor Edward C. Clark Papers, Texas State Library and Archives Commission.

5. William H. Graves, "The Five Civilized Tribes and the Beginning of the Civil War," *Journal of Cherokee Studies* 10 (Fall 1985): 205.

6. Graves, "The Five Civilized Tribes," 205.

7. James E. Harrison, James Bourland, Charles A. Hamilton to His Excellency Edward Clark, Governor of the State of Texas, U.S. War Department, *War of the Rebellion: Official Records of the Union and Confederate Armies* (Washington, 1880–1901): IV, 1, 322–24 (hereafter cited as *O.R.*).

8. *O.R.*, IV, 1, 323–24.

9. *O.R.*, IV, 1, 324.

10. *O.R.*, IV, 1, 324.

11. Graves, "The Five Civilized Tribes," 207–9; Tiya Miles, *Ties That Bind: The Story of an Afro-Cherokee Family in Slavery and Freedom* (Oakland: University of California Press, 2015), 186–87.

12. Miles, *Ties That Bind*, 186; Graves, "The Five Civilized Tribes," 207–9.

13. Graves, "The Five Civilized Tribes," 211; Miles, *Ties That Bind*, 188.

CHAPTER 12. JOHN BULL MAKES A CHOICE

1. Sven Beckert, *Empire of Cotton: A Global History* (New York: Alfred A. Knopf, 2015), 242–44; Edward E. Baptist, *The Half Has Never Been Told: Slavery and the Making of American Capitalism* (New York: Basic Books, 2014), 321–22.

2. Brian Schoen, *The Fragile Fabric of the Union: Cotton, Federal Politics, and the Global Origins of the Civil War* (Baltimore: Johns Hopkins University Press, 2009), 264–66; Beckert, *Empire of Cotton*, 261.

3. Beckert, *Empire of Cotton*, 261; Fladeland, *Men and Brothers*, 386.

4. Beckert, *Empire of Cotton*, 246–47; Schoen, *The Fragile Fabric of the Union*, 266.

5. Beckert, *Empire of Cotton*, 247–48.

6. Beckert, *Empire of Cotton*, 260.

CHAPTER 13. A SACRED EMBLEM OF THE BATTLE OF GLORIETA PASS

1. William Clarke Whitford, *Colorado Volunteers in the Civil War: The New Mexico Campaign in 1862* (Denver, CO: The State Historical and Natural History Society, 1906), 159; National Park Service, "The Battle of Glorieta Pass," *Pecos National Historical Park New Mexico*, https://www.nps.gov/peco/lear/historyculture/battle -of-glorieta-pass.htm/, accessed February 3, 2019. For the most thorough treatment of the Civil War in the West, see Megan Kate Nelson, *The Three-Cornered War:*

The Union, the Confederacy, and Native Peoples in the Fight for the West (New York: Scribner, 2020).

2. Kevin Waite, "Jefferson Davis and Proslavery Visions of Empire in the Far West," *The Journal of the Civil War Era* 6 (December 2016): 554; Megan Kate Nelson, "The Civil War from Apache Pass," *The Journal of the Civil War Era* 6 (December 2016): 514; National Park Service, "The Battle of Glorieta Pass."

3. As quoted in Thomas S. Edrington and John Taylor, *The Battle of Glorieta Pass: A Gettysburg in the West, March 26–28, 1862* (Albuquerque: University of New Mexico Press, 1998), 6–7.

CHAPTER 14. SAND CREEK MASSACRE NATIONAL HISTORIC SITE

1. Ari Kelman, *A Misplaced Massacre: Struggling Over the Memory of Sand Creek* (Cambridge, MA: Harvard University Press, 2013), xi, 32–42.

2. Jeff Broome, "The 1864 Hungate Family Massacre," *Wild West* 19 (June 2006): 48–53; Jeff Broome, "Indian Massacres in Elbert County Colorado: New Information on the 1864 Hungate and 1868 Dietemann Murders," *Denver Westerners Roundup* 60 (January–February 2004); Jerome A. Greene and Douglas D. Scott, *Finding Sand Creek: History Archeology, and the 1864 Massacre Site* (Norman: University of Oklahoma Press, 2004), 11.

3. Henry Littleton Pitzer and Robert Clairborne Pitzer, *Three Frontiers; Memories, and a Portrait of Henry Littleton Ptizer as Recorded by His Son* (Muscatine, IA: The Prairie Press, 1938), 163; Kellie Lee McKeehan, "'Be Sure to Get the First Shot': American Indians, Violence, and the Press in Colorado" (MA thesis, University of Nebraska Kearney, 2017), 80–81.

4. Alice Polk Hill, *Tales of Colorado Pioneers* (Denver: Pierson and Gardner, 1884), 80; Kelman, *A Misplaced Massacre*, 148; McKeehan, "'Be Sure to Get the First Shot,'" 82–83.

5. Kelman, *A Misplaced Massacre*, 66–68, 118, 147.

6. Greene and Scott, *Finding Sand Creek*, 15–20.

7. "Testimony of Colonel J. M. Chivington, April 26, 1865," in Joint Committee on the Conduct of the War, *Report of the Joint Committee on the Conducts of the War,* H.R. Rep. No. 38(2) (a865) part 3, Massacre of the Cheyenne Indians, 106.

8. Kelman, *A Misplaced Massacre*, 191–95; Greene and Scott, *Finding Sand Creek*, 20–21.

9. Kelman, *A Misplaced Massacre*, 175–76.

10. Kelman, "Remembering Sand Creek," 195–201.

CHAPTER 15. A TERRIBLE SLAUGHTER

1. Lewis H. Crandell, Diary, 1863, Lewis H. Crandell Papers, 1863, Pearce Civil War Collection, Navarro College, Corsicana, Texas; Report of Lieutenant Harry L. Haskell, U.S. War Department, *War of the Rebellion: Official Records of the Union and Confederate Armies* (Washington, 1880–1901): XVII, 1, 477 (hereafter cited as *O.R.*).

2. Carol Reardon and Tom Vossler, *The Gettysburg Campaign, June–July 1863* (Washington, DC: Center of Military History, United States Army, 2013), 19–31.

3. Reardon and Vossler, *The Gettysburg Campaign*, 23–27, 30–31; Haskell, *O.R.*, XVII, 1, 477.

4. Ezra D. Simmons, *A Regimental History: The One Hundred and Twenty-Fifth New York State Volunteers* (New York: E. D. Simmons, 1888), 101–2.

5. Reardon and Vossler, *The Gettysburg Campaign*, 31–46.

6. Crandell, Diary, Entry for July 2, 1863.

7. Simmons, *A Regimental History*, 112.

8. Reardon and Vossler, *The Gettysburg Campaign*, 46.

9. Crandell, Diary, Entry for July 2, 1863; Reardon and Vossler, *The Gettysburg Campaign*, 46–57.

10. Reardon and Vossler, *The Gettysburg Campaign*, 57–60.

11. Report of Brigadier General Alexander Hays, July 8, 1863, *O.R.*, 27, 1, 453; Reardon and Vossler, *The Gettysburg Campaign*, 57–61.

12. As quoted in James M. McPherson, *Battle Cry of Freedom: The Civil War Era* (New York: Oxford University Press, 1988), 664–65.

13. Records for Lewis H. Crandell, Levin Crandell, and Chauncey J. Crandell, all in *New York, Civil War Muster Roll Abstracts, 1861–1900*, New York State Archives; Simmons, *A Regimental History*, 350. Lincoln quoted in Reardon and Vossler, *The Gettysburg Campaign*, 61.

CHAPTER 16. "WE WILL PROVE OURSELVES MEN"

1. *Philadelphia Tribune*, February 11, 1890; November 8, 1985; February 13, 2001.

2. Kelly D. Mezurek, *For Their Own Cause: The 27th United States Colored Troops* (Kent, OH: Kent State University Press, 2016), 1, 39.

3. Eric Ledell Smith, "The Civil War Letters of Quartermaster Sergeant John C. Brock, 43rd Regiment, United States Colored Troops," in *Making and Remaking Pennsylvania's Civil War*, ed. William Blair and William Pencak (University Park: Pennsylvania State University Press, 2001), 144–45. Jeffry D. Wert, "Camp William Penn and the Black Soldier," *Pennsylvania History: A Journal of Mid-Atlantic Studies* 46 (October 1979), 336–37.

4. Wert, "Camp William Penn," 337–45.

5. Eric Ledell Smith, "Painted with Pride in the USA," *Pennsylvania Heritage* 27 (2001): 24–31. See also Richard A. Sauers, *Advance the Colors! Pennsylvania Civil War Battle Flags* (Capitol Preservation Committee, 1987), 40–57. Sauers discusses each of the eleven flags.

6. Wert, "Camp William Penn," 339.

7. Sauers, *Advance the Colors!*, 57.

8. Mezurek, *For Their Own Cause*, 1.

CHAPTER 17. CARING FOR THE WOUNDED

1. Patricia Hills, "Eastman Johnson's The Field Hospital: The U.S. Sanitary Commission, and Women in the Civil War," *Minneapolis Institute of Arts* 65 (1981): 66–81; "The Field Hospital. The Letter Home," Museum of Fine Arts Boston, Boston, Massachusetts, https://www.mfa.org/collections/object/the-field-hospital-33181/, accessed March 14, 2019.

2. Jeanie Attie, *Patriotic Toil: Northern Women and the American Civil War* (Ithaca, NY: Cornell University Press, 1998), 39–41, 52–54.

3. Judith Ann Giesberg, *Civil War Sisterhood: The U.S. Sanitary Commission and Women's Politics in Transition* (Boston: Northeastern University Press, 2000), 41–44; Attie, *Patriotic Toil*, 82–86.

4. Attie, *Patriotic Toil*, 39–41, 52–54.

5. Giesberg, *Civil War Sisterhood*, 41–44; David Gollaher, *Voice for the Mad: The Life of Dorothea Dix* (New York: Free Press, 1995), 409–10; Attie, *Patriotic Toil*, 82–86.

6. Hills, "Eastman Johnson," 73–75; Ira M. Rutkow, *Bleeding Blue and Gray: Civil War Surgery and the Evolution of American Medicine* (New York: Random House, 2005), 225–27.

7. Rutkow, *Bleeding Blue and Gray*, 228–33.

8. Judith E. Harper, "Juliet Opie Hopkins," in *Women during the Civil War: An Encyclopedia* (New York: Routledge, 2004), 196–98; "Artifact of the Month: Captain Sally Tompkins," *The American Civil War Museum*, February 2016, https://acwm .org/blog/february-2016-artifact-month-captain-sally-tompkins/, accessed March 14, 2019.

9. Susie King Taylor, *Reminiscences of My Life in Camp with the 33d United States Colored Troops Late 1st S.C. Volunteers* (Boston, 1902); Joycelyn K. Moody et al., "Susie King Taylor," in *American Women Prose Writers, 1870–1920*, ed. Sharon M. Harris et al. (Detroit, MI: Gale, 2000).

10. Drew Gilpin Faust, *This Republic of Suffering: Death and the American Civil War* (New York: Alfred A. Knopf, 2008), 12–13, 15, 77.

CHAPTER 18. "HIS NAME WAS BIDWELL PEDLEY"

1. Bidwell Pedley, Diary, 1863, Bidwell Pedley Papers, Pearce Civil War Collection, Navarro College, Corsicana, Texas.

2. Drew Gilpin Faust, *This Republic of Suffering: Death and the American Civil War* (New York: Alfred A. Knopf, 2008), 3, 55, 64–65.

3. The Civil War death toll has traditionally been numbered at 620,000. Recent scholarship places the number of losses at nearly 750,000. See Guy Gugliotta, "Civil War Toll Up by 20 Percent in New Estimate," *New York Times*, April 2, 2012.

4. Faust, *This Republic of Suffering*, 66, 69, 102; Walt Whitman, *Autobiographia; or, The Story of a Life by Walt Whitman, Selected from His Prose Writings* (New York: Charles L. Webster and Co., 1892), 101.

5. Faust, *This Republic of Suffering*, 65.

6. Faust, *This Republic of Suffering*, 127–28. Benjamin I. Scott's Muster Roll record for September to October 1862 shows the young soldier as "absent" and "Not heard

since the battle of Boonsboro, Maryland, Sept. 14th." Company Muster Roll, 18th
Virginia Infantry, Compiled Service Records of Confederate Soldiers Who Served in
Organizations from the State of Virginia, https://www.fold3.com/, accessed March
23, 2019.

7. Faust, *This Republic of Suffering*, 212–13, 238.

8. Florence Pedley Jones, undated manuscript, Bidwell Pedley Papers, Pearce Civil
War Collection, Navarro College; "Julia Eytcheson Marugg," *Find a Grave*, https://
www.findagrave.com/memorial/19437302/julia-marugg/, accessed March 23, 2019.

CHAPTER 19. "LET THEM SURRENDER AND GO HOME"

1. Grant as quoted in Joan Waugh, *U.S. Grant: American Hero, American Myth*
(Chapel Hill: University of North Carolina Press, 2009), 308.

2. Wilmer McLean, a native of Alexandria, Virginia, lived in Manassas, Virginia,
when the Civil War began in 1861. His home served as Confederate general P. G.
T. Beauregard's headquarters during the First Battle of Manassas along the banks of
Bull Run Creek. After the battle, McClean moved to the small village of Appomattox
Court House. It is said of McLean that the Civil War began in his backyard and
ended in his parlor. "Wilmer McLean," Appomattox Court House National Historical
Park, National Park Service, https://www.nps.gov/people/wilmer-mclean.htm,
accessed September 15, 2019.

3. Joan Waugh, "'I Only Knew What Was in My Mind': Ulysses. Grant and the
Meaning of Appomattox," *The Journal of the Civil War Era* 2 (September 2012): 324.
Whitman and Grant as quoted by Waugh. See also Kevin Levin, "Lee Accepts the
Surrender of Grant in His Vicksburg Boots," *Civil War Memory*, January 18, 2009,
http://cwmemory.com/2009/01/18/lee-accepts-the-surrender-of-grant-in-his
-vicksburg-boots/.

4. Charles McGrath, "Two Generals, Still Maneuvering: Exhibition Review,"
New York Times, October 17, 2008; David Meschutt, "Jean Leon Gerome Ferris,"
American National Biography Online, https://www-anb-org.ezproxy.baylor.edu
/view/10.1093/anb/9780198606697.001.0001/anb-9780198606697-e-1700278,
accessed September 15, 2019.

5. Jesse Grant Cramer, ed., *Letters of Ulysses S. Grant to His Father and His Youngest
Sister, 1857–1878* (New York: G. P. Putnam's Sons, 1912), 25.

6. Grant as quoted in Waugh, *U.S. Grant*, 53–56.

7. Grant as quoted in Waugh, "'I Only Knew What Was in My Mind,'" 324–25.

8. "General Orders No. 9," *Encyclopedia Virginia*, Virginia Humanities, https://www
.encyclopediavirginia.org/media_player?mets_filename=evm00002355mets.xml,
accessed April 2, 2019.

9. Caroline E. Janney, *Remembering the Civil War: Reunion and the Limits of
Reconciliation* (Chapel Hill: University of North Carolina Press, 2013), 43–44.

10. Joan Waugh, "Ulysses S. Grant, Historian," in *The Memory of the Civil War in
American Culture*, ed. Alice Fahs and Joan Waugh (Chapel Hill: University of North
Carolina Press, 2004), 15–17.

CHAPTER 20. LEE'S RIGHT ARM

1. Lee as quoted in James I. Robertson Jr., *Stonewall Jackson: The Man, the Soldier,
the Legend* (New York: Macmillan Publishing, 1997), 729–62.

2. As quoted in Robertson, *Stonewall Jackson*, 110–88.

3. As quoted in Robertson, *Stonewall Jackson*, 189–283.

4. Robert K. Krick, *The Smoothbore Volley That Doomed the Confederacy: The Death
of Stonewall Jackson and Other Chapters on the Army of Northern Virginia* (Baton
Rouge: Louisiana State University Press, 2002), 1–41.

CHAPTER 21. "THE BEAST"

1. Gerald M. Capers, *Occupied City: New Orleans Under the Federals, 1862–1865*
(Louisville: University Press of Kentucky, 1965), 60.

2. Keith Harris, "A Beastly Chamber Pot," *The Rogue Historian* blog, https://
theroguehistorian.com/keith-harris-history/chamber-pot, accessed August 1, 2019.

3. Capers, *Occupied City*, 56.

4. Arnold Blumberg, "Ben Butler's Draconian Move to Keep Maryland in the
Union Also Saved Washington," *Military History* 21 (October 2004): 24, 80; Capers,
Occupied City, 57–58.

5. Eric Foner, *The Fiery Trial: Abraham Lincoln and American Slavery* (New York:
W. W. Norton, 2010), 169–71; James Oakes, *Freedom National: The Destruction of
Slavery in the United States, 1861–1865* (New York: W. W. Norton, 2013), 93–103;
David W. Blight, *A Slave No More: Two Men Who Escaped to Freedom, Including
Their Own Narratives of Emancipation* (Orlando, FL: Harcourt, 2007), 133–34.

6. Chester G. Hearn, *When the Devil Came Down to Dixie: Ben Butler in New Orleans* (Baton Rouge: Louisiana State University Press, 1997), 34–36. John P. Bankhead as quoted on p. 35.

7. Hearn, *When the Devil Came Down to Dixie*, 36–37.

8. Benjamin F. Butler, *Autobiography and Personal Reminiscences of Major-General Benj. F. Butler: Butler's Book: A Review of His Legal, Political, and Military Career* (Boston: A. M. Thayer and Company, 1892), 414–18.

9. Jacqueline G. Campbell, "'The Unmeaning Twaddle about Order 28': Benjamin F. Butler and Confederate Women in Occupied New Orleans, 1862," *Journal of the Civil War Era* 2 (March 2012): 14–15; Butler, *Autobiography*, 418.

10. All as quoted in Campbell, "'The Unmeaning Twaddle about Order 28,'" 15–16.

11. Campbell, "'The Unmeaning Twaddle about Order 28,'" 21–24.

CHAPTER 22. "FATHER OF BLACK NATIONALISM"

1. Robert S. Levine, *Martin R. Delany: A Documentary Reader* (Chapel Hill: University of North Carolina Press, 2003), 1–20.

2. Dorothy Sterling, *The Making of an Afro-American: Martin Robison Delany, 1812–1885* (Garden City, NY: Doubleday and Company, 1971), 136–158; *Liberator*, May 21, 1852.

3. As quoted in Sterling, *Making of an Afro-American*, 159–218; Kellie Carter Jackson, *Force and Freedom: Black Abolitionists and the Politics of Violence* (Philadelphia: University of Pennsylvania Press, 2019), 59.

4. Delany as quoted in Sterling, *Making of an Afro-American*, 159–60.

5. Jackson, *Force and Freedom*, 103, 155; Levine, *Martin R. Delany*.

6. Levine, *Martin R. Delany*, 1–20.

7. Holly as quoted in Levine, *Martin R. Delany*, 3.

CHAPTER 23. "THOSE D–D BLACK HATTED FELLOWS"

1. Hat, Uniform, Pattern of 1858, Philander B. Wright Collection, Object Record, Object ID No. V1964.86, Wisconsin Veterans Museum, https://wisvetsmuseum. pastperfectonline.com/webobject/71D6E3DA-A10B-4932-9401-291103681890, accessed May 30, 2019; "The Iron Brigade and the Black Hat," Wisconsin Veterans

Museum blog, https://www.wisvetsmuseum.com/2014/the-iron-brigade-the-black
-hat/, accessed May 30, 2019. The red disk on Wright's hat indicates I Corps. The
Wisconsin Veterans Museum also holds the flag (Object ID No. V1964.219.38) and
the flag staff holder (Object ID No. V1964.87) carried by Wright at Gettysburg. See
https://wisvetsmuseum.pastperfectonline.com/byperson?keyword=Wright%2C+Phil
ander+B., accessed May 30, 2019.

2. Lance J. Herdegen, *The Iron Brigade in Civil War and Memory* (El Dorado Hills,
CA, 2012), 9–17; "Philo B. Wright," *The American Civil War Research Database*,
https://asp6new-alexanderstreet-com.ezproxy.baylor.edu/cwdb/cwdb.object.details
.aspx?handle=person&id=102002240, accessed June 20, 2019; *Chicago Tribune*, June
28, 1861.

3. The shell that killed Gardner is part of the permanent collection of the Wisconsin
Veterans Museum in Madison, Wisconsin.

4. Alan T. Nolan, *The Iron Brigade: A Military History* (Bloomington: Indiana
University Press, 1961), 52–54.

5. Herdegen, *The Iron Brigade*, 161–92.

6. Wright as quoted in Kevin Hampton, "Philander B. Wright Rediscovered," *The
Bugle: A Quarterly Publication of the Wisconsin Veterans Museum* 19 (Spring 2013): 7.

7. Program of the reunion and banquet of the Iron Brigade at the Chicago Athletic
Association, Michigan Avenue, Monday evening, August 27, 1900, Wisconsin
Veterans Museum Research Center, transcribed and available at "Origin of the Name
'Iron Brigade,'" The Civil War Roundtable of Milwaukee [Wisconsin], http://www
.milwaukeecwrt.org/iron-brigade-association/origin-of-the-name-iron-brigade/,
accessed March 4, 2019.

8. Herdegen, *The Iron Brigade*, 235–38. *Cincinnati Daily Commercial* as quoted in
Herdegen, *The Iron Brigade*, 237. See also Lance J. Herdegen, *The Men Stood Like
Iron: How the Iron Brigade Won Its Name* (Bloomington: Indiana University Press,
1997), 145–46, 244n12.

CHAPTER 24. LEE'S SHOCK TROOPS

1. Susannah J. Ural, *Hood's Texas Brigade: The Soldiers and Families of the
Confederacy's Most Celebrated Unit* (Baton Rouge: Louisiana State University Press,
2017), 245–46; Gregg S. Clemmer, *Valor in Gray: The Recipients of the Confederate
Medal of Honor* (Staunton, VA: Hearthside Publishing Company, 1996), 437;

"Athens Family Donates Rare Civil War Artifact to Texas Heritage Museum, Hill College," September 18, 2015, https://www.hillcollege.edu/news_archive/2015/09 /gold-star.html.

2. Douglas Southall Freeman, *R. E. Lee: A Biography* (New York: Scribner, 1977), II: 418.

3. Pender as quoted in Ural, *Hood's Texas Brigade*, 5.

4. Ural, *Hood's Texas Brigade*, 208–9, 212. See also Susannah U. Bruce, "The Fierce Pride of the Texas Brigade," HistoryNet, https://www.historynet.com/fierce-pride -texas-brigade.htm, accessed October 8, 2019.

5. Hunter as quoted in Ural, *Hood's Texas Brigade*, 5.

6. Manahan, Gaston, and Smither all as quoted in Bruce, "The Fierce Pride of the Texas Brigade." See also Ural, *Hood's Texas Brigade*, 42–43.

7. As quoted in Bruce, "The Fierce Pride of the Texas Brigade," and Ural, *Hood's Texas Brigade*, 80.

8. As quoted in Bruce, "The Fierce Pride of the Texas Brigade," and Ural, *Hood's Texas Brigade*, 163–65, 205–6.

9. Ural, *Hood's Texas Brigade*, 245.

10. Ural, *Hood's Texas Brigade*, 1–10.

CHAPTER 25. "WHAT IS TO BE DONE WITH THE PRISONERS?"

1. Benjamin G. Cloyd, *Haunted by Atrocity: Civil War Prisons in American Memory* (Baton Rouge: Louisiana State University Press, 2010), 1, 29.

2. Roger Pickenpaugh, *Captives in Gray: The Civil War Prisons of the Union* (Tuscaloosa: University of Alabama Press, 2009), 2.

3. Pickenpaugh, *Captives in Gray*, 27, 40.

4. Roger Pickenpaugh, *Captives in Blue: The Civil War Prisons of the Confederacy* (Tuscaloosa: University of Alabama Press, 2013), 1–34. *Richmond Whig* as quoted in Pickenpaugh.

5. Pickenpaugh, *Captives in Blue*, 27–28.

6. Cloyd, *Haunted by Atrocity*, 8–9.

7. Pickenpaugh, *Captives in Blue*, 134–56. Prisoners as quoted on 138, 143.

8. Pickenpaugh, *Captives in Blue*, 237; Cloyd, *Haunted by Atrocity*, 35.

CHAPTER 26. DAYS OF INFAMY AND DISGRACE

1. *Harper's Weekly*, July 25, 1863; August 1, 1863; Matthew Murphy, "'They deliberately set fire to it . . . simply because it was the home of unoffending colored orphan children': The New York Draft Riots and the Burning of the colored Orphan Asylum," *From the Stacks*, New York Historical Society, July 16, 2013, http://blog.nyhistory.org/burning-of-orphan-asylum/.

2. Susannah Ural Bruce, *The Harp and the Eagle: Irish-American Volunteers and the Union Army, 1861–1865* (New York: New York University Press, 2006), 42–81.

3. Bruce, *The Harp and the Eagle*, 82–189.

4. Bruce, *The Harp and the Eagle*, 136–41. Chandra Manning emphasizes the complex response to the Emancipation Proclamation. Manning, *What This Cruel War Was Over: Soldiers, Slavery, and the Civil War* (New York: Alfred A. Knopf, 2007), 86–87.

5. Bruce, *The Harp and the Eagle*, 173–74.

6. Leslie M. Harris, *In the Shadow of Slavery: African Americans in New York City, 1626–1863* (Chicago: University of Chicago Press, 2003), 277–86; *Harper's Weekly*, August 8, 1863.

CHAPTER 27. THE EVOLUTION OF THE UNION CAVALRY

1. Frank L. Klement, *Wisconsin in the Civil War: The Home Front and the Battle Front, 1861–1865* (Madison: The State Historical Society of Wisconsin, 1997), 91; "Horses Saddlery," Mine Creek Battlefield Historical Society," September 13, 2019, https://www.minecreek.info/historical-society/horses-saddlery.html/; *Wisconsin Volunteers: War of the Rebellion, 1861–1865, Arranged Alphabetically* (Madison, WI: Democrat Printing Company, 1914), 463. See also 1880 United States Federal Census, Wauwatosa, Milwaukee, Wisconsin, 446a.

2. Laurence D. Schiller, "The Evolution of the Union Cavalry," Essential Civil War Curriculum, June 2017, https://www.essentialcivilwarcurriculum.com/the-evolution-of-union-cavalry-1861-1865.html/; Edward G. Longacre, *Lincoln's Cavalrymen: A History of the Mounted Forces of the Army of the Potomac, 1861–1865* (Mechanicsburg, PA: Stackpole Books, 2000), 29–30.

3. Schiller, "The Evolution of the Federal Cavalry."

4. T. F. Dornblaser, *Sabre Strokes of the Pennsylvania Dragoons, in the War of 1861–1865, Interspersed with Personal Reminiscences* (Philadelphia: Lutheran Publication Society, 1884), 39–41.

5. Schiller, "The Evolution of the Federal Cavalry."

CHAPTER 28. "THE LAST THOUGHT OF A DYING FATHER"

1. Mark H. Dunkelman, *Gettysburg's Unknown Soldier: The Life, Death, and Celebrity of Amos Humiston* (Westport, CT: Praeger, 1999). "The Dead Soldier and the Daguerreotype" as quoted in Dunkelman, *Gettysburg's Unknown Soldier*, 142–43. Original article is from *American Presbyterian*, October 28, 1863. See also the series written by Errol Morris for the Opinionator: *New York Times*, March 29, 2009; March 30, 2009; March 31, 2009; April 1, 2009; April 2, 2009.

2. Dunkelman, *Gettysburg's Unknown Soldier*, 55–63.

3. As quoted in Dunkelman, *Gettysburg's Unknown Soldier*, 104.

4. Dunkelman, *Gettysburg's Unknown Soldier*; *Frank Leslie's Illustrated*, January 2, 1864. Alice as quoted in Dunkelman, *Gettysburg's Unknown Soldier*, 172–73.

5. Dunkelman, *Gettysburg's Unknown Soldier*, 213–27.

6. Mark H. Dunkelman, "Amos Humiston: Union Soldier Who Died at the Battle of Gettysburg," HistoryNet, https://www.historynet.com/amos-humiston-union-soldier-who-died-at-the-battle-of-gettysburg.htm, accessed August 30, 2019.

CHAPTER 29. "BREAD OR BLOOD!"

1. Stephanie McCurry, *Confederate Reckoning: Power and Politics in the Civil War South* (Cambridge, MA: Harvard University Press, 2010), 151–52.

2. McCurry, *Confederate Reckoning*, 166–67.

3. McCurry, *Confederate Reckoning*, 164, 175–76. Margaret Smith and the "Reglators" as quoted in McCurry, *Confederate Reckoning*, 164, 176.

4. F. N. Boney, *John Letcher of Virginia: The Story of Virginia's Civil War Governor* (Tuscaloosa: University of Alabama Press, 1966), 189; William Blair, *Virginia's Private War: Feeding Body and Soul in the Confederacy, 1861–1865* (New York: Oxford University Press, 1998), 69; Mary DeCredico and Jaime Amanda Martinez,

"Richmond during the Civil War," *Encyclopedia Virginia*, Virginia Humanities in partnership with the Library of Virginia, https://encyclopediavirginia.org/richmond _during_the_civil_war#start_entry, accessed August 19, 2019.

5. Blair, *Virginia's Private War*, 69; J. B. Jones, *A Rebel War Clerk's Diary at the Confederate States Capital* (Philadelphia, Pennsylvania, 1866), 252–80.

6. Jones, *A Rebel War Clerk's Diary*, 285–86.

7. *Staunton Spectator* (Virginia), April 7, 1863.

8. *New York Times*, April 8, 1863; *New York Daily Herald*, May 11, 1863; *New York Times*, April 21, 1863.

9. Blair, *Virginia's Private War*, 74–76; Michael B. Chesson, "Harlots or Heroines? A New Look at the Richmond Bread Riot," *Virginia Magazine of History and Biography* 92 (April 1984): 131–75.

CHAPTER 30. "POUNDING ON THE ROCK"

1. Because the image was found in Cecil County, Maryland, Civil War collector Ross J. Kelbaugh believes the unidentified soldier may have served in one of the seven USCT regiments recruited and organized in Maryland. See Ross J. Kelbaugh, *The Civil War in Maryland: An Exhibit of Rare Photographs from the Collections of the Maryland Historical Society and Its Members* (Baltimore, MD: Toomey Press, 2006), 36. In 2012, the genealogy magazine *The Kentucky Explorer* identified the family as Sergeant Samuel Smith, Co. D, 119th USCT, his wife Mollie, and daughters Mary and Maggie. However, the source or sources used to make the identification were not included in the article, making it impossible to verify the information. See *Kentucky Explorer* 27 (November 2012): 39. Since the publication of that article, several Civil War–related websites and forums have reprinted the identification, again without any sources given for the identification. A post on the American Civil War Forum provides data from the 1870 U.S. Census for Samuel Smith and his family; however, the data provided does not match the photographic evidence. According to the 1870 census entry, Samuel and Mollie had three children born before the Civil War: John (1855), Mary (1858), and Maggie (1861). Thus at the time this image was taken, the youngest child Maggie would have been two to four years old, while her older sister Mary would have been five to eight years old. In the photograph, the two girls appear to be twins, and neither child appears to be as young as Maggie would have been in 1863–1865. Also, John is missing from the photograph.

2. "Unidentified African American soldier in Union uniform with wife and two daughters," Library of Congress Prints and Photographs Division, http://www .loc.gov/pictures/item/2010647216/, accessed March 1, 2019; "The Campaign of 1864," The Civil War in America, November 1863–April 1865, Exhibitions, Library of Congress, http://www.loc.gov/exhibits/civil-war-in-america/november-1863 -april-1865.html, accessed March 1, 2019.

3. See, for example, Kevin Levin's discussion of Confederate soldier Andrew Chandler's portrait. Levin, *Searching for Black Confederates: The Civil War's Most Persistent Myth* (Chapel Hill: University of North Carolina Press, 2019), 12.

4. James G. Mendez, *A Great Sacrifice: Northern Black Soldiers, Their Families, and the Experience of the Civil War* (New York: Fordham University Press, 2019), 19–20; Leon F. Litwack, *Been in the Storm So Long: The Aftermath of Slavery* (New York: Vintage Books, 1980), 72; *Douglass' Monthly*, September 1861; November 1861. See also David W. Blight, *Frederick Douglass: Prophet of Freedom* (New York: Simon and Schuster, 2018), 335–54.

5. Mendez, *A Great Sacrifice*, 120–21; Nina Silber, *Daughters of the Union: Northern Women Fight the Civil War* (Cambridge, MA: Harvard University Press, 2005), 63–64; Julie L. Holcomb, "African Americans in the Civil War," in *Civil War: People and Perspectives* (Santa Barbara, CA: ABC-CLIO, 2009), 106–7.

6. Alfred M. Green as quoted in James M. McPherson, *The Negro's Civil War: How American Negroes Felt and Acted during the War for the Union* (Urbana: University of Illinois Press, 1982), 32; Mendez, *A Great Sacrifice*, 184.

CHAPTER 31. "I WANTED TO BE MY OWN GENERAL"

1. Ronald S. Coddington, "The Yellow Doc Raiders," Opinionator, *New York Times*, October 22, 2012, https://opinionator.blogs.nytimes.com/2012/10/22/the-yellow-doc -raiders/. See also Howel A. Rayburn, Compiled Service Records of Confederate Soldiers, fold3.com; Alan Thompson, "Howell A. 'Doc' Rayburn (1841?–1865?), in *Arkansas in Ink: Gunslingers, Ghosts, and Other Graphic Tales* (Little Rock: Butler Center for Arkansas Studies, 2014), 98–99; Neva Ingram Hunsicker, "Rayburn the Raider," *Arkansas Historical Quarterly* 7 (Spring 1948): 87–91.

2. Joseph M. Bailey, *Confederate Guerilla: The Civil War Memoir of Joseph M. Bailey*, ed. T. Lindsay Baker (Fayetteville: University of Arkansas Press, 2007), ix–xi.

3. Daniel E. Sutherland, *Savage Conflict: The Decisive Role of Guerrillas in the American Civil War* (Chapel Hill: University of North Carolina Press, 2009), xii.

4. Daniel E. Sutherland, "Guerillas: The Real War in Arkansas," *Arkansas Historical Quarterly* 52 (Autumn 1993): 262. Maddox and Bailey as quoted in Sutherland, "Guerillas," 262.

5. Stephanie McCurry, *Women's War: Fighting and Surviving the American Civil War* (Cambridge, MA: Belknap Press of Harvard University Press, 2019), 29.

6. Rebecca A. Howard, "No Country for Old Men: Patriarchs, Slaves, and Guerrilla War in Northwest Arkansas," *Arkansas Historical Quarterly* 75 (Winter 2016): 345–47.

7. Howard, "No Country for Old Men," 345.

8. Howard, "No Country for Old Men," 346–47.

9. As quoted in Michael A. Davis, "The Legend of Bill Dark: Guerrilla Warfare, Oral History, and the Unmaking of an Arkansas Bushwhacker," *Arkansas Historical Quarterly* 58 (Winter 1999): 426.

CHAPTER 32. ON HER OWN

1. *A Memorial and Biographical History of Ellis County Texas* (Chicago: Lewis Publishing Company, 1892), 114–15; 1860 United States Federal Census, Division 4, Ellis County, Texas, family number 148, Roll M653-1293, page 31, National Archives and Records Administration; 1860 United States Federal Census Slave Schedules, Ellis County, Texas, Roll M653, page 5, National Archives and Records Administration; Thomas C. Neel Historical Marker, Marker Number 11863, Ellis County, Texas, Texas Historical Commission, https://atlas.thc.state.tx.us/, accessed July 24, 2019; *Journal of the Secession Convention of 1861* (Austin, TX: Austin Printing Company, 1912), 432; Thomas C. Neel, Memorial Number 124038795, Find a Grave, https://www.findagrave.com/memorial/124038795/thomas-simpson -neel, accessed July 24, 2019; Thomas C. Neel, Will Record, September 10, 1863, Ellis County, Texas, County Clerk, Waxahachie, Texas.

2. John B. Latimer to Willia Latimer Neel, November 23, 1863, Neel Family Civil War Papers, 1833–1900, Texas General Land Office, Archives and Records, Austin, Texas.

3. Randolph B. Campbell, "Antebellum Texas," in *Handbook of Texas Online*, http:// www.tshaonline.org/handbook/online/articles/npa01, accessed July 27, 2019; Jerry Thompson, "Mexican Texans in the Civil War," in *Handbook of Texas Online*, http:// www.tshaonline.org/handbook/online/articles/pom02, accessed July 27, 2019.

4. Walter L. Buenger, "Secession," in *Handbook of Texas Online*, http://www
.tshaonline.org/handbook/online/articles/mgs02, accessed July 27, 2019.

5. Angela Boswell, "Introduction," in *Women in Civil War Texas: Diversity and Dissidence in the Trans-Mississippi*, ed. Deborah M. Liles and Angela Boswell (Denton: University of North Texas Press, 2016), 6–7.

6. Dorothy Ewing, "Caroline Sedberry, Politician's Wife," in *Women in Civil War Texas*, 39–56; Angela Boswell, "The Civil War and the Lives of Texas Women," in *The Fate of Texas: The Civil War and the Lone Star State*, ed. Charles D. Grear (Fayetteville: University of Arkansas Press, 2008), 75–77.

7. W. Caleb McDaniel, "Involuntary Removals: 'Refugeed Slaves' in Confederate Texas," in *Lone Star Unionism, Dissent, and Resistance: Other Sides of Civil War Texas*, ed. Jesus F. de la Teja (Norman: University of Oklahoma Press, 2016), 60–83.

8. Donald E. Reynolds, *Texas Terror: The Slave Insurrection Panic of 1860 and the Secession of the Lower South* (Baton Rouge: Louisiana State University Press, 2007); Wendell G. Addington, "Slave Insurrections in Texas," *Journal of Negro History* 35 (October 1950): 408–34; Donald E. Reynolds, "Reluctant Martyr: Anthony Bewley and the Texas Slave Insurrection Panic of 1860," *Southwestern Historical Quarterly* 96 (January 1993): 348–49; Donald E. Reynolds, "Texas Troubles," in *Handbook of Texas Online*, https://tshaonline.org/handbook/online/articles/vetbr, accessed July 27, 2019; Rebecca Sharpless, "'In Favor of our Fathers' Country and Government,'" in *Women in Civil War Texas*, 206–7. Matagorda *Gazette* and John H. Raegan as quoted in Addington, "Slave Insurrections in Texas," 420, 424–25.

9. Reynolds, *Texas Terror*, 8–10; Thompson, "Mexican Texans"; Jerry Thompson and Elizabeth Mata, "Mexican-Texan Women in the Civil War," in *Women in Civil War Texas*, 151–79.

10. W. Caleb McDaniel, "Involuntary Removals: 'Refugeed Slaves' in Confederate Texas," in *Lone Star Unionism, Dissent, and Resistance*, 60–83. Quotes are from 60, 61, and 78. For "Mammy Tilda," see "Faithful Old Servant Gone," *Waxahachie Daily Light*, April 3, 1903, https://texashistory.unt.edu/ark:/67531/metapth1070502/m1/1/zoom/?q="t.c. neel"&resolution=4&lat=3350.4901991610673&lon=2262.6357394722813, accessed July 6, 2019.

CHAPTER 33. "THE SPEECHLESS AGONY OF THE FETTERED SLAVE"

1. *The Emancipator*, November 23, 1837; Fred W. A. Smith, "U.S. Hard Times Tokens," *Antiques and Collecting* 112 (November 2007); Ellen Feingold, "The

Messages of Money," *Financial History*, no. 116 (Winter 2016): 20–23; "For the Love of Money: Blacks on US Currency," *Financial History*, no. 120 (Winter 2017): 20–23. Three pattern pieces were made of the kneeling male slave token, but the coin was never produced for circulation.

2. Teresa A. Goddu, "U.S. Antislavery Tracts and the Literary Imagination," in *The Cambridge Companion to Slavery in American Literature* (Cambridge: Cambridge University Press, 2016), 32–35; *Proceedings of the Anti-Slavery Convention of American Women, Hold in the City of New York, May 9th, 10th, 11th, and 12th, 1837* (New York: William S. Dorr, 1837), 14; Jean Fagan Yellin, *Women and Sisters: The Antislavery Feminists in American Culture* (New Haven, CT: Yale University Press, 1989), 5.

3. Clarkson as quoted in Yellin, *Women and Sisters*, 6. Thrale as quoted in Julie L. Holcomb, "Blood-Stained Sugar: Gender, Commerce and the British Slave-Trade Debates," *Slavery and Abolition* 35 (December 2014): 620.

4. Franklin as quoted in Cynthia S. Hamilton, "Hercules Subdued: The Visual Rhetoric of the Kneeling Slave," *Slavery & Abolition* 34 (December 2013): 635. The Pennsylvania Abolition Society is also known as the Pennsylvania Society for Promoting the Abolition of the Slave Trade.

5. See Elizabeth Margaret Chandler, "The Kneeling Slave," *Genius of Universal Emancipation*, June 1830; "Collection Box of the Massachusetts Anti-Slavery Society," Beinecke Rare Book and Manuscript Library," Yale University, https://brbl-dl.library .yale.edu/vufind/Record/3527252?image_id=1062609, accessed April 14, 2019.

6. Bernard F. Reilly Jr., "The Art of the Antislavery Movement," in *Courage and Conscience: Black and White Abolitionists in Boston*, ed. Donald M. Jacobs (Bloomington: Indiana University Press, 1993), 49, 51. See also Teresa A. Goddu, *Selling Antislavery: Abolition and Mass Media in Antebellum America* (Philadelphia: University of Pennsylvania Press, 2020). As Goddu notes, "Stowe's novel and related products mark[ed] the apex rather than the birth of antislavery mass media." Goddu, *Selling Antislavery*, 1.

CHAPTER 34. "THE LITTLE WOMAN WHO MADE THE GREAT WAR"

1. Harriet Beecher Stowe, *Uncle Tom's Cabin; or, Life among the Lowly*, The Splendid Edition, ed. David S. Reynolds (New York: Oxford University Press, 2011), 324, 327–

28; Peter Betjemann, "The Ends of Time: Abolition, Apocalypse, and Narrativity in Robert S. Duncanson's Literary Paintings," *American Art* 31 (Fall 2017): 99–106.

2. Louise L. Stevenson, "Virtue Displayed: The Tie-Ins of Uncle Tom's Cabin," *Uncle Tom's Cabin and American Culture*, ed. Stephen Railton, http://utc.iath.virginia .edu/interpret/exhibits/stevenson/stevenson.html, accessed April 30, 2019; "Uncle Tomitudes," *Putnam's Monthly*, January 1853, 97–102. Art critics of the time criticized Duncanson's painting as "An Uncle Tomitude" because it portrayed Tom as "a very stupid looking creature." *Clarksville Jeffersonian*, May 18, 1853. The *Clarksville Jeffersonian* review was reprinted from the *Cincinnati Gazette*.

3. Stowe, *Uncle Tom's Cabin*, 22, 251; "Literature of Slavery," *New Englander* 10 (November 1852): 591.

4. Briain Yothers, *Reading Abolition: The Critical Reception of Harriet Beecher Stowe and Frederick* Douglass (Rochester, NY: Camden House, 2016), 9; Josiah Henson, *An Autobiography of the Rev. Josiah Henson, (Mrs. Harriet Beecher Stowe's "Uncle Tom"). From 1789 to 1877*, ed. John Lobb (London: Christian Age Office, 1878). See also Harriet Beecher Stowe, *The Key to Uncle Tom's Cabin; Presenting the Original Facts and Documents Upon Which the Story Is Founded, Together with Corroborative Statements Verifying the Truth of the Work* (Boston: John P. Jewett and Company, 1854), http://utc.iath.virginia.edu/uncletom/key/kyhp.html, accessed May 16, 2019.

5. David S. Reynolds, *Mightier Than the Sword: Uncle Tom's Cabin and the Battle for America* (New York: W. W. Norton, 2011), 125.

6. Henry James, *A Small Boy and Others* (London: Macmillan, 1913), 167.

7. Yothers, *Reading Abolition*, 12; David S. Reynolds, "Introduction," *Uncle Tom's Cabin*, vii; Stevenson, "Virtue Displayed."

8. *The Southern Literary Messenger* 18 (October 1852): 638; *The Publishing History of* Uncle Tom's Cabin, *1852–2002* (Burlington, VT: Ashgate, 2007), 96.

9. Reynolds, *Mightier Than the Sword*, x–xi, 117, 128, 277; Daniel R. Vollaro, "Lincoln, Stowe, and the 'Little Woman/Great War' Story: The Making, and Breaking, of a Great American Anecdote," *Journal of the Abraham Lincoln Association* 30 (Winter 2009), https://quod.lib.umich.edu/j/jala/2629860.0030.104 /--lincoln-stowe-and-the-little-womangreat-war-story-the-making?rgn=main ;view=fulltext/.

CHAPTER 35. "IF YOU WANT MY FLAG, YOU'LL HAVE TO TAKE IT OVER MY DEAD BODY"

1. "Confederate Battle Flag of the 12th Texas Cavalry, Parson's Brigade," exhibit label, Texas Heritage Museum, Hillsboro, Texas; John Q. Anderson, ed., *Campaigning with Parsons' Texas Cavalry Brigade, CSA: The War Journals and Letters of the Four Orr Brothers, 12th Texas Cavalry* (Hillsboro, TX: Hill Junior College Press, 1967), 20; Anne J. Bailey, *Between the Enemy and Texas: Parsons's Texas Cavalry in the Civil War* (Fort Worth: Texas Christian University Press, 1989).

2. Susannah J. Ural, *Hood's Texas Brigade: The Soldiers and Families of the Confederacy's Most Celebrated Unit* (Baton Rouge: Louisiana State University Press, 2017), 126; "11th Regiment, NY Volunteer Infantry Regimental Color," New York State Military Museum and Veterans Research Center, NYS Division of Military and Naval Affairs, https://dmna.ny.gov/historic/btlflags/infantry/11thInfReg.htm, accessed June 16, 2020; 69th Regiment, NY Volunteer Infantry Regimental Color," New York State Military Museum, https://dmna.ny.gov/historic/btlflags/infantry/69t hInfRegColor2013.0022.htm, accessed June 16, 2020.

3. Robert Maberry Jr., *Texas Flags* (College Station: Texas A & M University Press, 2001), 64.

4. *Leavenworth* (Kansas) *Times*, June 23, 1861; *Evening Star* (Washington, DC), June 4, 1861; *Baltimore Sun*, July 1, 1861; *Philadelphia Inquirer*, May 7, 1861; *Fayetteville* (North Carolina) *Weekly Observer*, September 16, 1861; *Detroit Free Press*, September 7, 1861.

5. *New Orleans Daily Crescent*, May 20, 1861.

6. Maberry, *Texas Flags*, 74–78; Ural, *Hood's Texas Brigade*, 126; James A. Hathcock, "First Texas Infantry," *Handbook of Texas Online*, https://tshaonline.org/handbook /online/articles/qkf13, accessed May 29, 2019; Texas State Library and Archives Commission, "First Texas Infantry Regiment," *Historic Flags of the Texas State Library and Archives*, https://www.tsl.texas.gov/historicflags/4037FirstTexas.html, accessed May 29, 2019.

7. Ural, *Hood's Texas Brigade*, 126; "'No Man Can Take Those Colors and Live': The Epic Battle Between the 24th Michigan and 26th North Carolina at Gettysburg," *American Battlefield Trust*, https://www.battlefields.org/learn/articles/no-man-can -take-those-colors-and-live, accessed May 29, 2019.

8. E. B. Qiner, *Military History of Wisconsin* (Chicago: Clarke and Company, 1866), 423–24; *Chicago Tribune*, August 31, 1861; Wisconsin Veteran's Museum, "1st

Wisconsin Infantry & Their Flag," Forward: Wisconsin's Civil War Battle Flags, http://www.wisconsinbattleflags.com/units-flags/1st-wisconsin.php, accessed May 26, 2019.

9. Robert E. Bonner, *Colors and Blood: Flag Passions of the Confederate South* (Princeton, NJ: Princeton University Press, 2004), 19–22. Quotes are from 20–21.

10. Tim Marshall, *A Flag Worth Dying For: The Power and Politics of National Symbols* (New York: Scribner, 2016), 23–24; Nashville Public Library, "Nashville and Old Glory," Off the Shelf blog, June 8, 2015, http://nashvillepubliclibrary.org /offtheshelf/tag/william-driver/; *The Tennessean* (Nashville, Tennessee), June 11, 2008; "History," *Barbara Fritchie House*, http://barbarafritchie.org/history/, accessed May 14, 2019. Whittier used the German of spelling of Fritchie's name.

CHAPTER 36. SETTING THE BEAT FOR WAR

1. Robert E. Bonner, *Colors and Blood: Flag Passions of the Confederate South* (Princeton, NJ: Princeton University Press, 2004), 30.

2. L. Fanshaw, "The Southern Marseillaise" (New Orleans, LA: P. P. Werlein and Halsey, 1861); F. W. Rosier, "The Virginian Marseillaise" (Richmond, VA: George Dunn and Company, 1863).

3. J. L. Power, *Proceedings of the Mississippi State Convention, Held January 7th to 26th, A.D. 1861. Including the Ordinances, as Finally Adopted, Important Speeches, and a List of Members, Showing the Postoffice, Profession, Nativity, Politics, Age, Religious Preference, and Social Relations of Each* (Jackson, MS: Power and Cadwallader, Book and Job Printers, 1861), 16; *The Confederate Veteran* 19 (1911): 478; *Weekly Clarion-Ledger* (Jackson, Mississippi), February 14, 1895; *The Daily Oklahoman* (Oklahoma City), April 25, 1916. For a brief period in 1860 and 1861, the lone star became the South's secession symbol. Confederate states adopted lone star flags to emphasize their withdrawal from the Union. See Robert Maberry Jr., *Texas Flags* (College Station: Texas A & M University Press, 2011), 55.

4. Bonner, *Colors and Blood*, 30–31; Edward Young McMorries, *History of the First Regiment, Alabama Volunteer Infantry, C.S.A.* (Montgomery, AL: Brown, 1904), 22; Christian McWhirter, *Battle Hymns: The Power and Popularity of Music in the Civil War* (Chapel Hill: University of North Carolina, 2012), 74.

5. The lyrics of "The Homespun Dress" are reprinted in McWhirter, *Battle Hymns*, 83.

6. McWhirter, *Battle Hymns*, 90, 105–8; William O. Stoddard, *Inside the White House in War Times* (New York: C. L. Webster and Company, 1880), 18–19.

7. J. L. Geddes, "The Bonnie Flag with the Stripes and Stars" (Saint Louis, MO: Balmer and Weber, 1863).

8. McWhirter, *Battle Hymns*, 109; Jessica Ann Dauterive, "'Bonnie Blue Flag': The Most Dangerous Song of the Civil War," New Orleans Historical, https://neworleanshistorical.org/items/show/806, accessed June 1, 2019.

9. McWhirter, *Battle Hymns*, 76–77.

CHAPTER 36. TEXTBOX — *THE BONNIE BLUE FLAG*

1. Harry Macarthy, "The Bonnie Blue Flag" (New Orleans, LA: A. E. Blackmar and Brother, 1861).

CHAPTER 37. THE GREAT LOCOMOTIVE CHASE

1. Russell S. Bonds, *Stealing the General: The Great Locomotive Chase and the First Medal of Honor* (Yardley, PA: Westholme Publishing, 2007). The Great Locomotive Chase is the subject of two movies: Buster Keaton's silent comedy *The General* and Walt Disney's *The Great Locomotive Chase*, starring Fess Parker. The *General* is on exhibit at the Southern Museum of Civil War and Locomotive History (https://www.southernmuseum.org/) in Kennesaw, while the *Texas* is exhibited at the Atlanta History Center (https://www.atlantahistorycenter.com/explore/exhibitions/texas-locomotive, accessed October 12, 2019). Freelance writer Rich Grant traced the Great Locomotive Chase in 2017. See Grant, "Following the Great Locomotive Chase: A 120-Mile Journey Tracing the Civil War's Greatest Adventure," *HuffPost*, May 11, 2017, https://www.huffpost.com/entry/following-the-great-locomotive-chase_b_591378e2e4b0d928baa249d7/. Several raiders published recollections of their adventures, most notably William Pittenger. See Pittenger, *Daring and Suffering: A History of the Great Railroad Adventure* (Philadelphia: J. W. Daughaday Publishers, 1863).

2. John E. Clark, *Railroads in the Civil War: The Impact of Management on Victory and Defeat* (Baton Rouge: Louisiana State University Press, 2004), 15.

3. Christopher R. Gabel, *Railroad Generalship: Foundations of Civil War Strategy* (Fort Leavenworth, KS: U.S. Army Command and General Staff College, 1997), 18.

CHAPTER 38. A SCIENTIFIC FOUNDATION FOR MEDICAL CARE

1. There were two major amputation techniques: the flap method and the circular method. Of the two, "the flap method was a more elegant procedure; it created a flap of skin to close the raw stump, which allowed quicker healing but took longer to perform." Surgeons preferred the circular method, which cut straight through the limb and the left the amputation site open, because it was faster and easier to perform in poorly lit regimental field hospitals. See Alfred J. Bollet, *Civil War Medicine, Challenges and Triumphs* (Tucson: Galen Press, Ltd. 2002), 149–52.

2. George A. Otis and D. L. Huntington, *The Medical and Surgical History of the War of the Rebellion* (Washington, DC: Government Printing Office, 1883), 6:595–97. See also Augustine K. Russell, Service Record [Electronic Document], Compiled Service Records of Volunteer Union Soldiers Who Served in Organizations from the State of Massachusetts; Carded Records Showing Military Service of Soldiers Who Fought in Volunteer Organizations during the American Civil War, 1890–1912; Records of the Adjutant General's Office, 1762–1984, Record Group 94; National Archives Building, Washington, DC.

3. Ira M. Rutkow, "The *Medical and Surgical History of the War of the Rebellion, 1861–1865*," *Archives of Surgery* 133 (July 1998): 783.

4. Shauna Devine, "'To Make Something Out of the Dying in This War': The Civil War and the Rise of American Medical Science," *Journal of the Civil War Era* 6 (June 2016): 152–53; Otis and Huntington, *Medical and Surgical History of the War of the Rebellion*, 6:899–902.

5. Lance J. Herdegen, *The Iron Brigade in Civil War and* Memory (El Dorado Hills, CA: Savas Beatie LLC, 2012), 23–30; George Otis, *The Second Wisconsin Infantry, with Letters and Recollections by Other Members of the Regiment*, ed. Alan D. Goff (Dayton, OH: Press of Morningside Bookshop, 1984), 33–34; Otis and Huntington, *Medical and Surgical History of the War of the Rebellion*, Appendix to Part 1, 1:2–3; Ira M. Rutkow, *Bleeding Blue and Gray: Civil War Surgery and the Evolution of American Medicine* (New York: Random House, 2005), 18–28, quote is from 21–22.

6. Shauna Devine, *Learning from the Wounded: The Civil War and the Rise of American Medical Science* (Chapel Hill: University of North Carolina Press, 2014), 14.

7. Shauna Devine, "'Examined at the University of Pennsylvania': Dr. Fulton, His Professional Milieu, and Military Medicine, 1862–1864," in *Civil War Medicine: A Surgeon's Diary*, ed. Robert D. Hicks (Bloomington: Indiana University Press, 2019),

271–72; Guy R. Hasewaga, "'We Got Up and Began to Pack Our Medicines': What Dr. Fulton Prescribed," *Civil War Medicine*, 291.

8. Surgeon General's Office, Circular No. 2, May 21, 1862, http://resource.nlm.nih .gov/101534229, accessed June 9, 2019; Devine, *Learning from the Wounded*, 29–38.

9. Devine, *Learning from the Wounded*, 27–28; Devine, "'To Make Something Out of the Dying in This War,'"150.

10. Otis and Huntington, *Medical and Surgical History of the War of the Rebellion, Part III, Volume II*, 899–902.

CHAPTER 39. "A CURIOUS MARINE MONSTER"

1. David Hunter Strother, *A Virginia Yankee in the Civil War: The Diaries of David Hunter Strother*, ed. Cecil D. Eby Jr. (Chapel Hill: University of North Carolina Press, 1961), 147. See also Katherine Bentley Jeffrey, ed., *Two Civil Wars: The Curious Shared Journal of a Baton Rouge Schoolgirl and a Union Sailor on the USS Essex* (Baton Rouge: Louisiana State University Press, 2016).

2. Brendan Wolfe, "Anaconda Plan," *Encyclopedia Virginia*, Virginia Foundation for the Humanities, May 9, 2011, https://www.encyclopediavirginia.org/anaconda_plan.

3. See Spencer C. Tucker, *Blue and Gray Navies: The Civil War Afloat* (Annapolis, MD: Naval Institute Press, 2006); Spencer C. Tucker, Paul G. Pierpaoli, and William E. Whyte, eds., *The Civil War Naval Encyclopedia*, 2 vols. (Santa Barbara, CA: ABC-CLIO, 2010).

4. William E. Whyte III, "Cairo-class River Ironclads," in *The Civil War Naval Encyclopedia*, 93–94.

5. Spencer C. Tucker, *Unconditional Surrender: The Capture of Forts Henry and Donelson* (Abilene, TX: McWhiney Foundation Press, 2001); B. Franklin Cooling, *Forts Henry and Donelson: The Key to the Confederate Heartland* (Knoxville: University of Tennessee Press, 1987).

CHAPTER 40. THE SILK DRESS BALLOON

1. J. H. Easterby, "Captain Langdon Cheves, Jr., and the Confederate Silk Dress Balloon," *South Carolina Historical and Genealogical Magazine* 45 (January 1944): 1–11; Thomas Paone, "The Most Fashionable Balloon of the Civil War," Smithsonian National Air and Space Museum, November 3, 2013, https://airandspace.si.edu /stories/editorial/most-fashionable-balloon-civil-war/.

2. Eugene B. Block, *Above the Civil War: The Story of Thaddeus Lowe, Balloonist, Inventor, Railway Builder* (Berkeley, CA: Howell-North Books, 1966), 17–18. Franklin as quoted in Block.

3. As quoted in F. Stansbury Haydon, *Aeronautics in the Union and Confederate Armies, with a Survey of Military Aeronautics Prior to 1861* (Baltimore, MD: Johns Hopkins University Press, 1941), 1:167.

4. As quoted in Frank Moore, ed., *The Rebellion Record: A Diary of American Events* (New York: G. P. Putnam, 1861), 1:108.

5. Block, *Above the Civil War*, 62, 68–76, 93–94. Heintzelman as quoted in Block, *Above the Civil War*, 103.

PART IX. EMANCIPATION

1. David W. Blight, *A Slave No More: Two Men Who Escaped to Freedom, Including Their Own Narratives of Emancipation* (Orlando, FL: Harcourt, 2007), 132, 139–40.

CHAPTER 41. FREEDOM'S FORT

1. Henry Louis Gates Jr., "The Black Roots of Memorial Day," *The Root*, May 26, 2014, https://www.theroot.com/the-black-roots-of-memorial-day-1790875788/; Eric Foner, *The Fiery Trial: Abraham Lincoln and Slavery* (New York: W. W. Norton, 2010), 169; "History," *Fort Monroe: Where Freedom Lives*, https://fortmonroe.org/about/fort-monroe/history/, accessed June 30, 2019; Christopher Beagan, "Freedom's Fortress," *Fort Monroe National Monument*, National Park Service, https://www.nps.gov/articles/featured_stories_fomr.htm, accessed June 30, 2019. See also Cassandra L. Newby-Alexander, *An African American History of the Civil War in Hampton Roads* (Charleston, SC: History Press, 2010).

2. James Oakes, *Freedom National: The Destruction of Slavery in the United States, 1861–1865* (New York: W. W. Norton, 2013), 95. See also David W. Blight, *A Slave No More: Two Men Who Escaped to Freedom, Including Their Own Narratives of Emancipation* (Orlando, FL: Harcourt, 2007), 132. Writing about the Civil War escapes of Wallace Turnage and John Washington, enslaved men from Alabama and Virginia respectively, Blight writes, "Without the Union armies and navies neither man would have achieved freedom when he did. But they never would have gained their freedom without their own courageous initiative, either."

3. Amy Murrell Taylor, *Embattled Freedom: Journeys through the Civil War's Refugee Camps* (Chapel Hill: University of North Carolina Press, 2018), 3, 5; Oakes, *Freedom National*, 88–89; Blight, *A Slave No More*, 133.

4. Oakes, *Freedom National*, 95–97; Blight, *A Slave No More*, 133. Butler as quoted in Oakes and Blight.

5. Oakes, *Freedom National*, 98.

6. Murrell Taylor, *Embattled Freedom*, 3, 5; Oakes, *Freedom National*, 89; Blight, *A Slave No More*, 133.

CHAPTER 42. AN ABOLITION WAR

1. Harold Holzer, Edna Medford, and Frank J. Williams, *The Emancipation Proclamation: Three Views, Social, Political, Iconographic* (Baton Rouge: Louisiana State University Press, 2006), 116; Mark Neeley and Harold Holzer, *The Union Image: Popular Prints of the Civil War North* (Chapel Hill: University of North Carolina Press, 2000), 231.

2. Michael Vorenberg, *The Emancipation Proclamation: A Brief History with Documents* (Boston: Bedford/St. Martin's, 2010), 14–15; Manisha Sinha, *The Slave's Cause: A History of Abolition* (New Haven, CT: Yale University Press, 2016), 584; David W. Blight, *A Slave No More: Two Men Who Escaped to Freedom, Including Their Own Narratives of Emancipation* (Orlando, FL: Harcourt, 2007), 138–41.

3. Henry M. Turner, "Reminiscences of the Proclamation of Emancipation," *African Methodist Episcopal Church Review* 29 (January 1913): 213–14. See also Andre E. Johnson, "Who Was Bishop Henry McNeal Turner?" *Rhetoric, Race, and Religion*, October 7, 2012, https://www.patheos.com/blogs/rhetoricraceandreligion/2012/10/who-was-bishop-henry-mcneal-turner.html; Andre E. Johnson, "Bishop Turner's #Emancipation and King's Dream: Reflections on the #MarchonWashington," *Rhetoric, Race, and Religion*, August 28, 2013, https://www.patheos.com/blogs/rhetoricraceandreligion/2013/08/bishop-turners-emancipation-and-kings-dream-reflections-on-the-marchonwashington.html/.

4. Vorenberg, *The Emancipation Proclamation*, 18.

CHAPTER 43. TROUBLED REFUGE

1. Jacobs as quoted in David W. Blight, Gregory P. Downs, and Jim Downs, "Introduction," in *Beyond Freedom: Disrupting the History of Emancipation*, ed. David W. Blight and Jim Downs (Athens: University of Georgia Press, 2017), 1.

2. Chandra Manning, *Troubled Refuge: Struggling for Freedom in the Civil War* (New York: Alfred A. Knopf, 2016), 99.

3. Manning, *Troubled Refuge*, 79, 92.

4. Manning, *Troubled Refuge*, 106.

5. Glymph, "Black Women and Children," 125.

6. Blight, Downs, and Downs, "Introduction," 4; for the phrase "incubators of revolutionary revival," see Abigail Cooper, "'Lord, Until I Reach My Home': Inside the Refugee Camps of the American Civil War" (PhD diss., University of Pennsylvania, 2015), 3. Thavolia Glymph describes refugee camps as sites of "unspeakable violence" where "the making of freedom unfolded . . . under warlike conditions." See Glymph, "Black Women and Children in the Civil War," in *Beyond Freedom*, 121–35. Quotes are from 123 and 127.

CHAPTER 44. A NEW BIRTH OF FREEDOM

1. "The Thirteenth Amendment," in *Smithsonian Civil War: Inside the National Collection*, ed. Neil Kagan and Stephen G. Hyslop (Washington, DC: Smithsonian Books, 2013), 292.

2. Julian as quoted in "The Thirteenth Amendment," 292.

3. See, for example, Richard Rothstein, *The Color of Law: A Forgotten History of How Our Government Segregated America* (New York: Liveright Publishing, 2017).

CHAPTER 44. TEXTBOX—THIRTEENTH AMENDMENT

1. "Abolition of Slavery," Interactive Constitution, National Constitution Center, https://constitutioncenter.org/interactive-constitution/amendment/amendment-xiii, accessed October 1, 2019.

CHAPTER 45. HELP ME FIND MY PEOPLE

1. Brenda E. Stevenson, "'Us never had no big funerals or weddin's on de place': Ritualizing Black Marriage in the Wake of Freedom," in *Beyond Freedom: Disrupting the History of Emancipation*, ed. David W. Blight and Jim Downs (Athens: University of Georgia Press, 2017), 55.

2. Franks as quoted in Stevenson, "'Us never had no big funerals,'" 40. Veney as quoted in Heather Andrea Williams, *Help Me to Find My People: The African*

American Search for Family Lost in Slavery (Chapel Hill: University of North Carolina Press, 2012), 64–65.

3. Amy Murrell Taylor, *Embattled Freedom: Journeys through the Civil War's Slave Refugee Camps* (Chapel Hill: University of North Carolina Press, 2018), 35.

4. Taylor, *Embattled Freedom*, 245–46; Williams, *Help Me to Find My People*, 185.

5. All as quoted in Abigail Cooper, "'Away I Goin' to Find My Mamma': Self-Emancipation, Migration, and Kinship in Refugee Camps in the Civil War Era," *Journal of African American History* 102 (September 2017): 454.

6. Cooper, "'Away I Goin' to Find My Mamma,'" 444, 453–54, 463.

7. Rose Herera's story is detail in Adam Rothman, *Beyond Freedom's Reach: A Kidnapping in the Twilight of Slavery* (Cambridge, MA: Harvard University Press, 2015).

8. Rothman, *Beyond Freedom's Reach*, 119. More than nine hundred of these "Information Wanted" ads have been digitized, transcribed, and made available online through the website Last Seen: Finding Family after Slavery, a joint project of the department of history at Villanova University and Mother Bethel AME Church, available online at http://informationwanted.org/, accessed October 25, 2019.

PART X. LEGACY

1. Ta-Nehisi Coates, "The Case for Reparations," *Atlantic Monthly* (June 2014).

CHAPTER 46. "I WON'T BE RECONSTRUCTED"

1. Historians differ on Shelby's location at the time of Lee's surrender. Conger Beasley Jr. places him in Arkansas, while Art Leatherwood places him in Texas. See John N. Edwards, *Shelby's Expedition to Mexico: An Unwritten Leaf of the War*, ed. Conger Beasley Jr. (Fayetteville: University of Arkansas Press, 2002), xix; Art Leatherwood, "Shelby Expedition," *Handbook of Texas Online*, http://www .tshaonline.org/handbook/online/articles/qms01, accessed September 18, 2019.

2. Smith and Shelby as quoted in Noah Andre Trudeau, *Out of the Storm: The End of the Civil War, April–June 1865* (Boston: Little, Brown and Company, 1994), 336, 339.

3. Smith as quoted in Trudeau, *Out of the Storm*, 339–40.

4. Carter as quoted in Ron Soodalter, "The Confederados," *America's Civil War* (September 2013): 65.

5. "God Ol' Rebel Soldier," Poetry and Music of the War between the States, https://www.civilwarpoetry.org/confederate/songs/rebel.html/, accessed July 24, 2020. "The Unreconstructed Rebel" as quoted in "General Joseph Orville (Jo) Shelby, Waverly, Mo.," Waymarking.com, https://www.waymarking.com/waymarks/WMKZCQ_General_Joseph_Orville_JO_Shelby_Waverly_Mo, accessed September 18, 2019. See also Joseph Melvin Thompson, "I Won't Be Reconstructed: Good Old Rebels, Civil War Memory, and Popular Song" (MA thesis, Oxford, University of Mississippi, 2013).

CHAPTER 47. MEMORIALIZING THE DEAD

1. David W. Blight, *Race and Reunion: The Civil War in American Memory* (Cambridge, MA: Harvard University Press, 2001), 70; Ethan J. Kytle and Blain Roberts, *Denmark Vesey's Garden: Slavery and Memory in the Cradle of the Confederacy* (New York: New Press, 2018), 52–57.

2. "First Confederate Memorial Day, Petersburg, VA," catalog record, The American Civil War Museum, https://moconfederacy.pastperfectonline.com/photo/5F0B396C-7B3B-4F78-BEA7-970577235890, accessed September 14, 2018.

3. Blight, *Race and Reunion*, 71.

4. Caroline E. Janney, *Remembering the Civil War: Reunion and the Limits of Reconciliation* (Chapel Hill: University of North Carolina Press, 2013), 121, 125.

5. Janney, *Remembering the Civil War Dead*, 44, 46.

6. Caroline E. Janney, *Burying the Dead but Not the Past: Ladies' Memorial Associations and the Lost Cause* (Chapel Hill: University of North Carolina Press, 2008), 198.

CHAPTER 48. RECONCILIATION AND REUNION

1. See, for example, *St. Louis* (Missouri) *Post-Dispatch*, June 30, 1938; *Billings* (Montana) *Gazette*, July 1, 1938; *Iola* (Kansas) *Daily Register and Evening News*, June 28, 1938; *Medford* (Oregon) *Mail Tribune*, July 27, 1938.

2. David W. Blight, *Race and Reunion: The Civil War in American Memory* (Cambridge, MA: Harvard University Press, 2001), 9.

3. Caroline E. Janney, *Remembering the Civil War: Reunion and the Limits of Reconciliation* (Chapel Hill: University of North Carolina Press, 2013), 174–76.

4. Janney, *Remember the Civil War*, 266–69.

5. Rebekah N. Oakes, "Old War, New Deal: Commemorative Landscapes, the National Park Service, and the 7th Anniversary of the War" (MA thesis, West Virginia University, 2015), 68, 77. Roy as quoted in Oakes, "Old War, New Deal," 68.

6. Fergus M. Bordewich, "We Have Found One Another Again as Brothers," *The Imperfect Union*, July 16, 2013, http://www.fergusbordewich.com/blog/?p=113/.

CHAPTER 49. THE BLACK CONFEDERATE STORY

1. Kevin M. Levin, *Searching for Black Confederates: The Civil War's Most Persistent Myth* (Chapel Hill: University of North Carolina Press, 2019), 12–14. See also Kevin Levin, "Searching for Black Confederates," presentation at the National Archives, Washington, DC, September 2019, https://www.youtube.com/watch?time_continue =735&v=Xoe2-PhKK1I&feature=emb_logo/.

2. Levin, *Searching for Black Confederates*, 3–4.

3. Levin, *Searching for Black Confederates*, 148.

4. Andy Hall, "Famous 'Negro Cooks Regiment' Found ¾ in My Own Backyard!" *Dead Confederates*, August 8, 2011, https://deadconfederates.com/2011/08/08 /famous-negro-cooks-regiment-found-in-my-own-backyard/.

5. Levin, *Searching for Black Confederates*, 135–36.

6. Levin, *Searching for Black Confederates*, 140. Two notable exceptions are Harvard scholars Henry Louis Gates and John Stauffer. See Levin, *Searching for Black Confederates*, 171–74.

7. Levin, *Searching for Black Confederates*, 176, 184.

CHAPTER 50. STONE MOUNTAIN

1. James W. Loewen, *Lies Across America: What Our Historic Sites Get Wrong* (New York: The New Press, 1999), 262; Debra McKinney, "Stone Mountain: A Monumental Dilemma," *Intelligence Report*, Spring 2018, https://www.splcenter.org /fighting-hate/intelligence-report/2018/stone-mountain-monumental-dilemma?gclid =CjwKCAjw34n5BRA9EiwA2u9k3-DzM8N-Xz8wUM2MeqIxsNExs0_4phXQNH9 _AZLQH1ZO3u7WSB8i0BoCwhIQAvD_BwE/.

2. Richard Fausset, "Stone Mountain: The Largest Confederate Monument Problem in the World," *New York Times*, October 18, 2018.

AFTERWORD

1. Annette Gordon-Reed, "Foreword," in *Racism in America: A Reader* (Cambridge, MA: Harvard University Press, 2020), xvii–xviii; Kevin Levin, "Confederate Monuments Are Coming Down with No End in Sight," *Civil War Memory*, June 21, 2020, http://cwmemory.com/2020/06/21/confederate-monuments-are-coming-down-with-no-end-in-sight/.

2. Robin Pogrebin and Julia Jacobs, "Floyd Case Forces Arts Groups to Enter the Fray," *New York Times*, June 7, 2020, https://www.nytimes.com/2020/06/07/arts/museums-theaters-protests.html/.

3. Gordon-Reed, "Foreword," xvii.

Selected Bibliography

GENERAL WORKS

Blair, William. *Virginia's Private War: Feeding Body and Soul in the Confederacy, 1861–1865*. New York: Oxford University Press, 1998.

Blight, David W. "Decoration Days: The Origins of Memorial Day in North and South." In *The Memory of the Civil War in American Culture*, edited by Alice Fahs and Joan Waugh. Chapel Hill: University of North Carolina Press, 2004.

Blight, David W., and Jim Downs, eds. *Beyond Freedom: Disrupting the History of Emancipation*. Athens: University of Georgia Press, 2017.

Cashin, Joan E. *War Matters: Material Culture in the Civil War Era*. Chapel Hill: University of North Carolina Press, 2018.

———, eds. *The War Was You and Me: Civilians in the American Civil War*. Princeton, NJ: Princeton University Press, 2002.

Clinton, Catherine, and Nina Silber, eds. *Divided Houses: Gender and the Civil War*. New York: Oxford University Press, 1992.

Faust, Drew Gilpin. *This Republic of Suffering: Death and the American Civil War*. New York: Alfred A. Knopf, 2008.

Forbes, Ella. *African American Women during the Civil War*. New York: Garland Publishing, 1998.

Gallman, J. Matthew, ed. *The Civil War Chronicle: The Only Day-by-Day Portrait of America's Tragic Conflict as Told by Soldiers, Journalists, Politicians, Farmers, Nurses, Slaves, and Other Eyewitnesses.* New York: Gramercy Books, 2000.

Glymph, Thavolia. *Out of the House of Bondage: The Transformation of the Plantation Household.* New York: Cambridge University Press, 2008.

Harris, Leslie M. *In the Shadow of Slavery: African Americans in New York City, 1626–1863.* Chicago: University of Chicago Press, 2003.

Heidler, David S., and Jeanne T. Heidler, eds. *Encyclopedia of the American Civil War: A Political, Social, and Military History.* Santa Barbara, CA: ABC-CLIO, 2000.

Janney, Caroline E. *Remembering the Civil War: Reunion and the Limits of Reconciliation.* Chapel Hill: University of North Carolina Press, 2013.

Kagan, Neil, and Stephen G. Hyslop. *Smithsonian Civil War: Inside the National Collection.* Washington, DC: Smithsonian Books, 2013.

Kendi, Ibram X. *Stamped from the Beginning: The Definitive History of Racist Ideas in America.* New York: Bold Type Books, 2016.

Manning, Chandra. *Troubled Refuge: Struggling for Freedom in the Civil War.* New York: Alfred A. Knopf, 2016.

———. *What This Cruel War Was Over: Soldiers, Slavery, and the Civil War.* New York: Alfred A. Knopf, 2007.

McCurry, Stephanie. *Confederate Reckoning: Power and Politics in the Civil War South.* Cambridge, MA: Harvard University Press, 2010.

———. *Women's War: Fighting and Surviving the American Civil War.* Cambridge, MA: The Belknap Press of Harvard University Press, 2019.

McPherson, James M. *Battle Cry of Freedom: The Civil War Era.* New York: Oxford University Press, 1988.

Mendez, James G. *A Great Sacrifice: Northern Black Soldiers, Their Families, and the Experience of the Civil War.* New York: Fordham University Press, 2019.

Sinha, Manisha. *The Slave's Cause: A History of Abolition.* New Haven, CT: Yale University Press, 2016.

Stewart, James Brewer. *Holy Warriors: The Abolitionists and American Slavery.* New York: Hill and Wang, 1997.

Ural, Susannah J. *Don't Hurry Me Down to Hades: The Civil War in the Words of Those Who Lived It*. New York: Osprey Publishing, 2013.

Wallenstein, Peter, and Bertram Wyatt-Brown. *Virginia's Civil War*. Charlottesville: University of Virginia Press, 2005.

PART I: CAUSES

Baptist, Edward E. *The Half Has Never Benn Told: Slavery and the Making of American Capitalism*. New York: Basic Books, 2014.

Berry, Daina Ramey. *The Price for Their Pound of Flesh: The Value of the Enslaved, from Womb to Grave, in the Building of a Nation*. Boston: Beacon Press, 2017.

Carton, Evan. *Patriotic Treason: John Brown and the Soul of America*. New York: Free Press, 2006.

Etcheson, Nicole. *Bleeding Kansas: Contested Liberty in the Civil War Era*. Lawrence: University Press of Kansas, 2004.

Freeman, Joanne B. *The Field of Blood: Violence in Congress and the Road to Civil War*. New York: Farrar, Straus and Giroux, 2018.

Hinks, Peter P. *To Awaken My Afflicted Brethren: David Walker and the Problem of Antebellum Slave Resistance*. University Park: Pennsylvania State University Press, 1997.

Holcomb, Julie L. *Moral Commerce: Quakers and the Transatlantic Boycott of the Slave Labor Economy*. Ithaca, NY: Cornell University Press, 2016.

Jackson, Kellie Carter. *Force and Freedom: Black Abolitionists and the Politics of Violence*. Philadelphia: University of Pennsylvania Press, 2019.

Jewett, Clayton E., and John O. Allen. *Slavery in the South: A State-by-State History*. Westport, CT: Greenwood Press, 2004.

Johnson, Walter. *Soul by Soul: Life Inside the Antebellum Slave Market*. Cambridge, MA: Harvard University Press, 1999.

Jordan, Ryan. *Slavery and the Meetinghouse: The Quakers and the Abolitionist Dilemma, 1820–1865*. Bloomington: Indiana University Press, 2007.

Maizlish, Stephen E. *A Strife of Tongues: The Compromise of 1850 and the Ideological Foundations of the American Civil War*. Charlottesville: University of Virginia Press, 2018.

Mayer, Henry. *All on Fire: William Lloyd Garrison and the Abolition of Slavery*. New York: St. Martin's Griffin, 1998.

Newman, Richard S. *The Transformation of American Abolitionism: Fighting Slavery in the Early Republic*. Chapel Hill: University of North Carolina Press, 2002.

Quarles, Benjamin. *Black Abolitionists*. New York: Oxford University Press, 1969.

Schermerhorn, Calvin. *The Business of Slavery and the Rise of American Capitalism, 1815–1860*. New Haven, CT: Yale University Press, 2015.

Tomek, Beverly C. *Colonization and Its Discontents: Emancipation, Emigration, and Antislavery in Antebellum Pennsylvania*. New York: New York University Press, 2011.

PART II: POLITICS

Blackett, R. J. M. *The Captive's Quest for Freedom: Fugitive Slaves, the 1850 Fugitive Slave Law, and the Politics of Slavery*. New York: Cambridge University Press, 2018.

Edgerton, Douglas R. *Year of Meteors: Stephen Douglas, Abraham Lincoln, and the Election That Brought on the Civil War*. New York: Bloomsbury Press, 2010.

Fladeland, Betty. *Men and Brothers: Anglo-American Antislavery Cooperation*. Urbana: University of Illinois Press, 1972.

Foner, Eric. *The Fiery Trial: Abraham Lincoln and American Slavery*. New York: W. W. Norton, 2010.

Harris, William C. *Lincoln and the Border States: Preserving the Union*. Lawrence: University of Kansas Press, 2011.

Harrold, Stanley. *Border War: Fighting over Slavery before the Civil War*. Chapel Hill: University of North Carolina Press, 2010.

Holcomb, Julie L., ed. *Southern Sons, Northern Soldiers: The Civil War Letters of the Remley Brothers, 22nd Iowa Infantry*. DeKalb: Northern Illinois University Press, 2004.

Holt, Michael F. *The Election of 1860: A Campaign Fraught with Consequences*. Lawrence: University Press of Kansas, 2017.

Horton, James Oliver, and Lois E. Oliver. *Black Bostonians: Family Life and Community Struggle in the Antebellum North*. Revised edition. New York: Homes and Meier, 1999.

Kantowitz, Stephen. *More Than Freedom: Fighting for Black Citizenship in a White Republic, 1829–1889.* New York: Penguin Books, 2012.

Murphy, Angela F. *The Jerry Rescue: The Fugitive Slave Law, Northern Rights, and the American Sectional Crisis.* New York: Oxford University Press, 2015.

Warde, Mary Jane. *When the Wolf Came: The Civil War and the Indian Territory.* Fayetteville: University of Arkansas Press, 2013.

PART III: BATTLEFIELD

Alberts, Don E. *The Battle of Glorieta: Union Victory in the West.* College Station: Texas A & M University Press, 1998.

Bowden, J. J. *The Exodus of Federal Forces from Texas, 1861.* Austin, TX: Eakin Press, 1986.

Brown, Thomas J. *Dorothea Dix: New England Reformer.* Cambridge, MA: Harvard University Press, 1998.

Edrington, Thomas S., and John Taylor. *The Battle of Glorieta Pass: A Gettysburg in the West, March 26–28, 1862.* Albuquerque: University of New Mexico Press, 1998.

Gollaher, David. *Voice for the Mad: The Life of Dorothea Dix.* New York: Free Press, 1995.

Hess, Earl J. *Pickett's Charge: The Last Attack at Gettysburg.* Chapel Hill: University of North Carolina Press, 2001.

Holcomb, Julie L. "From Enslaved to Liberators: African Americans and the Civil War." In *Civil War: People and Perspectives,* edited by Lisa Tendrich Frank and Peter C. Mancall, 95–112. Santa Barbara, CA: ABC-CLIO, 2009.

Humphreys, Margaret. *Marrow of Tragedy: The Health Crisis of the American Civil War.* Baltimore, MD: Johns Hopkins University Press, 2013.

Jacquette, Henrietta Stratton. *Letters of a Civil War Nurse: Cornelia Hancock, 1863–1865.* Lincoln: University of Nebraska Press, 1998.

Kelman, Arie. *A Misplaced Massacre: Struggling Over the Memory of Sand Creek.* Cambridge, MA: Harvard University Press, 2013.

Levin, Kevin M. *Remembering the Battle of the Crater: War as Murder.* Lexington: University Press of Kentucky, 2012.

Nelson, Megan Kate. *The Three-Cornered War: The Union, the Confederacy, and Native Peoples in the Fight for the West*. New York: Scribner, 2020.

Pfanz, Harry W. *Gettysburg: The First Day*. Chapel Hill: University of North Carolina Press, 2001.

Pryor, Elizabeth Brown. *Clara Barton: Professional Angel*. Philadelphia: University of Pennsylvania Press, 1987.

Scott, Donald, Sr. *Camp William Penn*. Images of America Series. Charleston, SC: Arcadia Publishing, 2008.

———. *Camp William Penn, 1863–1865*. Atglen, PA: Schiffer Military History, 2012.

Scott, Robert. *Glory, Glory, Glorieta: The Gettysburg of the West*. Boulder: Johnson Books, 1992.

Smith, David Paul. *Frontier Defense in the Civil War: Texas' Rangers and Rebels*. College Station: Texas A & M University Press, 1992.

Toler, Pamela D. *Heroines of Mercy Street: The Real Nurses of the Civil War*. New York: Little, Brown, and Company, 2016.

Trudeau, Noah Andre. *Like Men of War: Black Troops in the Civil War, 1862–1865*. Boston: Little, Brown, and Company, 1998.

Wert, Jeffry D. *Gettysburg, Day Three*. New York: Simon and Schuster, 2001.

Whitlock, Flint. *Distant Bugles, Distant Drums: The Union Response to the Confederate Invasion of New Mexico*. Boulder: University Press of Colorado, 2006.

PART IV: OFFICERS

Adelke, Tunde. *Without Regard to Race: The Other Martin Robison Delany*. Jackson: University Press of Mississippi, 2009.

Capers, Gerald M. *Occupied City: New Orleans Under the Federals, 1862–1865*. Louisville: University Press of Kentucky, 1965.

Carmichael, Peter S. *Audacity Personified: The Generalship of Robert E. Lee*. Baton Rouge: Louisiana State University Press, 2004.

Davis, William C. *Crucible of Command: Ulysses S. Grant and Robert E. Lee, the War They Fought, the Peace They Forged*. Boston, MA: Da Capo Press, 2014.

Freeman, Douglas Southall. *R.E. Lee*. New York: Charles Scribner, 1934–1937.

Hearn, Chester G. *When the Devil Came Down to Dixie: Ben Butler in New Orleans.* Baton Rouge: Louisiana State University Press, 1997.

Hettle, Wallace. *Inventing Stonewall Jackson: A Civil War Hero in History and Memory.* Baton Rouge: Louisiana State University Press, 2011.

Levine, Robert S., ed. *Martin R. Delany: A Documentary Reader.* Chapel Hill: University of North Carolina Press, 2003.

———. *Martin Delany, Frederick Douglass, and the Politics of Representative Identity.* Chapel Hill: University of North Carolina Press, 1997.

Pryor, Elizabeth Brown. *Reading the Man: A Portrait of Robert E. Lee through His Private Letters.* New York: Viking Press, 2007.

Robertson, James I., Jr. *Stonewall Jackson: The Man, the Soldier, the Legend.* New York: Macmillan, 1997.

Simpson, Brooks D. *Let Us Have Peace: Ulysses S. Grant and the Politics of War and Reconstruction, 1861–1868.* Chapel Hill: University of North Carolina Press, 1991.

———. *Ulysses S. Grant: Triumph over Adversity, 1822–1865.* Boston, MA: Houghton Mifflin, 2000.

Sterling, Dorothy. *The Making of an Afro-American: Martin Robison Delany, 1812–1885.* Garden City, NY: Doubleday, 1971.

Waugh, Joan. "Ulysses S. Grant, Historian." In *The Memory of the Civil War in American Culture,* edited by Alice Fahs and Joan Waugh. Chapel Hill: University of North Carolina Press, 2004.

———. *U.S. Grant: American Hero, American Myth.* Chapel Hill: University of North Carolina Press, 2009.

White, Ronald C. *American Ulysses: A Life of Ulysses S. Grant.* New York: Random House, 2017.

PART V: SOLDIERS

Baggett, James Alex. *Homegrown Yankees: Tennessee's Union Cavalry in the Civil War.* Baton Rouge: Louisiana State University Press, 2009.

Bernstein, Iver. *The New York City Draft Riots: Their Significance for American Society and Politics in the Age of the Civil War.* New York: Oxford University Press, 1990.

Bruce, Susannah Ural. *The Harp and the Eagle: Irish-American Volunteers and the Union Army, 1861–1865*. New York: New York University Press, 2006.

Clemmer, Gregg S. *Valor in Gray: The Recipients of the Confederate Medal of Honor*. Staunton, VA: Herathside Publishing Company, 1996.

Cloyd, Benjamin G. *Haunted by Atrocity: Civil War Prisons in American Memory*. Baton Rouge: Louisiana State University Press, 2010.

Herdegen, Lance J. *The Iron Brigade in Civil War and Memory: The Black Hats from Bull Run to Appomattox and Thereafter*. El Dorado Hills, CA: Savas Beatie, 2012.

———. *The Men Stood Like Iron: How the Iron Brigade Won Its Name*. Bloomington: Indiana State University Press, 1997.

Klement, Frank L. *Wisconsin in the Civil War: The Home Front and the Battle Front, 1861–1865*. Madison: The State Historical Society of Wisconsin, 1997.

Longacre, Edward. *Lincoln's Cavalrymen: A History of the Mounted Forces of the Army of the Potomac, 1861–1865*. Mechanicsburg, PA: Stackpole Books, 2000.

Pickenpaugh, Roger. *Captives in Blue: The Civil War Prisons of the Confederacy*. Tuscaloosa: University of Alabama Press, 2013.

———. *Captives in Gray: The Civil War Prisons of the Union*. Tuscaloosa: University of Alabama Press, 2009.

Schecter, Barnet. *The Devil's Own Work: The Civil War Draft Riots and the Fight to Reconstruct America*. New York: Walker and Company, 2005.

Ural, Susannah J. *Hood's Texas Brigade: The Soldiers and Families of the Confederacy's Most Celebrated Unit*. Baton Rouge: Louisiana State University Press, 2017.

PART VI: HOME FRONT

Attie, Jeanie. *Patriotic Toil: Northern Women and the American Civil War*. Ithaca, NY: Cornell University Press, 1998.

Baum, Dale. "Slaves Taken to Texas for Safekeeping during the Civil War." In *The Fate of Texas: The Civil War and the Lone Star State*, edited by Charles D. Grear, 83–103. Fayetteville: University of Arkansas Press, 2008.

Cimbala, Paul A., and Randall M. Miller. *The Northern Home Front during the Civil War*. Santa Barbara, CA: Praeger, 2017.

Davis, Michael A. "The Legend of Bill Dark: Guerrilla Warfare, Oral History, and the Unmaking of an Arkansas Bushwhacker." *Arkansas Historical Quarterly* 58 (Winter 1999): 414–29.

Dunkelman, Mark H. *Gettysburg's Unknown Soldier: The Life, Death, and Celebrity of Amos Humiston.* Westport, CT: Praeger, 1999.

Faust, Drew Gilpin. *Mothers of Invention: Women of the Slaveholding South in the American Civil War.* New York: Vintage Books, 1997.

Frank, Lisa Tendrich. *The Civilian War: Confederate Women and Union Soldiers During Sherman's March.* Baton Rouge: Louisiana State University Press, 2015.

Giesberg, Judith. *Army at Home: Women and the Civil War on the Northern Homefront.* Chapel Hill: University of North Carolina Press, 2009.

Giesberg, Judith, and Randall M. Miller, eds. *Women and the American Civil War: North-South Counterpoints.* Kent, OH: Kent State University Press, 2018.

Holcomb, Julie L. "African Americans in the Civil War." In *Civil War: People and Perspectives,* edited by Lisa Tendrich Frank. Santa Barbara, CA: ABC-CLIO, 2009.

Howard, Rebecca A. "No Country for Old Men: Patriarchs, Slaves, and Guerrilla War in Northwest Arkansas." *Arkansas Historical Society* 75 (Winter 2016): 336–54.

Liles, Deborah M., and Angela Boswell, eds. *Women in Civil War Texas: Diversity and Dissidence in the Trans-Mississippi.* Denton: University of North Texas Press, 2016.

McCaslin, Richard B., and Jesus F. de la Teja. *A Texas Reign of Terror: Anti-Unionist Violence in North Texas.* Norman: University of Oklahoma Press, 2016.

McDaniel, W. Caleb. "Involuntary Removals: 'Refugeed Slaves' in Confederate Texas." In *Lone Star Unionism, Dissent, and Resistance: Other Sides of Civil War Texas,* edited by Jesus F. de la Teja. Norman: University of Oklahoma Press, 2016.

McKnight, Brian Dallas. *The Guerilla Hunters: Irregular Conflicts during the Civil War.* Baton Rouge: Louisiana State University Press, 2017.

Paradis, James M. *African Americans and the Gettysburg Campaign.* Lanham, MD: Scarecrow Press, 2005.

Reynolds, Donald E. *Texas Terror: The Slave Insurrection Panic of 1860 and the Secession of the Lower South.* Baton Rouge: Louisiana State University Press, 2007.

Silber, Nina. *Daughters of the Union: Northern Women Fight the Civil War.* Cambridge, MA: Harvard University Press, 2005.

Stowe, Steven M. *Keep the Days: Reading the Civil War Diaries of Southern Women.* Chapel Hill: University of North Carolina Press, 2018.

Sutherland, Daniel E. "Guerrillas: The Real War in Arkansas." *Arkansas Historical Quarterly* 52 (Autumn 1993): 257–85.

———. *A Savage Conflict: The Decisive Role of Guerillas in the American Civil War.* Chapel Hill: University of North Carolina Press, 2009.

Whites, LeeAnn, and Alecia P. Long, eds. *Occupied Women: Gender, Military Occupation, and the American Civil War.* Baton Rouge: Louisiana State University Press, 2009.

PART VII: SYMBOLS

Bonner, Robert E. *Colors and Blood: Flag Passions of the Confederate South.* Princeton, NJ: Princeton University Press, 2004.

Boyd, Steven R. *Patriotic Envelopes of the Civil War: The Iconography of Union and Confederate Covers.* Baton Rouge: Louisiana University State Press, 2010.

Coski, John M. *The Confederate Battle Flag: America's Most Embattled Emblem.* Cambridge, MA: Belknap Press of Harvard University Press, 2005.

Finley, Cheryl. *Committed to Memory: The Art of the Slave Ship Icon.* Princeton, NJ: Princeton University Press, 2018.

Guyatt, Mary. "The Wedgwood Slave Medallion: Values in Eighteenth-Century Design." *Journal of Design History* 13 (2000): 96–97.

Hamilton, Cynthia S. "Hercules Subdued: The Visual Rhetoric of the Kneeling Slave." *Slavery and Abolition* 34 (December 2013): 631–52.

Lapsansky, Phillip. "Graphic Discord: Abolitionist and Antiabolitionist Images." In *The Abolitionist Sisterhood: Women's Political Culture in Antebellum America,* edited by Jean Fagan Yellin and John C. Van Horne, 201–30. Ithaca, NY: Cornell University Press, 1994.

Maberry, Robert, Jr. *Texas Flags.* College Station: Texas A & M University Press, 2001.

Marshall, Tim. *A Flag Worth Dying For: The Power and Politics of National Symbols*. New York: Scribner, 2016.

McWhirter, Christian. *Battle Hymns: The Power and Popularity of Music in the Civil War*. Chapel Hill: University of North Carolina, 2012.

Parfait, Claire. *The Publishing History of* Uncle Tom's Cabin, *1852–2002*. Burlington, VT: Ashgate, 2007.

Reilly, Bernard F., Jr. "The Art of the Antislavery Movement." In *Courage and Conscience: Black and White Abolitionists in Boston*, edited by Donald M. Jacobs, 47–73. Bloomington: Indiana University Press, 1993.

Reynolds, David S. *Mightier Than the Sword: Uncle Tom's Cabin and the Battle for America*. New York: W. W. Norton, 2011.

Stowe, Harriet Beecher. *Uncle Tom's Cabin; or, Life Among the Lowly*. The Splendid Edition. Edited by David S. Reynolds. New York: Oxford University Press, 2011.

Sumrall, Alan K. *Battle Flags of Texas in the Confederacy*. Austin, TX: Eakin Press, 1995.

Trodd, Zoe. "Am I Still Not a Man and a Brother? Protest Memory in Contemporary Antislavery Visual Culture." *Slavery and Abolition* 34 (June 2013): 338–52.

Wood, Marcus. *Blind Memory: Visual Representations of Slavery in England and America, 1780–1865*. New York: Routledge, 2000.

Yorthers, Brian. *Reading Abolition: The Critical Reception of Harriet Beecher Stowe and Frederick Douglass*. Rochester, NY: Camden House, 2016.

PART VIII: TECHNOLOGY

Block, Eugene B. *Above the Civil War: The Story of Thaddeus Lowe, Balloonist, Inventor, Railway Builder*. Berkeley, CA: Howell-North Books, 1966.

Bollet, Alfred J. *Civil War Medicine, Challenges and Triumphs*. Tucson: Galen Press, Ltd., 2002.

Bonds, Russell S. *Stealing the General: The Great Locomotive Chase and the First Medal of Honor*. Yardley, PA: Westholme Publishing, 2007.

Clark, John E. *Railroads in the Civil War: The Impact of Management on Victory and Defeat*. Baton Rouge: Louisiana State University Press, 2004.

Cooling, B. Franklin. *Forts Henry and Donelson: The Key to the Confederate Heartland*. Knoxville: University of Tennessee Press, 1987.

Crouch, Tom D. *The Eagle Aloft: Two Centuries of the Balloon in America*. Washington, DC: Smithsonian Institution Press, 1983.

Davis, William C. *Duel Between the First Ironclads*. Mechanicsburg, PA: Stackpole Books, 1994.

Devine, Shauna. *Learning from the Wounded: The Civil War and the Rise of American Medical Science*. Chapel Hill: University of North Carolina Press, 2014.

———. "'To Make Something Out of the Dying in This War': The Civil War and the Rise of American Medical Science." *Journal of the Civil War Era* 6 (June 2016).

Dictionary of American Naval Fighting Ships. Washington, DC: U.S. Government Printing Office, Naval Department, 1960.

Evans, Charles Morgan. *War of the Aeronauts: The History of Ballooning in the Civil War*. Mechanicsburg, PA: Stackpole Books, 2002.

Gabel, Christopher R. *Railroad Generalship: Foundations of Civil War Strategy*. Fort Leavenworth, KS: U.S. Army Command and General Staff College, 1997.

Hess, Earl J. *Civil War Logistics: A Study of Military Transportation*. Baton Rouge: Louisiana State University Press, 2017.

Hicks, Robert D., ed. *Civil War Medicine: A Surgeon's Diary*. Bloomington: Indiana University Press, 2019.

Humphreys, Margaret. *Marrow of Tragedy: The Health Crisis of the American Civil War*. Baltimore, MD: Johns Hopkins University Press, 2013.

Meredith, Roy, and Arthur Meredith. *Mr. Lincoln's Military Railroads: A Pictorial History of the United States Civil War Railroads*. New York: W. W. Norton, 1979.

Rhode, Michael G., and James T. H. Connor. "'A Repository for Bottled Monsters and Medical Curiosities': The Evolution of the Army Medical Museum." In *Defining Memory: Local Museums and the Construction of History in America's Changing Communities*. Lanham, MD: AltaMira Press, 2007.

Rutkow, Ira M. *Bleeding Blue and Gray: Civil War Surgery and the Evolution of American Medicine*. New York: Random House, 2005.

———. "The *Medical and Surgical History of the War of the Rebellion, 1861–1865*." *Archives of Surgery* 133 (July 1998): 783.

Schroeder-Lein, Glenna R. *The Encyclopedia of Civil War Medicine*. London: Routledge, 2008.

Thomas, William G. *The Iron Way: Railroads, the Civil War, and the Making of Modern America*. New Haven, CT: Yale University Press, 2011.

Tucker, Spencer C. *Unconditional Surrender: The Capture of Forts Henry and Donelson*. Abilene, TX: McWhiney Foundation Press, 2001.

Tucker, Spencer C., Paul G. Pierpaoli, and William E. Whyte, eds. *The Civil War Encyclopedia*. 2 volumes. Santa Barbara, CA: ABC-CLIO, 2010.

Turner, George Edgar. *Victory Rode the Rails: The Strategic Place of Railroads in the Civil War*. Indianapolis, IN: Bobbs-Merrill, 1953.

Ward, James A. *That Man Haupt: A Biography of Herman Haupt*. Baton Rouge: Louisiana State University Press, 1973.

PART IX: EMANCIPATION

Blight, David W. *A Slave No More: Two Men Who Escaped to Freedom, Including Their Own Narratives of Emancipation*. Orlando, FL: Harcourt, 2007.

Cooper, Abigail. "'Away I Goin' to Find My Mamma': Self-Emancipation, Migration, and Kinship in Refugee Camps in the Civil War Era." *Journal of African American History* 102 (September 2017): 444–67.

Crockett, Norman L. *The Black Towns*. Lawrence: The Regents Press of Kansas, 1979.

Holzer, Harold, Edna Greene Medford, and Frank J. Williams. *The Emancipation Proclamation: Three Views*. Baton Rouge: Louisiana State University Press, 2006.

Lang, Andrew F., ed. *In the Wake of War: Military Occupation, Emancipation, and Civil War America*. Baton Rouge: Louisiana State University Press, 2017.

McDaniel, W. Caleb. *Sweet Taste of Liberty: A True Story of Slavery and Restitution in America*. New York: Oxford University Press, 2019.

Newby-Alexander, Cassandra L. *An African American History of the Civil War in Hampton Roads*. Charleston, SC: History Press, 2010.

Oakes, James. *Freedom National: The Destruction of Slavery in the United States, 1861–1865.* New York: W. W. Norton, 2013.

Schwalm, Leslie A. *A Hard Fight for We: Women's Transition from Slavery to Freedom in South Carolina.* Urbana: University of Illinois Press, 1997.

Taylor, Amy Murrell. *Embattled Freedom: Journeys through the Civil War's Slave Refugee Camps.* Chapel Hill: University of North Carolina Press, 2018.

Vorenberg, Michael. *The Emancipation Proclamation: A Brief History with Documents.* Boston: Bedford/St. Martin's, 2010.

Weicksel, Sarah Jones. "Fitted Up for Freedom: The Material Culture of Refugee Relief." In *War Matters: Material Culture in the Civil War Era,* edited by Joan E. Cashin. Chapel Hill: University of North Carolina Press, 2018.

Williams, Heather Andrea. *Help Me to Find My People: The African American Search for Family Lost in Slavery.* Chapel Hill: University of North Carolina Press, 2012.

PART X: LEGACY

Blight, David W. *Beyond the Battlefield: Race, Memory, and the American Civil War.* Amherst: University of Massachusetts Press, 2002.

———. *Race and Reunion: The Civil War in American Memory.* Cambridge, MA: Harvard University Press, 2001.

Edwards, John N. *Shelby's Expedition to Mexico: An Unwritten Leaf of the War.* Fayetteville: University of Arkansas Press, 2002.

Fahs, Alice, and Joan Waugh, eds. *The Memory of the Civil War in American Culture.* Chapel Hill: University of North Carolina Press, 2004.

Freeman, David B. *Carved in Stone: The History of Stone Mountain.* Macon, GA: Mercer University Press, 1997.

Horowitz, Tony. *Confederates in the Attic: Dispatches from the Unfinished Civil War.* New York: Pantheon Books, 1998.

Janney, Caroline E. *Burying the Dead but Not the Past: Ladies' Memorial Associations and the Lost Cause.* Chapel Hill: University of North Carolina Press, 2008.

Jones, Christopher L. "Deserting Dixie: A History of Emigres, Exiles, and Dissenters from the American South, 1866–1925." PhD dissertation. Brown University, 2009.

Kytle, Ethan J., and Blain Roberts. *Denmark Vesey's Garden: Slavery and Memory of the Cradle of the Confederacy*. New York: The New Press, 2018.

Levin, Kevin M., ed. *Interpreting the Civil War at Museums and Historic Sites*. Lanham, MD: Rowman and Littlefield Publishers, 2017.

———. *Searching for Black Confederates: The Civil War's Most Persistent Myth*. Chapel Hill: University of North Carolina Press, 2019.

Levine, Bruce. *Confederate Emancipation: Southern Plans to Free and Arm Slaves during the Civil War*. New York: Oxford University Press, 2006.

Phillips, Jason. *Diehard Rebels: The Confederate Culture of Invincibility*. Athens: University of Georgia Press, 2010.

Rister, Carol Coke. "Carlota, a Confederate Colony in Mexico." *Journal of Southern History* 11 (February 1945): 33–50.

Soodalter, Ron. "The Confederados." *America's Civil War*, September 2013: 61–65.

Trudeau, Noah Andre. *Out of the Storm: The End of the Civil War, April–June 1865*. Boston: Little, Brown and Company, 1994.

Index

Page references for figures are italicized.

About the Author

Julie L. Holcomb is the author of *Moral Commerce: Quakers and the Transatlantic Boycott of the Slave Labor Economy* (Cornell University Press, 2016) and the editor of *Southern Sons, Northern Soldiers: The Civil War Letters of the Remley Brothers, 22nd Iowa Infantry* (Northern Illinois University Press, 2004). In addition to her books, Holcomb has published widely in a variety of academic and popular venues. Within the field of Civil War history, she has published entries in several reference works published by ABC-CLIO, including *Civil War: Perspectives in American Social History*, *Encyclopedia of the Material Culture of Slave Life*, and *Women in the American Civil War*. Holcomb has published essays for the online publications *Essential Civil War Curriculum* and *The Ultimate History Project* and had an essay published in *The Fate of Texas: The Civil War and the Lone Star State* (University of Arkansas, 2008). Holcomb serves as the editor of *Quaker History*, the peer-reviewed journal published by the Religious Society of Friends.

Holcomb is associate professor in museum studies at Baylor University in Waco, Texas, where she teaches courses in collections management, archival management, ethics, and preventive conservation. Prior to her appointment at Baylor, Holcomb was the director of the Pearce Civil War and Western Art Museums in Corsicana, Texas. In that position, she worked with the donors, Charles and Peggy Pearce, to increase the size and scope of the collection in preparation for the 2004 opening of the Pearce Collections Museum. During her eight-year tenure with the Pearce Collections, Holcomb increased the size of the Civil War collection from three thousand to seventeen thousand objects, manuscripts, and other materials and expanded the scope of the collection to include the antebellum and Reconstruction eras and the home front all the while maintaining the original emphasis on Northern and Southern military history. As director of the Pearce Museum, Holcomb supervised all aspects of the museum and archives, including acquisitions, public programming, exhibit development, marketing and outreach, research services, and the volunteer and internship programs.

Holcomb received her bachelor of arts in history and creative writing from Pacific University, Forest Grove, Oregon (1999); her master of library and information science, with a specialization in archives and records management, from the University of Texas at Austin (2000); and her PhD in transatlantic history from the University of Texas at Arlington (2010).